TRACKS ON THE TRAIL

TRACKING POP

SERIES EDITORS: JOCELYN NEAL, JOHN COVACH,
ROBERT FINK, AND LOREN KAJIKAWA

TRACKS ON THE TRAIL

Popular Music, Race, and the US Presidency

DANA GORZELANY-MOSTAK

UNIVERSITY OF MICHIGAN PRESS
ANN ARBOR

For questions or permissions, please contact um.press.perms@umich.edu

Published in the United States of America by the
University of Michigan Press
Printed and bound by CPI Group (UK) Ltd, Croydon, CR0 4YY

First published October 2023

A CIP catalog record for this book is available from the British Library.

Library of Congress Cataloging-in-Publication data has been applied for.

ISBN 978-0-472-07616-1 (hardcover : alk. paper)
ISBN 978-0-472-05616-3 (paper : alk. paper)
ISBN 978-0-472-90350-4 (open access ebook)

DOI: https://doi.org/10.3998/mpub.12654659

The University of Michigan Press's open access publishing program is made possible thanks to
additional funding from the University of Michigan Office of the Provost and the generous support of contributing libraries.

CONTENTS

Digital materials related to this title can be found on the Fulcrum platform via the
following citable URL: https://doi.org/10.3998/mpub.12654659

ACKNOWLEDGMENTS

This project has been an enormous undertaking that I cannot compare to any other in my career, and it would not have been possible without the support of many mentors, friends, colleagues, family, and students. To begin, I would like to thank the hundreds of folks who have been involved with the Trax on the Trail project over the past seven years. The conversations surrounding this website and research project, and our mission to cultivate a more critical and discerning ear among the public, have shaped much of the content in this book. The Trax project would not exist without the creative vision of Naomi Graber and Jim Deaville, two colleagues I am fortunate enough to also call close friends. I am indebted to the many contributors who have penned essays, recorded podcasts, and developed educational materials for the website, and to the Georgia College & State University students who have worked to track music on the trail over the past two elections, especially Sarah Kitts, Cannon McClain, Sarah Griffin, and Haley Strassburger. Trailheadz, I salute you! Thank you to my colleagues across the country who have welcomed me into their institutions (sometimes through the front door, and sometimes virtually) to speak about campaign music. These experiences have always challenged me and pushed my thinking in new directions. Thanks especially to William Cheng, Loren Kajikawa, Laura Moore Pruett, Peter Kupfer, Emily Abrams Ansari, Carl Leafstedt, Daniel Goldmark, Naomi Graber, and Joan Campbell Huguet.

The ideas I explore here began as papers presented in various forums over the past few years. I am grateful to the Society for American Music, the American Musicological Society, and the International Association for the Study of Popular Music for giving me the opportunity to share my work and receive invaluable feedback from a robust community of dedicated scholars. Several colleagues have been kind enough to weigh in on drafts of my work in this book, and I am tremendously grateful for their input. Thank you to Justin Patch, Stefanie Sevcik, Remi Chiu, and Naomi Graber (again). This book did not have much of a structure until Sheryl Kaskowitz tackled the introduction with her unparalleled developmental editing skills. I am also deeply grateful to Erin K. Maher, a brilliant scholar and copyeditor, who in short order copyedited this book in its entirety.

During my time at Georgia College & State University, I have been fortunate to have my research supported by several offices on campus. The bulk of the work on this book was completed in the summer of 2021 with funding from the Provost's Summer Research Fellows Grant. I have also received several Faculty Research Grants and funding from the Office of the Dean, the Department of Music, and most recently, the Vertically Integrated Projects Program. My sincerest thanks to Dean Eric Tenbus, Provost Costas Spirou, Associate Provost Jordan Cofer, music department chair Don Parker, former music department chair Sergio Ruiz, and former College of Arts & Sciences dean Ken Proctor for their unwavering support of all of my research endeavors.

I first met David Brackett when I started my PhD in 2006, and he later served as my dissertation adviser. He has been a constant source of support, encouragement, and inspiration over the past sixteen years. His brilliance is only matched by his kindness, and I have been fortunate to have his guidance and his friendship all of these years.

I was hopeful that the University of Michigan Press would accept my book because I knew I wanted to work with Loren Kajikawa. I am deeply grateful for his thoughtful feedback and guidance through each step of this process. I would also like to thank senior acquisitions editor Sara Cohen, the editorial board, and my anonymous reviewers for their careful reading of my work and their invaluable suggestions, which I know greatly enriched and added nuance to my work.

I am fortunate to have a large community of friends here at Georgia College & State University who are supportive, snarky, all-around brilliant and amazing people, especially the folks in the veggie dinner group, the game group, and the Department of Music. This book took shape while Jenny Flaherty, Alyssa Harris, Amber Kaufman, and Paul Hindemith were my roommates. My life and work are all the more rich because you all are in it. I must also mention my "work wife," Jennifer Flory (aka The Floogle)—thank you for always being on the assist with your encouragement, tech support, and willingness to grab a mediocre meal on a moment's notice.

Last, I would like to thank my family. This book is dedicated to my parents, Stan and Connie, who financed college, music lessons, and several lost dental apparatuses, and to my sister, Jen, who has alternately been my sidekick, side bank, and a steadfast source of support. I was born first, but you are and always will be the Number 1. Thank you Mom, Dad, and Stweebs for making my life extraordinary.

Introduction

On June 3, 1992, presidential hopeful Bill Clinton performed a saxophone rendition of Elvis Presley's "Heartbreak Hotel" on *The Arsenio Hall Show*.[1] In doing so, he aligned himself with perhaps the most recognizable music celebrity of all time—a cultural icon whom rock critic Greil Marcus described as "the country's most extreme embodiment of possibility and disruption, of renewal and defeat."[2] The young Democrat from Hope, Arkansas, never concealed his fandom, referring to Elvis as "the major cultural figure of [his] childhood," and the press frequently alluded to affinities between musician and politician.[3] While Clinton invoked young Elvis in his interviews and rally playlist, his *Arsenio* performance, complete with shaded glasses (indoors) and bland but hokey improvisations, actually revealed just as many affinities with late Elvis—that is, the neutered, ballad-singing, safe, sequined Elvis who entered the Las Vegas arena to the strains of *Also Sprach Zarathustra*.[4]

In this moment of musical engagement, Bill Clinton was constructing not merely *his* presidential identity, but the identity of the American presidency as well. On the surface, such musicking (to use Christopher Small's term) would seem to crystallize the candidate's cool quotient, hip dad character, or "man of the people" persona.[5] On a less explicit level, such moments of musical engagement operate as aural articulations of race and racial identity that tether the candidate to specific values, insights, communities, histories, and embodied knowledge. How might the gendered and racialized discourses that surround Elvis's music and persona be mapped onto Clinton as their identities become enmeshed in this iconic moment? Novelist Toni Morrison tapped Clinton as the "first Black president," citing his saxophone chops as one such indicator of this identity.[6] While his

Fig. 1. Bill Clinton performs "Heartbreak Hotel" on *The Arsenio Hall Show*. AP Images / Reed Saxon.

upbringing undergirded this assertion, indeed Clinton's music tastes and dispositions completed the package by providing an apt aural counterpoint. Thus, Bill Clinton's star turn on *Arsenio* represents a moment where music and race coalesced in the formation of his presidential identity. If we are to consider the American presidency as both a symbol and an index of American masculinity, and by extension whiteness, how might music serve as a vehicle for performing identities both within and outside of this "standard," and what value might these articulations offer candidates and the constituencies with which they wish to communicate?[7]

Presidential campaigns were noisy affairs long before Elvis, Bill Clinton, Bill Clinton's sax, and late-night television. Brass bands and glee clubs; the sounds of Frank Sinatra and Simon & Garfunkel; the strains of a crowd erupting in their own rousing cadence; a candidate's impromptu performance on the keys—all have left an imprint on the campaign soundscape over the past 180 years.[8] Whether live, broadcast via media, or piped through a set of AirPods, music can regulate the emotions of listeners, communicate ideas about candidates, and serve as a catalyst for community building in physical and virtual spaces. The roles of textual and visual media in the constitution of presidential identity are generally acknowledged and well theorized, but the persuasive power of sound in its ubiquity and multivalence is sometimes omitted from the equation. We can hear the music, yet it is inaudible. Building on earlier research that explores sound, listening, and music making on the campaign trail, *Tracks on the Trail: Popular Music, Race, and the US Presidency* centers race, offering a critical evaluation of *how* presidential candidates harness racialized sounds to assert authority, identity, affiliation, and cultural competence.[9] While conversations regarding "official" campaign music, such as rally setlists and candidate playlists, dominate traditional media channels, this book extends the conversation to incorporate "unofficial" campaign music in the form of remixes, newly composed songs, and parodies, taking into consideration the ways in which digital formats and technologies of interactivity have cultivated new modes of political engagement that have transformed the campaign soundscape. Bringing sounds both official and unofficial into the analytical fold, this book considers how the racialization of sound intersects with other markers of difference, ultimately shaping the public discourse surrounding candidates, popular music, and the meanings attached to race in the twenty-first century.

As race is a social construct rather than an inborn set of genetic traits or physiological attributes, the meanings attached to it are perpetually shifting and highly contingent upon historical, cultural, and geographic contexts.[10] This extends to sound as well, whether it be rooted in linguistic markers or musical utterances. There are no direct correlations between specific sounds and racial identities. Rather, any correlations are established in contexts where sound—through performance, acts of listening, or discourse—becomes racialized. This book does not position race or racialized sound as a monolith, but rather draws on the work of previous scholars who have developed meaningful frameworks for demystifying music's processes of racialization and interrogated the ties of such processes to the legacies of imperialism and colonialism.

Drawing on musical performance and literary production in the nineteenth and twentieth centuries, Jennifer Lynn Stoever explores sound as a marker of difference and (after W. E. B. Du Bois) theorizes what she calls "the sonic color line," a "socially constructed boundary that racially codes sonic phenomena such as vocal timbre, accents, and musical tones."[11] Focusing specifically on voice, Nina Sun Eidsheim challenges the notion that timbre and vocality can be reliable markers of racial difference.

Instead, she focuses on the effects of training and environment on the sound of the voice and issues a call to replace a reliance on perceptions of innate ability with a more critical approach to interpretation, as listeners' race-based assessments hold the potential to discriminate and uphold White supremacy.[12] Both Stoever and Eidsheim center the listener in the process of racialization and the production of racial subjectivities.

Similarly accounting for mediation and the attendant gulf between sound and its source of production, Karl Hagstrom Miller and David Brackett both trace correlations between sound and racial identity to recording technologies developed at the beginning of the twentieth century. Miller starts by debunking some of the origin myths surrounding the emergence of blues and country music, which were previously thought to have developed as two distinct streams, despite the similarities between them. The separation, he argues, was the deliberate work of folklorists who perpetuated the notion of a southern folk music uncontaminated by "foreign," commercial influences and a record industry that imagined rigid marketing categories—"race records" for African Americans and "old-time music" for White people. This maintenance of a de facto racial color line reinforced the Jim Crow divide in the South, and although southern musicians played a wide variety of music regardless of race or regional identity, thus challenging the racialized categorization of music, these categories persist in the popular imagination.[13] Brackett argues that the impulse to categorize in this manner *predated* sound recording, and while the impulse to connect genres to specific audiences persists, such homological models often ring false.[14]

Ultimately such studies validate Ronald Radano and Philip V. Bohlman's contention that music facilitates aesthetic and discursive constructions of race, which is in turn a fundamental element in the construction of music, as well as Josh Kun's bold claim that "there is no history of racial formation in the Americas that is not a history of popular music, and there is no history of inter-American popular music without a history of racial formation."[15] Parties who select music for candidates or create music in homage to them often perpetuate the mythos, stereotypes, and historical inaccuracies that scholars such as Stoever, Eidsheim, Miller, and Brackett have attempted to dismantle and remediate. Similarly, those who listen often fall prey to selective hearing or mishearing when they attempt to hear race in music on the campaign trail. Therefore, studies that examine the racialization of vocal production or categories of music, unveiling the political exigencies and agendas that underlie these processes, provide both a model and a springboard for this work.

LESSONS FROM BILL CLINTON

Bill Clinton was *not* the first presidential candidate to capitalize upon racialized sounds, their tangled histories, and their complex web of meanings on the campaign trail. However, his *Arsenio* performance and broader music strategy represent a crucial moment in the formation of Clinton's presidential identity and his successful bid, and they also serve as a referential snapshot in the history of music on the trail.[16] Paul Begala once claimed, "A presidential campaign is like a film. . . . It never comes together until it's scored and tracked."[17] Indeed, Clinton's senior strategist understood the power of a well-placed song, and while candidates rarely assign experts to the task, there is ample evidence to suggest that presidential hopefuls acknowledge music's communicative capabilities and cultural capital, and that they therefore plot a musical course of action or strategy as a part of their campaign plan.[18] Writing in 1992, the *Washington Post*'s David Maraniss lauded Clinton's *Arsenio* appearance, claiming it was a "lesson in how to electioneer in the brave new world of American politics."[19] Indeed, this "lesson" schooled future candidates, including those addressed in the first three chapters of this book: Barack Obama, Ben Carson, and Kamala Harris. In addition to establishing a foundation and framework for the analysis of racialized sounds within the context of the presidential campaign, the Clinton music strategy also illustrates the inner workings of three additional strands of inquiry relevant to all five case studies discussed in this book: nostalgia, identity, and genre.

Weighing in on the affinities between Clinton and his idol, journalist Maureen Dowd mused over Clinton's "trademark 'Elvis' look," which to her "convey[ed] an appealing combination of decency and deviltry."[20] Like Elvis, Clinton simultaneously embodied both decency *and* deviltry, and such contradictions played out in his campaign soundscape more broadly. While drawing on the devilish, rebellious Elvis allowed the candidate to offer a "safe" market-controlled form of rebellion filtered through the lens of 1960s nostalgia, the decent, domesticated Elvis of later years allowed him to assume a respectable and sentimental stance. Reliance on spectacle, or camp, and the accompanying depletion of musical authenticity and masculine virility may have worked against Elvis, but this narrative allowed the icon to "perform" cultural work for Clinton in 1992.[21] In the late-show context, Clinton did *not* attempt to create an authentic performance or even an homage to his boyhood hero. Whether it be lip biting, Elvis worshiping, or sax swinging, Clinton was *not* Clinton performing Elvis, but rather Clinton consciously performing Clinton-as-Elvis.

That is to say, Elvis and the mythos that surrounded him offered the public a common language and matrix of cultural associations through which they could see and hear Bill Clinton from Arkansas as presidential candidate. To solidify this connection, Clinton regularly opined on his love of rock and roll and especially Elvis on the campaign trail. His running mate, Senator Al Gore, acknowledging the same affinities as Dowd, even told Democratic National Convention attendees that "it had always been his dream to come 'to Madison Square Garden and be the warm-up act for Elvis.'"[22] Not surprisingly, the Elvis banter became a linchpin for incumbent candidate President George H. W. Bush, who stated at the Republican National Convention, "He [Clinton] says he's for balanced budgets. But he came out against the amendment. He's like that on a lot of issues, first on one side, then the other. He's been spotted in more places than Elvis Presley. . . . I guess you'd say his plan really is 'Elvis economics.' America will be checking into the 'Heartbreak Hotel.'"[23] Whereas Bush tried to make Elvis a liability, Clinton consistently tried to make him an asset, stating, "I don't think Bush would have liked Elvis very much, and that's just another thing that's wrong with him."[24] With this comment, Clinton positioned Elvis fandom as the litmus test that determined the difference between Bush and himself, a distinction that extended to their respective constituencies. In this light, disliking Elvis (or Clinton-as-Elvis) was tantamount to disliking America, or at least certain parts of it.

With the *Arsenio* performance, we see the candidate engaging with a tradition closely aligned with Black Americans (the blues) as a means of asserting hipness, while he simultaneously reminds us that he is not all that hip. This contradiction played out in the reception of his performance. Maraniss weighed in on Clinton's second *Arsenio* song, "God Bless the Child":

> The scene left contrasting impressions: one of Clinton as a hipster, the first baby boomer candidate, in tune with the *Zeitgeist*; the other of Clinton as a metaphor for all politicians these days, diminished by cultural forces that have ren-

dered them little more than sidemen in the band. . . . His *Arsenio* performance was almost flawless. The reason was also the answer to a question Clinton's ever-curious traveling press corps had been asking grumpily over the last few days—where the heck is Clinton? He was in a secluded hotel room listening to Billie Holiday tapes to get the rhythms right for his rendition of "God Bless the Child."[25]

Entertainment Weekly polled bona fide saxophone players to assess the performance as well. David Sanborn claimed, "He doesn't really play like a President. I think Lester Young—'Pres'—had that covered. I think Clinton plays like a Governor of Arkansas."[26] Phil Woods agreed that something was lacking: "I think his sax soul needs some work. I think he should get with Ray Charles and get on the road. He should take a sabbatical with a band and learn how to go to the bathroom out the window of the bus at 80 miles per hour. That would help."[27] Maraniss, Sanborn, and Woods all allude to Clinton's ineptness in one fashion or another, and two hint toward his advanced age. Each takes a subtle jab at the lack of authenticity in Clinton's performance, with such critiques rooted in presumed racial difference. Maraniss focuses on Clinton's active rehearsal schedule to prepare for the second piece that he performed on the show, "God Bless the Child," seeming to suggest that Clinton lacks innate musical knowledge or instincts. In specifically citing *rhythm*, he may be hinting toward prevalent stereotypes that essentialize Black musicality. Sanborn alludes to jazz saxophonist Lester Young's nickname, "Pres," to confirm that a (Black) saxophonist already holds the presidential title, suggesting that although Clinton may become *pres*ident, he simply does not have the aptitude required to be *Pres*. In advising that this title already has a holder, Sanborn may also be taking a dig at Clinton's act as derivative and lacking in creativity. By contrast, Woods focuses on the notion that Clinton's "soul" needs training—that he does not share the values or background of real bluesmen and can only learn through experience, in this case, on a tour bus with Ray Charles. At least according to Woods, Clinton plays like a White boy.

Riffing on Andrew Ross, Ingrid Monson describes hipness as follows: "To be hip . . . is to be 'in the know,'[28] not to be duped by the world around one, and to react with dignity and 'cool' when faced with an assault on one's being."[29] As a blues player, Clinton was *not* "in the know"; however, since the *Arsenio* performance came about during a period of his campaign where he was being pummeled by his competitors, one could argue that he does meet the definition of hipness in that he was reacting to hostility with "dignity and cool," which came in the form of fronting a band. But Clinton attempted to forge that "cool" by identifying with Black culture, and some were quick to criticize the facade. In a 2000 *Village Voice* piece titled "Proxy Music," Eric Weisbard draws an analogy between twentieth-century politicians' appropriation of rock and pop culture and nineteenth-century candidates' reliance on minstrelsy for their campaign music.[30] Citing Clinton's *Arsenio* appearance, Jimmy Carter's alliance with southern rockers, and George H. W. Bush's "performance" (with Lee Atwater) of the blues at his 1989 inaugural festivities, Weisbard claims, "Rock, or its Uncle Sambo ancestor blackface minstrelsy, has been used to sell presidents ever since Jackson dispelled the notion that presidents should manifest the patrician dignity of the Founding Fathers."[31] Weisbard focuses on alliances and appropriation, but he expresses discomfort with White candidates' problematic engagement with music bearing racial connotations. Although the earlier "reviews" by Maraniss, Sanborn, and Woods couch the Clinton-as-bluesman performance in humorous barbs, subtle hints of uneasiness bubble to the surface.

Ultimately, Clinton's whiteness forms the crux of the late-night spectacle. The shades, the floral tie, the corny improvisations, and the ungainliness of the performance all remind the listener that Clinton is impersonating a White man impersonating a Black man. Thus, Clinton's performance almost takes on the aural and visual markers of camp in that it is "deliberately exaggerated and theatrical in style." And there is a second aspect of camp, what Susan Sontag calls a "victory of 'style' over 'content,'" that we might consider here.[32] The *Village Voice*'s Richard Goldstein weighed in on Clinton-as-Elvis, stating, "Clinton's Elvis has little to do with the transcendent aspects of the King, and much to do with what made that cat from Tupelo a star. . . . He set a style for male sexuality that was at once ecstatic and needy—a far cry from the strong silent type."[33] The "neediness" certainly comes across in Clinton's performance. "Heartbreak Hotel" offers the first-person perspective of a forlorn man who has been deserted by the object of his affection. In the absence of lyrics, Clinton evokes the wails and cries of the male protagonist with his improvisatory gestures. His musical channeling of that vulnerability would seem to run counter to efforts to appear "presidential" or to assert traditional manhood, but the presentation of sentimentality and a softer form of masculinity might account for part of his appeal to women, as Goldstein notes. While aspects of Clinton's performance may have wooed women voters and appealed to some Black audiences, the campiness and amateurism of the act worked to reaffirm Clinton's identity as a White candidate, whose Black musical disguise (like the minstrel's mask or even the Elvis impersonator's costume) can be discarded at will.[34]

The *Arsenio* spot was neither the beginning nor the end of Clinton's musical engagement. In addition to amusing television viewers with his sax-playing and energizing rally-goers with his "official" campaign theme song, Fleetwood Mac's "Don't Stop" (1977), the Arkansas governor offered an expansive playlist of popular songs—mainly rock from the 1960s and 1970s—at his many appearances on the trail.[35] The practice of using unaltered popular songs as campaign songs predates Clinton, but 1992 was the first time the press made a consistent and conscious effort to note such usage at campaign rallies (Table 1). Rather than choosing contemporary chart-toppers, Clinton's team selected songs that had reached the height of their popularity almost two or three decades earlier.[36] Shortly before Clinton's campaign moved into full swing, nostalgia had become an increasingly visible component of marketing, advertising, and entertainment media, which often targeted baby boomers (a substantial voting bloc and powerful consumer demographic) and senior citizens.[37] In their study of the biological and environmental factors that shape the formation of musical taste, Morris B. Holbrook and Robert M. Schindler found that people tend to favor the music that was popular when they were young adults, and they continue to find pleasure in this music throughout their lives.[38] While nostalgia was once focused on specific places (such as the home), celebrities, films, and music from one's past can also be objects of nostalgia.[39] Through the consumption of these objects, subjects experience feelings of safety, contentment, and belonging. Nostalgia for adolescence and early adulthood appears to be the strongest, and people are most prone to nostalgia during transitional periods in the life cycle, especially the middle age and retirement years.[40] Clinton's own cohort (baby boomers), whom he targeted with his campaign messaging and self-presentation, was highly susceptible to nostalgia-laden messages. Moreover, Clinton's strategists emphasized his small-town southern roots and branded him as the "poster child" of the 1960s, so in this regard, the playlist tied into not only the nostalgic narratives that fomented around his campaign, but also his campaign platform and ideological orientation.[41] As baby boomers actively engaged with Clinton's music (*their* music) at live events, they renewed their belonging to a certain group, and reaffirmed their collective identity by way of their shared nostalgic experience.[42]

Connections between presidential candidates and specific genres, and by extension, specific genre audiences frequently emerge in discussions of candidate playlists and candidates' own musings over their music tastes. Consider the following headlines:

Clinton Proves Himself a Rock and Roll President[43]

Is Obama Really the Hip-Hop President?[44]

Sorry Obama but Donald Trump is America's First Hip-Hop President[45]

Beto Wants to Be Our First Punk President[46]

As Samuel Popkin notes, voters use such cues (in Clinton's case, an affinity with rock and roll) to make inferences about which candidates share their worldview and thus will be more likely to institute policies that directly benefit them.[47] So what might classic rock signal to the potential Clinton voter? During the early 1990s, the classic rock radio format gained momentum with the baby boomer demographic, mirroring a larger effort to commodify the cultural artifacts of the 1960s. Although rock music is anticommercial in principle, Lawrence Grossberg argues that the genre was subjected to an endless cycle of co-optation by hegemonic forces and resistance by musicians and fans culturally invested in the genre.[48] Rock even became a discourse appropriated for the articulation of public memory at events such as the fall of the Berlin Wall and various professional sporting events, including the World Cup in soccer.[49] Subsequently, the boundary between center (dominant culture) and periphery (subculture) became effaced as the dominant culture subsumed the baby boomer generation, a sizable cohort that held the potential to shape the nation's political and economic future. Grossberg suggests that the desire to placate the baby boomer "threat" played a role in this co-optation. This sociocultural shift profoundly impacted what he refers to as rock's "affective power," and the genre's status as nostalgia neutralized its capacity to function as a symbol of rebellion. Although the structures of earlier styles remained on a surface level, the quest for commercial success and popular appeal solidified

Table 1. Bill Clinton's 1992 campaign playlist

Song	Artist	Date	Genre
Blue Suede Shoes	Elvis Presley	1956	pop/rock
Don't Be Cruel	Elvis Presley	1956	pop/rock
Hound Dog	Elvis Presley	1956	pop/rock
Jailhouse Rock	Elvis Presley	1957	pop/rock
Twist and Shout	The Beatles	1963	pop/rock
Surfin' U.S.A.	Beach Boys	1963	pop/rock
My Guy	Mary Wells	1964	pop/rock, R & B
Good Vibrations	Beach Boys	1966	pop/rock
Oh Happy Day	Edwin Hawkins Singers	1968	religious
Revolution	The Beatles	1968	pop/rock
All Along the Watchtower	Jimi Hendrix	1968	pop/rock
Here Comes the Sun	The Beatles	1969	pop/rock
Power to the People	John Lennon	1971	pop/rock
Lean on Me	Bill Withers	1972	R & B
Takin' Care of Business	Bachman-Turner Overdrive	1974	pop/rock
Scarlet Begonias	Grateful Dead	1974	pop/rock
Margaritaville	Jimmy Buffett	1977	pop/rock
Don't Stop	Fleetwood Mac	1977	pop/rock
Sweet Home Chicago	Blues Brothers	1980	R & B
Born in the U.S.A.	Bruce Springsteen	1984	pop/rock
The Boy in the Bubble	Paul Simon	1986	pop/rock
Graceland	Paul Simon	1986	pop/rock
U Can't Touch This	MC Hammer	1990	rap
Right Here, Right Now	Jesus Jones	1990	pop/rock
We Shall Be Free	Garth Brooks	1992	country

rock's *adherence* to the dominant culture.[50] Rock *is* a mass-marketed commodity, yet the purchase of rock music has "produced intense feelings of freedom, rebellion, marginality, oppositionality, uniqueness, and authenticity."[51] Thus, in 1992, Clinton's classic rock lineup retained the residue of these intense feelings, yet simultaneously evoked the safety and security of an idealized past, signified the satisfaction of consuming familiar objects, and recalled events that exude American pride and patriotism in the collective social memory.

Just as rock's rebellious and liberatory potential became neutralized, so too did the more radical cultural and political leanings of the 1960s that Clinton deftly sidestepped in his campaign messaging. As Philip Abbott notes, during the 1992 campaign, Clinton focused his recollections on the "happy Sixties"—the period before the death of John F. Kennedy, which also preceded the loss of life in Vietnam and the Watergate scandal that led to profound anxiety, cynicism, and disillusionment. A 1963 photo of teen-aged Clinton shaking hands with the young president became a powerful symbol of torch passing, with Clinton positioned as heir to the legacy of Camelot and son of the New Frontier.[52] The Clinton strategy hinged upon the public's misreading, or at least selective reading of the 1960s. Although Abbott does not specifically mention music other than Elvis, I would argue that Clinton's rally playlist, with acts such as the Beach Boys, the Beatles, and Mary Wells, offered an aural analogue to his recollections of the happy sixties and solidified Clinton's optimism and idealism.

But a candidate's self-professed affinity for a music genre can just as easily misfire. For example, the day after declaring his presidential candidacy in 2015, Senator Ted Cruz (R-TX) made the following statement in an interview with *CBS This Morning*:

> I grew up listening to classic rock, and I'll tell you sort of an odd story. My music taste changed on 9/11, and it's a very strange. . . . I actually intellectually find this very curious, but on 9/11, I didn't like how rock music responded. And country music, collectively, the way they responded, it resonated with me, and I have to say, it just is a gut level. I had an emotional reaction that says, "These are my people," and so ever since 2001, I listen to country music, but I'm an odd country music fan because I didn't listen to it prior to 2001.[53]

Journalists and other commenters online were amused by Cruz's expedient genre shifting, and in many instances chuckled at his contrived efforts to pander to his party's base supporters through declaring his affection for "their music." Cruz, who made a point of positioning himself as a party outsider, likely held the perception that country music was the favored genre for most Republicans. In his CBS anecdote, he adheres to an overly simplistic reading of country music as embracing traditional values, patriotism, and a Christian worldview (not to mention whiteness), and rock, on the other hand, as more antiestablishment, self-indulgent, promiscuous, and commercial. Indeed, the industry moguls' efforts to segregate sound, as noted by Brackett and Miller, persist in the present day, and Cruz was ready to harness this divide to meet his political goals.

Candidates and parties alike often lack a nuanced understanding of the myriad ways audiences identify with genres—their sounds, histories, associations, and connotations. These ruptures often serve as a springboard for those who wish to position music genres as a divining rod for seeking insight into a candidate, their values, and their policy stances, and those who would use this same information to map a critique of music onto policy. Despite efforts to align candidates with genres, the very elasticity of such categories and their fluid boundaries, not to mention the slippage between them, opens a minefield for presidential candidates. As Brackett notes, "The range of genre-identity relations does not arise as a natural or biological connection (even in the most seemingly straightforward cases of homology) but rather must be sutured together through the repetition of social practices in which a generic label brings together categories of people."[54] While classic rock and Clinton appeared a natural fit because of the candidate's age, knowledge, and long-established connection with the genre as both fan and musician, Cruz plus country didn't quite sell. As authenticity—the perception that someone is honest and real as opposed to fake or insincere—holds sway with voters, it is not surprising that purportedly contrived music tastes are sometimes met with scorn or even outright hostility.[55]

When candidates such as Clinton and Cruz affiliate themselves with an artist, a genre, a song, or a playlist, they tend to work under the assumption that the public will interpret or hear the music as they do. But in recent years, the public has turned a more discerning ear to candidate-music pairings: as seen with Cruz, and as we will later see with Kamala Harris and Ben Carson, candidates have been censured for their superficial understanding of music and the fan communities for which the music is meaningful. Culture critics such as Theodor W. Adorno, who limit popular music's value to its status as a mass-produced commodity, claim that the producers of popular music and the music's inherent qualities manipulate listeners "into a system of response mechanisms wholly antagonistic to the ideal of individuality in a free, liberal society."[56] However, scholars like Grossberg, Richard Middleton, and Simon Frith challenge the notion that popular music promotes the suppression of individual identities and exists only to reinforce capitalist structures. As Frith has argued, popular music "gives us a way of being in the world, a way of making sense of it."[57] Josh Kun similarly claims that "the emotion and the sensibility that music offers is what leads to a change in who we are, who we want to be, and how we want the world to be. . . . Music gives us the feelings we need to get where we want to go."[58] Popular songs offer up rich histories, associated cultural texts, a complex web of connotations, and audiences already culturally invested in them.[59] That is to say, a song or a group of songs can communicate a political message, an ideological orientation, a worldview, or a set of values, and this affective and persuasive power resides in its sounds, not just the semantic content of its lyrics. But this meaning is in perpetual flux, as it is both dialogically constituted and socially and historically contingent.[60] Popular music cannot simply be reduced to its ability to carry a message—and this is where journalists (and candidates) who fixate on lyrics usually miss the mark. As Frith and Kun suggest, songs can serve as the vehicle through which people experience their emotions.[61] Popular music performance and fandom can be a site for empowerment, self-exploration, self-definition, and community building. Just as Clinton drew on rhetorical traditions to construct authority in his political speeches, he relied on the multivalence, openness, expressive capabilities, and flexibility of popular music to invent such authority in the auditory realm.[62]

OUTLINE OF CHAPTERS

This book begins with the election of 2008, a logical starting point for a study on race, music, and the US presidency for two reasons.[63] To begin, this year witnessed the ascendancy of the first Black US president. Barack Obama's election and the subsequent eight years of his presidency profoundly impacted national conversations regarding race. Some saw the Obama presidency as heralding the beginning of a postracial society, where meritocracy would supersede racial identity, while others argued that the persistence of structural racism and "colorblind" rhetoric continued to limit opportunities for people of color. According to Eduardo Bonilla-Silva, efforts in racial discourses to center the individual and maintain a stance of "colorblindness" have only impeded the country's ability to promote open discussion and to fight racial inequality.[64] Michael Tesler similarly contests the myth of a postracial society, arguing that the Obama presidency actually made race *more* visible and accessible in the minds of the public. Subsequently, racial attitudes inflected everything, from party identification to policy preferences, to perceptions surrounding the breed of dog owned by the Obamas.[65]

National conversations on race did not end with Obama. Before the unexpected rise of business mogul-cum-celebrity Donald Trump, being

"White" meant, in the popular American imagination, that one was unmarked or devoid of a racialized identity, but as the campaign unfolded, White became a racial category, albeit a contested one.[66] Many thinkpieces in 2016 and beyond opined on the meaning of whiteness in the age of Donald Trump. Ta-Nehisi Coates even went so far as to call Trump "the first white president."[67] In 2020, the Democratic side welcomed a highly diverse pool of presidential hopefuls, which included several women (including Kamala Harris, who is addressed in chapter 3), Black and Latino candidates, and an openly gay candidate. Moreover, social movements such as #MeToo and Black Lives Matter; polemical conversations regarding border control and immigration policy; debates surrounding the removal of Confederate statues; the Covid-19 pandemic, which disproportionately impacted people of color; and more recently, discord over the alleged teaching of critical race theory in public schools all pushed conversations regarding race (and the ways in which race intersects with class, gender, and citizenship status) into the public consciousness.[68]

These conversations coincided with the largest upward transfer of wealth since the late nineteenth century and the weakening of institutions that guarded against it, including labor unions, progressive taxation policies, consumer protections, social welfare programs, and antidiscrimination laws.[69] Institutions that historically assumed the mantle of racial activism were compromised in their ability to address the needs of racially subordinated groups.[70] Stagnant wages, privatization, and deregulation impacted not only the lower class but the middle class as well, diluting the protections historically afforded to Whites who found themselves in a similar state of precarity, albeit not at the same level of material loss experienced by people of color.[71] In 2016 and 2020 such conditions and the attendant societal shifts offered an opening for Donald Trump, "who summons a racial populism to sustain the fantasy that economic inequality and the vulnerability it produces can be avenged through attacks on immigrants and people of color."[72] Ultimately, Trump's demagoguery posed a challenge to the ethos of liberal democracy in that he persuaded his White followers to center their own precarity rather than acknowledge the connections they share with people they perceive as different from them.[73]

Barack Obama's image was conceived as much in sound as it was in word and image. Encounters with pop culture, especially music, played a central role in the cultivation of his identity, but the voting public was equally interested in engaging with his candidacy through music. The availability of YouTube sparked an upsurge in the production of newly composed campaign music, such as the viral videos "Crush on Obama" (addressed in chapter 1) and "Yes We Can." The video-sharing hub offered a democratized platform and free access to a virtual audience. The public could upload videos of music performed at campaign rallies or fund-raising concerts, share links, post commentary, generate their own video montages with unaltered songs (chapter 5), or create their own candidate-themed music (chapter 4). Thus the 2008 election cycle marks a turn in which voters came to embody the roles of consumer *and* creator of the political message.[74]

Tracks on the Trail: Popular Music, Race, and the US Presidency is divided into five chapters, each of which turns a critical eye and ear to a specific instance of music on the campaign trail between 2008 and 2020. While this study is not comprehensive, I have aimed for breadth with regards to genre, including hip-hop, R&B, classical crossover, gospel, patriotic, pop, rock, and country. The types of musical engagement considered are similarly broad, encompassing official music in the form of candidate playlists, rally and launch event setlists, and candidate interviews, as well as unofficial music in the form of newly composed campaign songs, mash-ups, parodies, and remixes. Successful and unsuccessful candidates from both major parties make an appearance. In order to assemble a nuanced picture of the campaign soundscape, I draw on a diverse collection of sources, which includes newspapers, blogs, news shows, comedy television, footage of campaign events, candidate websites and autobiographies, music-streaming and video-sharing sites, and conversations across social media. Research traversing the fields of musicology, political science, gender studies, sound studies, psychology, media studies, and sociology offers a framework for investigating the complexities of the twenty-first-century campaign soundscape. Although this book includes some detailed musical analyses, its primary focus is on digital ethnography and cultural analyses with an interdisciplinary and intersectional bent.

The first chapter, "Keepin' It Real (Respectable): Barack Obama's Music Strategy and the Formation of Presidential Identity," addresses the unique challenges the Illinois senator faced as presidential candidate and the music strategy he developed to navigate these challenges. Theories on race and political communication and research on hip-hop and politics are blended with close music analysis in order to shed light on how Obama negotiated his multiracial identity through the medium of sound.[75] As a

Black candidate seeking young, first-time voters, Obama was obliged to engage with hip-hop in a meaningful way, but such engagement presented a political minefield, as he also sought the support of older Black voters and women. Obama found a balance by outwardly embracing the creativity, energy, entrepreneurship, and potential of hip-hop while cautiously calling out some of its more unsavory messages and lifestyles. Adopting a cool dad posture, he positioned himself as a cautious admirer rather than an insider. These personae were also cultivated in interviews where Obama discussed his music tastes and through rallies featuring playlists straight out of his own formative years—the sounds of 1960s and 1970s R & B. The soulful hits of Stevie Wonder, Jackie Wilson, and Aretha Franklin allowed Obama to tap into the benefits of a nostalgic soundtrack and forge a connection with older Black voters who were the architects of the civil rights movement. The romantic themes of this music also appealed to communities of female voters who had their own crushes on Obama, a sentiment expressed not only through the viral hit "Crush on Obama," but also thorough other remixes celebrating Obama's most iconic moments on the trail. Taking into consideration the candidate's position on hip-hop culture, his professed old-school music tastes, and the discourses his musical engagement precipitated on social media, this chapter shows how the candidate used music as a point of reference through which he could affirm his cultural blackness and project a Black identity that was both "real" and "respectable."

"Anatomy of a Campaign Launch: Heal, Inspire, Revive, *Erase* with Ben Carson," the book's second chapter, focuses on a specific event: Ben Carson's 2016 campaign launch. Carson, a Republican and esteemed neurosurgeon, avoided the typical launch event script and instead staged a concert at the Music Hall Center for the Performing Arts in Detroit—a site associated with cultural renewal. The event featured a slate of musical performances that evoked his slogan "Heal, Inspire, Revive," words that resonate in medical and spiritual parlance and effectively highlight both his Christian identity and his impressive accomplishments in medicine. Veritas, a White Christian classical-crossover male quintet, and Selected of God, a Black gospel choir that came into the public's view with their 2011 performance in a Super Bowl commercial, each performed a set of numbers before joining Carson onstage for a reprise of "Battle Hymn of the Republic." Carson, following in the footsteps of Clinton and Obama, harnessed the power of nostalgia, but rather than selecting the sounds of his own formative years, he chose Eminem's iconic track "Lose Yourself," a gospel tune, a show tune, and a medley of classic patriotic songs. In the absence of a cadre of speakers, music became the medium through which Carson constructed his vision of the nation's past, present, and future. A close reading of the campaign-launch concert reveals how Carson's campaign team recontextualized and reframed music and performance traditions in order to construct a narrative that aligned with the candidate's own biography and campaign platform. Specifically, Carson elevated his forefathers, the Christian faith, and postracial ideologies while deploying rhetorical (and musical) strategies that precipitated the erasure of Black narratives that were incongruent with his racially transcendent strategy.[76]

"Kamala Harris, Rap Genius?" the third chapter, adopts an intersectional approach to address the unique challenges women candidates face in asserting a musical identity. Harris, the daughter of an Indian scientist and a Jamaican economist, declared her candidacy for the presidency on Martin Luther King Day in 2019. Within the first three weeks of her campaign, she notably engaged with music on three occasions: a mixtape on *The Late Show with Stephen Colbert*, a Twitter video where she grooves out to Cardi B, and a *Breakfast Club* interview where she mentions Tupac and Snoop Dogg. Each instance of musical engagement unleashed a torrent of negative criticism, with many Twitter users questioning Harris's relatability, authenticity, and electability. In this chapter, research on the communication strategies of intersectional candidates and the cultivation of community on Black Twitter is combined with theories on the coalescence of sound, race, and gender in order to analyze Harris's musical engagement and the negative responses it generated among Black voters.[77] Ultimately, this chapter shows that although musicking bestows cultural capital on male politicians such as Bill Clinton and Barack Obama, it becomes yet another minefield of double standards for women candidates, and especially Black women.

The fourth chapter, "Girls 'Keep America Great': Singing the *White Stuff* for Donald Trump," turns to the "unofficial," newly composed campaign music that regularly circulates across various social media platforms during election season. Camille & Haley, a sister songwriting duo from Oklahoma, first made waves in political circles in 2012 when they released a song for then-presidential candidate Rick Santorum. The country-pop act entered the spotlight again in June 2020 with "Keep America Great," a pro-Trump music video filmed in Tulsa outside the BOK Center, the site where Trump held his first "post-Covid" rally. A MSNBC reporter posted a clip of Camille & Haley's performance on Twitter, where it boasts over twenty-nine million views. In 2020, female artists only sparsely populated the official Trump playlist, and even homemade YouTube videos in support of Trump were generally created for and by men, making acts such as Camille & Haley unusual. Drawing on research that investigates race, evangelicalism, and voter behavior, this chapter explores how patriotism, Christian identity, and White middle-class girlhood converge in the performances of Camille & Haley.[78] Moreover, this chapter offers a close reading of the reception surrounding their videos and accompanying media to shed light upon young women's musical engagement with electoral politics in the twenty-first century. These analyses reveal how girl groups such as Camille & Haley espouse Christian nationalist ideologies that appeal to White evangelicals yet neutralize the virulence of the messaging by invoking seemingly innocuous nostalgic sentiments and performing traditional femininity.

The fifth chapter, "Settling the Score: Pop Songs, Protest, and Punishment," tracks the circulation of pop songs in online chatter engaging with the Black Lives Matter movement. During a summer 2020 protest in Portland, Oregon, bystanders captured the moment when a Molotov cocktail set a protester's feet on fire. Dan Scavino, White House deputy chief of staff and director of social media, tweeted footage of the incident with Kenny Loggins's song "Footloose" added, and his post was later retweeted by President Donald Trump. The "Footloose" video, viewed 3.4 million times within forty-eight hours of its posting, garnered responses from supporters and detractors alike and inspired others in the Twitterverse to add their own "soundtracks" to the bystanders' footage.[79] As the hearty exchange of songs, GIFs, images, and one-liners unfolded, virtual spectators bore witness to (and reveled in) the protester's punishment. But who was this protester and what did he represent to the digital mob who celebrated his retribution? Drawing on research in the areas of political communication and internet trolling culture, this chapter follows the chain of musical responses inspired by Scavino's and Trump's tweets and investigates how humor is generated through acts of musical substitution.[80] Moreover, Daniel Martinez HoSang and Joseph E. Lowndes's concept of "racial transposition" and theories on punishment contextualize the phenomenon of digital lynching and reveal the role sound can play in driving political polarization across online platforms.[81]

We are at a crucial moment in US history where humanities-based inquiry can play a role in restoring and amplifying truth, or at least offer a primer that demystifies the role of sound in the art of persuasion or the sowing of discord. *Tracks on the Trail: Popular Music, Race, and the US Presidency* promotes a critical evaluation of *how* music and sound shape our perceptions of presidential candidates, and I believe this knowledge will contribute to the cultivation of a more just, accessible, and inclusive society. While the 2020 election cycle would indicate a shift in the face of American leadership—the election introduced an impressive roster of candidates who were *not* White males, one of whom was elected vice president—the work is far from over. Since 2016, the US has experienced a significant surge in reported hate crimes, and while current research does not prove Trump's election caused this increase, the data does suggest a link between Trump's presidency and racist attitudes and behaviors, which regularly emerge when issues such as immigration policy and critical race theory enter public discourse.[82] Currently, the very concept of "truth" is under fire. Trump is often positioned as the grand purveyor of "alternative facts," but broader factors that emerged during his campaign and presidency—highly partisan news media, regular assaults on the press, foreign interference and its robust role in perpetuating falsehoods, and social media circulating and amplifying misinformation and conspiracy theories—have all worked in concert to animate a segment of the population that shuns the notion of objective truth even in the face of incontrovertible evidence. Moreover, the vilification of expertise and anti-intellectualism evident in conversations on issues such as vaccination and climate change suggest that the social and political climate that aided Trump's rise will not disappear anytime soon. If we are to accept HoSang and Lowndes's assertion that "the idea of 'race' has shaped every aspect of political development in U.S. history structurally, institutionally, and culturally," a close study of music and race on the campaign trail becomes all the more vital.[83]

Nota bene: many of the tweets cited in this book are no longer available as they have been taken down due to copyright violation or suspension of the user's account. All quotations from social media and comments from news and video-sharing sites are copied verbatim without correcting spelling/grammar/punctuation.

CHAPTER 1

Keepin' It Real (Respectable)

Barack Obama's Music Strategy and the
Formation of Presidential Identity

There's only one thing different about Barack Obama when it comes to being a Democratic presidential candidate. He's half African-American. Whether that will make any difference, I don't know. I haven't heard him have a strong crackdown on economic exploitation in the ghettos. Payday loans, predatory lending, asbestos, lead. What's keeping him from doing that? Is it because he wants to talk white? . . . He wants to show that he is not a threatening . . . another politically threatening African-American politician. He wants to appeal to white guilt. You appeal to white guilt not by coming on as black is beautiful, black is powerful. Basically, he's coming on as someone who is not going to threaten the white power structure, whether it's corporate or whether it's simply oligarchic. And they love it. Whites just eat it up.

—RALPH NADER TO *ROCKY MOUNTAIN NEWS*, JUNE 2008[1]

Politicians often reveal their musical tastes in interviews or through their selection of a campaign playlist. Jimmy Carter tuned in to Bob Dylan during his downtime, Ronald Reagan capitalized on the popularity of Lee Greenwood's "God Bless the U.S.A.," and George W. Bush's "iPod One" contained country music and classic rock with "a little bit of hard core and honky tonk," a playlist *Rolling Stone* journalist Joe Levy called "safe," "reliable," and "loving."[2] Appearing live, guitar in hand, Bruce Springsteen "brought on [John] Kerry like a rock star" at several rallies in 2004.[3] And in 2008, harnessing the power of YouTube and the cultural phenomenon of reality talent contests, Hillary Clinton demonstrated digital proficiency and her own pop culture cred by launching a "Choose Our Campaign Song" contest via video announcement, through which the selection of her one official campaign song would be left up to her constituents.[4]

Under most circumstances, politicians' personal music tastes or rally playlists on the campaign trail would not be a source of much controversy or even serious inquiry. But in a corporatized electoral landscape where the fields of politics and popular culture are inextricably intertwined, and where every aspect of the candidate's public and private life is subjected to intense scrutiny enabled by the emergence of Web 2.0 technologies, nontraditional texts (such as music) play an increasingly significant role in selling a presidential candidate. During the 2008 presidential primary race, this confluence of political and popular culture was especially apparent in the campaign of newcomer Barack Obama, a candidate whom Naomi Klein later described as "the first U.S. president who is also a superbrand."[5] The contents of Obama's iPod were not just a human-interest story, but also a litmus test to determine his cultural blackness as well as his acceptability as a candidate, even though the public acknowledged the performative dimension of such disclosures. The personal (represented here by music preference) was definitely political.

Barack Hussein Obama II was born in Honolulu in 1961 to a White American mother from Kansas and a Black Kenyan father. After his parents' divorce, the young "Barry" spent some of his formative years in Indonesia living with his mother, her second husband (a Muslim of Javanese descent), and his half sister, as well as in Hawaii with his maternal grandparents. After receiving a bachelor of arts degree from Columbia University in New York, Obama worked as a community organizer on Chicago's South Side. In 1988, he began his studies at Harvard Law School, where he was later selected as the first Black president of the *Harvard Law Review*. Returning to Chicago, he served as a law and government fellow and then lecturer at the University of Chicago Law School, and as a civil rights attorney, before being elected to the Illinois Senate in 1996 and the US Senate in 2004. In the wake of his well-received 2004 speech at the Democratic National Convention, he became one of the party's rising stars. On February 10, 2007, he declared his intentions to seek the presidency of the United States.

From the beginning, Barack Obama was an unconventional candidate. He was multiracial and the son of a Black father who did not share the traditional narrative of enslavement in the United States.[6] The majority of his childhood elapsed outside of the contiguous United States, and his relatives hail from Kenya, Kansas, and Indonesia—in 2006 he described his extended family gatherings as being "like a little mini-United Nations."[7]

While most Black leaders were rooted in the Black church, Obama, who was raised in nonreligious households, did not make a declaration of Christian faith until the late 1980s when he attended Trinity United Church of Christ in Chicago.[8] Moreover, unlike many Black politicians before him, he did not hold leadership roles in the church. At the time he declared his candidacy, he was only forty-five years old, considerably younger than most first-time presidential candidates. Last, he held no familial wealth or connections and had a solidly middle-class upbringing.[9] In his memoir, *Dreams from My Father: A Story of Race and Inheritance* (1995), he ruminated on his family's history, his religious journey, and his own internal conflicts regarding his racial identity.[10] Jerry Harris and Carl Davidson argue that "Obama's personal history is grounded in the multicultural and global reality of today's world."[11] But it was Obama's personal history that caused pundits, politicians, and the public alike to question his blackness, his religion, his citizenship, and his legitimacy as a presidential candidate.

Ralph Nader's incendiary musings serving as the epigraph to this chapter bring the "Is he Black enough?" question into focus. The presidential candidate opined on whether Obama being "half African-American" would compel him to focus his sights on the economic and environmental issues disproportionately affecting Black communities. He treated such a notion with skepticism, as in his mind, Obama was too preoccupied with currying the favor of Whites and even attempted to "talk white" in order to neutralize fears that his candidacy would pose a threat to the White establishment. What Nader failed to acknowledge was the extra layer of pressure on Black public figures to conform to the politics of respectability; they must embrace dominant cultural norms in their presentation in order to achieve widespread acceptance.[12] Nader is an independent activist, but people across the ideological spectrum raised questions regarding Obama's racial identity and its role in shaping his political views. Some Black voters found that their commitment to racial loyalty was dissonant with their need to critique the candidate's policies and politics that did little by way of improving Black lives.

The issue of Obama's blackness also intersects with his religious identity. In March 2008, resurrected soundbites of Obama's pastor, Rev. Dr. Jeremiah Wright, in which he makes what some perceived as anti-American remarks, aired on ABC News and then made the rounds via other news outlets.[13] In a sermon just days after September 11, 2001, Wright suggested that the attacks at the World Trade Center and Pentagon were retribution for violence perpetrated abroad by Americans—the bombings of Hiroshima and Nagasaki and American state-sponsored terrorism against Palestinians and Black South Africans.[14] Although some thought Obama's personal connection with Wright would sink his campaign, he came back just days later with the "A More Perfect Union" speech, where he distanced himself from Wright's inflammatory rhetoric but did not denounce him, offering instead an explanation for how his preacher of two decades fit into what Max Perry Mueller describes as a "lineage of Jeremiah-like, truth-telling justice fighters."[15] Moreover, Obama acknowledged the ways in which racial inequality shaped his own history and is imbricated in the history of the nation, but used the speech as an opportunity to address anger and resentment on the parts of both Black *and* White Americans.[16] As Anthony Pinn notes, Obama "acknowledged racial inequality, but instead tamed the angry [*sic*] over injustice by de-racializing social pain and making it a more general American response that speaks to all suffering."[17] With these universalizing gestures, Obama distanced himself from Black-church radicalism and created an authentic (but non-alienating) racial performance while giving a nod to his own Black and White heritage. And he continued this strategy throughout his campaign, placing his focus on religious pluralism, with an emphasis on the moral and ethical tenets that traverse religious traditions.[18]

Obama's history with Reverend Wright, suspicion regarding his birth certificate, and accusations that he was secretly a Muslim heightened his presumed "foreignness" in the minds of some of his detractors. Architects of the birther movement, which later included Donald Trump, went so far as to challenge the legitimacy of Obama's candidacy. Although these claims emerged from the margins, they did not stay there. Polls in 2009 showed that 24% of those surveyed believed Obama was *not* from the United States and 14% were unsure; another poll showed that 11% believed Obama to be a Muslim.[19] Situating such conspiratorial claims within broader racial logics that demarcate the boundaries of citizenship, Vincent Pham argues that "birther discourses re-inscribe political power and access to the presidency by essentializing loyalty, legitimacy, and allegiance through the rhetoric and logic of the 'natural-born' citizen, untarnished by foreignness."[20]

Since the end of his presidency, scholars across various fields have grappled with Obama's legacy and have retrospectively turned a critical lens to the racial framework from which Obama campaigned and the ways in which he negotiated his own identity and the racial politics that shaped the public's reception to his candidacy.[21] Taking into consideration the unique challenges that Obama faced due to his multiracial identity and complex personal and political background, and the central role media spectacles played in his image formation, this chapter investigates the candidate's engagement with music in 2008 and the discourses it both reflected and engendered in live and virtual contexts.[22] I explore three facets of the primary campaign soundscape: (1) the candidate's engagement with hip-hop—its artists, audiences, and values; (2) the intersections between his professed music tastes and his biography; and (3) the playlists he used at rallies and the factors that allowed this soundtrack to solidify his own identity as a candidate as well as forge alliances with women voters and Black voters, the two constituencies he needed to win over in order to defeat his Democratic rival, Hillary Clinton. Positioning research on the intersections of racial and gender identities in American presidential politics as a critical and contextual frame, I show how Obama's music strategy allowed him to project a Black identity that was both "real" and "respectable."

OBAMA: THE HIP-HOP PRESIDENT

Rap and hip-hop, Murray Forman argues, are "inextricably entwined with race, cultural politics, ideology, and communication in contemporary America.'"[23] Politicians such as Ronald Reagan, George H. W. Bush, Bill Clinton, George W. Bush, John Kerry, and many others have been the unwitting targets of hip-hop verses over the past three decades. However, the relationship between hip-hop and electoral politics was an ambivalent one pre-2008, and, as Shaun Ossei-Owusu maintains, the skepticism and mistrust directed toward the Obama candidacy by some hip-hop devotees might be explained by "hip-hop's historically indignant attitude toward the state."[24] The genre did briefly become a talking point on the campaign trail in June 1992 when presidential hopeful Bill Clinton famously admonished rap artist Sister Souljah (née Lisa Williamson) for expressing what he perceived to be Black extremist viewpoints in the wake of the Los Angeles riots. In a May 1992 interview with the *Washington Post*, she stated,

> I mean, if black people kill black people every day, why not have a week and kill white people? You understand what I'm saying? In other words, white people,

this government and that mayor were well aware of the fact that black people were dying every day in Los Angeles under gang violence. So, if you're a gang member and you would normally be killing somebody, why not kill a white person? Do you think that somebody thinks that white people are better, or above dying, when they would kill their own kind?[25]

The candidate condemned her remarks at a meeting of Jesse Jackson's Rainbow Coalition: "Her [Sister Souljah's] comments before and after Los Angeles were filled with the kind of hatred that you do not honor today and tonight.... If you took the words white and black and reversed them, you might think David Duke was giving that speech."[26] Alluding to her status as a well-informed and respected rap artist and Black social activist, Sister Souljah fired back at Clinton (and the *Post*) for taking her comments out of context and called his authenticity and morality into question.[27] Indeed, this exchange between politician and artist mirrors broader ideological and cultural battles over hip-hop's potential transformative power and legitimacy as a form of social critique, and it substantiates Tricia Rose's claim that hip-hop functions as a lens through which we gauge the status of race and the state of race relations in America.[28]

Although in the 1990s candidates such as Clinton could safely denounce rap artists without fear of political fallout (these remarks likely increased his stock among White working- and middle-class voters), by the dawn of the twenty-first century, hip-hop had transcended racial and economic boundaries and emerged as a transnational, multi-billion-dollar industry with artists and producers who possessed serious political clout. (While hip-hop is a global phenomenon that boasts a diverse fan base, the genre maintains its symbolic connection with Black urban youth.)[29] As Black politician Adam Clayton Powell IV asserted in 2006, the hip-hop generation "dominate[s] everything [culture, music, and economics] except politics, because they generally have not been participating."[30] The industry's engagement with electoral politics reached its height in 2008 with Obama's historic candidacy. Although Russell Simmons (and others in the community) occasionally questioned Obama's ability to effectively address Black issues, he and Sean Combs, as well as other hip-hop artists, such as Jay-Z, Young Jeezy, LL Cool J, Common, Ludacris, and Talib Kweli, endorsed the candidate, performed at rallies and concerts on his behalf, or name-dropped him in their songs. (Travis L. Gosa refers to these tracks and mixtapes as "Obama-Hop.")[31]

Highly visible celebrity artists organized some of these events, but others were the fruits of grassroots community initiatives.

A substantial slice of the "hip-hop generation" embraced Obama, but how did Obama feel about hip-hop?[32] Not surprisingly, the question of hip-hop's cultural value emerged in several interviews with Obama during the 2008 election cycle. The candidate was in a position where he needed to reach out to the hip-hop community but was faced with the predicament of engaging with artists and a genre that, in the eyes of many (both Black and White), glorified drug culture, urban violence, consumer fetishism, and misogyny. At this time, conflict and controversy swirled within the hip-hop community as well: Who does hip-hop represent? Is it politically relevant?

Obama engaged with hip-hop's controversies (what Rose calls the "hip hop wars") when he brought his stance on the genre into the political fray early in 2007. At a fundraising event for the South Carolina Legislative Black Caucus, he criticized radio shock jock Don Imus for referring to the Rutgers University women's basketball team as "nappy-headed hos" during an edition of *Imus in the Morning*.[33] Obama then shifted the focus away from Imus to offer a broader critique:

> We've got to admit to ourselves, that it was not the first time that we heard the word "ho." Turn on the radio station. There are a whole lot of songs that use the same language. . . . We've been permitting it in our homes, and in our schools and on iPods. If it's not good for Don Imus, I don't know why it's good for us. If we don't like other people to degrade us, why are we degrading ourselves?[34]

Obama's attack on rap lyrics bears quite a few affinities with Clinton's uninformed indictment of Sister Souljah in 1992. Both candidates directed their remarks to gatherings of Black political leaders, and both offered universalizing rhetoric that constructs an analogy between the bad behavior of White men and their purported Black counterparts: Clinton established a parallel between the alleged hate speech of Sister Souljah and that of David Duke, a White nationalist and 1992 Republican presidential candidate. Similarly, Obama linked hip-hop artists' degrading language directed toward their sisters to Imus's use of the word "ho" to describe a team of female athletes. In making such comparisons, both candidates failed to acknowledge either the institutionalized inequalities and material realities that fuel hip-hop or the role that hyperbole and parody have historically played in various Black cultural practices. Shortly after the Caucus event, Simmons called out the candidate on his indictment of lyrics, claiming, "What we need to reform is the conditions that create these lyrics. Obama needs to reform the conditions of poverty."[35]

In later appearances over the course of the primary campaign, the candidate addressed the issue of lyrics in a more nuanced manner that demonstrated a greater awareness and appreciation of Black urban cultures. In a 2008 BET interview with Jeff Johnson, the candidate attempted to draw a division between hip-hop's art and its message:

> Honestly, I love the art of hip-hop; I don't always love the message of hip-hop. There are times where, even on the ones that I, even with the artists I named, the artists I love, you know, there's a message that is not only sometimes degrading to women, not only uses the N-word a little too frequently, but also, it's something I'm really concerned about, it's always talking about material things. You know, always talking about how I can get something, you know, how, you know, I've got more money, more, you know, cars, more, and . . . I think the potential for them [hip-hop artists] to deliver a message of extraordinary power that gets people thinking. I mean, you know, the thing about hip-hop today is, it's smart, I mean, you know, a lot—it's insightful. The way that they can communicate a complex message in a very short space, is remarkable. . . . . I understand folks want to be rooted in the community. They want to be down, but what I always say is that, you know, hip-hop is not just a mirror of what is. It should also be a reflection of what can be.[36]

By privileging the creativity inherent in the process of composition (the art) over the lyrical content (the message), Obama shields himself from critics of the genre, while acknowledging the larger systemic failures that gave rise to the social conditions many hip-hop artists explicate in their music. The candidate also makes a plea for art's ethical obligation to envisage a brighter future rather than merely fixate on the present. Rootedness in the community (or keepin' it real), he implies, can be compatible with this imagined future. Moreover, with this statement he refrains from directly criticizing hip-hop performers and instead positions these artists and their fan communities as holding the potential, through their cultural practice, to initiate the changes he envisions. And this vision did come to fruition, albeit for a short period. Travis L. Gosa and Erik Nielson's research documents "the 'Obamafication of rap': a

brief renaissance of socially conscious lyrics and the widespread participation of celebrity rappers in the political process."[37]

In July 2008, Obama made similar remarks in an interview with Jann
Wenner of *Rolling Stone*, stating, "I am troubled sometimes by the misogyny and materialism of a lot of rap lyrics, but I think the genius of the
art form has shifted the culture and helped to desegregate music. . . . It
would be nice if I could have my daughters listen to their music without
me worrying that they were getting bad images of themselves."[38] Again,
the candidate acknowledges the objectionable lyrical content, but uses
the word "art" to describe the genre and positions hip-hop's "genius"
alongside its ability to promote desegregation. The candidate also plays
the role of concerned father, once again praising the art's potential while
implying that it still needs to rethink its representation of women. The
wise father figure may have also held sway with the hip-hoppers themselves. Journalist Gabe Meline writes, "Hip-hop can think of Obama as
a really, really cool dad. He'll trust hip-hop to be good, and it'll occasionally live up to that trust. It'll do things he disapproves of, but he'll be
tolerant, with measured criticism."[39]

In assuming the father role, Obama also established generational distance, a strategy he deployed in other interviews as well. In September
2008, *MTV News* asked the candidate how he felt about the hip-hop community's excitement over his candidacy. Obama responded by highlighting the gap between his own teenage years and hip-hop's infancy, stating
"I'm a little older than hip-hop culture. I was there at the beginning, but I
was already getting older."[40] He admitted to shuffling Jay-Z and Kanye on
his iPod, but positioned himself as an onlooker who has enjoyed watching "this hip-hop generation" grow. Although Obama does not technically
fall into Bakari Kitwana's definition of the hip-hop generation, a cohort
that includes Black Americans born between 1965 and 1984, he did indeed
come of age during the era of hip-hop.[41] In any case, hip-hop's "really cool
dad" chose instead to identify himself as an "old school" guy who prefers
the iconic Black performers of the 1960s and 1970s, a point he expressed in
an interview with Hot 97 radio.[42]

Despite the distancing strategies and cautious admission of fandom,
the candidate at times subtly hinted that he was indeed "in the know"
(although not too much) with regard to hip-hop. Obama sauntered onstage
to "Crazy in Love," the anthem of hip-hop's supercouple Beyoncé and Jay-
Z, during an October 2007 appearance on *The Ellen DeGeneres Show*.[43]

In the BET interview where he criticized rap's message, he also praised Jay-Z's lexical virtuosity because, "as Jay would say, 'he's got flow,'" and referred to the mogul's album *American Gangster* as "tight."[44] With these accolades, the candidate not only drops his knowledge, but also demonstrates his allegiance to the community by appropriating hip-hop vernacular. Although on several occasions the candidate expressed vexation over the artists' penchant for materialism, he praised the business acumen of hip-hop producers in the *Rolling Stone* interview: "I know Jay-Z. I know Ludacris. I know Russell Simmons. I know a bunch of these guys. They are great talents and great businessmen, which is something that doesn't get emphasized enough."[45] Indeed, an entrepreneurial spirit and strong work ethic imbues Obama-endorsing artists with an air of respectability.[46]

However, Obama may have wished to retract his praise of Ludacris's business sense shortly after this interview. In late July, the artist released "Politics as Usual," a track that included derisive remarks about Hillary Clinton, George W. Bush, and John McCain. Quick to respond, the Obama team deemed the song offensive not only to the individuals directly targeted in its lyrics, but also "to all of us who are trying to raise our children with the values we hold dear." Once again pinpointing the message rather than the artist, Obama's spokesman Bill Burton stated, "While Ludacris is a talented individual he should be ashamed of these lyrics."[47] Tricia Rose has called out social critics who take a stance against the sexism in hip-hop yet publicly demonstrate their support for the artists who promote it.[48] Obama might be considered a part of this camp. His contradictory actions irked potential voters, many of whom lodged their complaints online. Citing the candidate's need for youth votes as a reason why Obama would keep the artist in his coterie, one retorted, "Obama will publicly condemn Ludacris and privately pat him on the back—then say, 'I'm just messing with you man.'"[49]

In his attempts to frame himself as "in the know," the candidate did not limit himself to interviews or controversies where hip-hop momentarily became the topic of focus. In a speech the day after the ABC News debate where, according to Obama, opponent Hillary Clinton played "the textbook Washington game," the younger senator demonstrated his attitude toward her acrimonious barbs by physically brushing the metaphorical dirt off his shoulders. He nonchalantly remarked, "When you're running for the presidency, then you've gotta expect it, and, you know, you just gotta kinda let it . . . you know, you know. That's what you gotta do."

Obama's shoulder-brushing gesture, which blogger Spencer Ackerman cited as "perhaps the coolest subliminal cultural reference in the history of American politics," alludes to "Dirt off Your Shoulder," a 2003 Jay-Z hit.[50] With this physical cue—a prime example of the candidate's deft code-switching—Obama not only safely pays homage to a hip-hop standard and its artist, but also forms an alliance with the genre and its community by appropriating and recontextualizing a message in the song that he could agree with—that is, the choice to confront hostility in a nonaggressive manner.[51] And as the candidate wittily demonstrates, a decision to take the higher ground can be made in the realm of politics, just as it can on the street. By appropriating this multivalent gesture, Obama embraces the respectable side of street culture while remaining removed from the actual language of the song—and rejects the more nefarious aspects of street life: crime and violence.[52]

The candidate delivered this gesture to an audience primarily consisting of young White voters; however, he most likely did so with the knowledge that many of these youngsters came of age around the same time as *The Black Album*, and that the clip would quickly go viral.[53] Shortly after the April 17 speech, his campaign placed the video clip on YouTube, and the mashups quickly followed.[54] In one popular mashup, "Barack Gets That Dirt off His Shoulders," footage from Obama's speech is interspersed with video clips of various detractors criticizing the candidate, while Jay-Z's 2003 album serves as the backing track. One clip includes Clinton commenting on Obama's relationship with Jeremiah Wright, and in another, she dismisses some of her opponent's remarks as "elitist" and "out of touch." When Obama reaches the point in his speech with the "dirt off your shoulder" gesture, the music shifts from "Moment of Clarity" to "Dirt off Your Shoulder" as he brushes off superimposed images of Hillary Clinton, Bill Clinton, Charles Gibson, George Stephanopoulos, and of course, the kitchen sink.[55]

Another mashup based on the same speech, "Obama Dirt off Your Shoulder Remix," alternates footage of the candidate's gesture with his enviable "Crazy in Love" dance moves displayed on *The Ellen DeGeneres Show*.[56] After the video flashes a photo of Obama proudly standing in front of a towering Superman statue, "Dirt off Your Shoulder" fades out and Jay-Z's "99 Problems" begins. With the phrase "I got ninety-nine problems but a bitch ain't one," the creator juxtaposes close-up, still images of a choleric-appearing Clinton with more footage of Obama dancing. The still images of Clinton's contorted, unnatural facial expressions make her appear as a caricature of the stereotypical, militant feminist man-hater detractors wished to portray her as, whereas Obama becomes more relatable as the viewer watches his casual, fluid grooves captured in the video footage. These dance moves, like Bill Clinton's Elvis-inspired sax-blowing fifteen years earlier, affirm the candidate's coolness and pop culture cred. Stylish photos of the rapper Ghostface Killah (Dennis Coles), singer Morrissey, and actress Scarlett Johansson appear with the text "VOTING FOR OBAMA" on the bottom of the screen. An image of an overweight, long-haired, shirtless man lounging on his bed surrounded by guitars, guns, and ammo with the text "VOTING FOR MCCAIN" comes next. Thus, the mashup establishes a comparison between Obama's cool, hip, and sexy supporters, and Republican candidate John McCain's purportedly portly, gun-toting "redneck" supporters. With these images, the creator unabashedly constructs stereotypes of race, gender, and even class: Black men have rhythm, feminists are angry, and poor Whites cling to their guns. He also pairs images of "heroic" gangstas (including Obama) with images of objectified women and positions the viewer/voter as both a witness to the unfolding spectacle and a potential arbiter of taste: flat-chested women support Clinton, and voluptuous women endorse Obama (in this case, Natalie Portman and Scarlett Johansson, respectively). Using a hip-hop-influenced filmic aesthetic, images are appropriated, recontextualized, and collaged to create a counternarrative within campaign discourses—in this narrative, Obama becomes a "real" hip-hop icon. He has the smooth moves, the superhuman strength, and the decorative women, and no one can stand in his way.[57]

According to the *New York Times*, viewers spent 14.5 million hours watching the Obama campaign's official content created for YouTube.[58] But the candidate's supporters (and detractors) were more than just passive spectators. On his campaign website, Obama offered voters sophisticated participatory frameworks that facilitated user invention and interactivity, and this spilled over into the musical realm.[59] "Yes We Can" is the most well-known music video of the 2008 campaign, but countless others created by the public circulated online.[60] Music videos, newly composed songs, and mashups (like those created by users "jarts" and "Bill3948") drew from preexisting material, including candidate speeches, images, and songs. One blogger even referred to 2008 as the "year of the campaign song."[61] The video responses to the "Dirt off Your Shoulder" speech I cite here are just a few of the many instances where YouTube's participatory, video-based culture facilitated the construction of a dialogically constituted campaign soundscape.

OBAMA: THE "OLD SCHOOL" GUY

Although the accessibility of social media and the availability of user-generated content sites have democratized the soundscape to some extent, candidates continue to control their sonic image by divulging their musical tastes and by selecting campaign playlists for their rallies and other appearances. Indeed, Obama needed to target the hip-hop generation (a cohort with historically low participation in electoral politics), but his success in the primary was also to some extent contingent on his ability to draw in older Black voters. Obama's rally playlists and personal playlists affirmed both his realness and respectability, while also solidifying his relationship with this constituency.

Establishing a narrative that positioned Obama's candidacy as an extension of the civil rights movement was a significant thread of his overarching strategy. Obama was multiracial and spent some of his formative years abroad; therefore, he did not share the same background or experience the same struggles as the Black American political luminaries who paved the way for his success. In March 2007, shortly after announcing his candidacy, Obama merged his biography with the saga of the civil rights movement as he spoke at the Selma Voting Rights March Commemoration at Brown Chapel A.M.E. Church in Alabama, the departure point for the 1965 Selma to Montgomery marches. In his speech, he discussed how the lives of his father (who was able to study in the United States because of Kennedy's policies) and his mother (who was permitted to marry his father), as well as his own aspirations for an education and political office, were made possible by the men and women who fought for civil rights in the 1960s. (The accuracy of this narrative was later questioned.)[62] With the aplomb of a Black preacher, he drew a parallel between the biblical heroics of Moses and the accomplishments of civil rights leaders (past and present), a rhetorical strategy adopted by Martin Luther King Jr. and other Black church leaders who often imagined biblical heroes as their partners in struggle.[63] Drawing on the common narratives of liberation theology, Obama extended the lineage by positioning himself and his audience as "the Joshua Generation," citizens who possess the moral imperative to continue the battle "not just on behalf of African Americans but on behalf of all of America."[64] Although Obama began with the battles pertaining to civil rights, he positioned this historically specific struggle within larger, more universal struggles to ensure and preserve American freedoms. In doing so, he bolstered his "political blackness" for aging Black voters, the cohort defined by the civil rights movement, while still maintaining the relevance of the fight for (in a generalized sense) the public at large.[65] Like Bill Clinton before him, Obama's "reaccentuation of rhetorical traditions in a performative display of practical wisdom" allowed him to construct rhetorical authority, thereby affirming his legitimacy as a spokesperson for the Black community.[66]

Personal and public playlists aided Obama in this quest for legitimacy. The presidential hopeful opined on his tastes in interviews for *Rolling Stone*, BET, MTV, Hot 97, and *Vibe*, as well as in a *Blender* article that polled both Obama and Republican opponent John McCain on their top ten favorite songs.[67] Although Daniel Blim rightly describes the candidate's tastes as an eclectic mix with broad appeal, Table 2 shows that Black music of the 1960s and 1970s dominated his list of preferences.[68] The Black performers Obama admires offer star personas and generic connotations that conjure up clusters of beneficial associations. For example, Miles Davis and John Coltrane, regarded as jazz innovators, reached the height of their success and recognition during the 1960s, the era when jazz accumulated significant cultural capital. But even setting aside the specifics of these canonized performers, the nostalgic music has something of value to offer the "old school" candidate. As Murray Forman has posited, the flexibility of the term "old school" allows it to be strategically deployed in generational contexts whereby it can project onto an individual values or virtues that connect them to something of enduring cultural value, rather than the ephemeral tastes of the present moment.[69] Obama's enduring soundtrack musically aligned him with the values of the civil rights movement.

When creating rally playlists, the Obama team likely took their cues from the candidate's list of favorites—his "public" music was an extension of his private tastes. (The Xs in Table 2 indicate artists Obama cited in interviews who were also represented on his rally playlists.)[70] This continuity is significant, considering the flak Hillary Clinton received for the list of songs her team preselected for her "Choose Our Campaign Song" contest ballot; critics questioned whether or not the ballot faithfully reflected her own musical interests. At rallies, Obama offered a diverse soundtrack overall—he used perennial candidate favorites U2, Bruce Springsteen, and Brooks & Dunn, among others. The contents of the rally playlist shifted over the course of the campaign, and the candidate's team likely took into consideration the expected audience, the state of the campaign, and local preferences when making these decisions. However, as one playlist from a January 2008 event shows, R & B formed the backbone of his rally soundscape (Table 3).[71] Although not included on the list for this event, Curtis Mayfield's "Move on Up" (1970), Aretha Franklin's "Think" (1968), The Staple Singers' "I'll Take You There" (1972), and Jackie Wilson's "(Your Love Keeps Lifting Me) Higher and Higher" (1967) were in steady rotation as well. Of the twenty-one tracks on this rally playlist, ten can be classified as R & B hits from the 1960s or 1970s. With the exception of the songs by Natasha Bedingfield, India.Arie, and U2, the entire list comprises songs that predate 2003. Like Bill Clinton before him, Obama fashioned his nostalgic campaign playlist with the sounds of his own coming of age.

Noting the affinities between Obama's message of hope and change and the ideals of Chicago soul performers Sam Cooke, Curtis Mayfield, and the Staple Singers, one *Chicago Sun-Times* journalist even went so far as to claim that "the unbending spirit of the 1960s and '70s Chicago soul movement helped put Obama on that stage [in Grant Park for his victory speech]."[72] Indeed, the hip-hop generation embraced Obama as their own, but so did fans of soul, who even started their own "Soul Music Lovers For Obama" group on his campaign website with the rallying call, "From the inner cities to the suburbs, Sen. Obama unites us like the music we love." Although millennials may have associated Obama's cool posture with the swagger of a rap icon, Mavis Staples saw an earlier model: Obama, she claimed, "has that same walk Sam [Cooke] did with [the gospel group] the Soul Stirrers."[73]

Rally playlists also aligned Obama with the ethos of Motown. With its slick, polished production style and fusion of pop and R & B, the genre appealed to a broad market while simultaneously bringing professional recognition to Black artists as well as affording them artistic self-determination. Institutionalized racism and exploitation still persisted alongside practices that precipitated the integration and assimilation of Black artists, but Motown, its crossover music, and its artists have retrospectively come to signify the breakdown of firmly entrenched social divisions as well as the promotion of interracial understanding—the central initiatives of the civil rights movement.[74] In his live appearances for

Table 2. Barack Obama's taste in music, 2007–8. This table shows the music preferences Obama declared in interviews with *Rolling Stone*, BET, MTV, Hot 97, *Vibe*, and *Blender*

Artist cited in interview	Cited artist also represented on rally playlist	Song or album cited in interview	Genre
Beyoncé			R & B
John Coltrane			jazz
Common			rap
Sheryl Crow	X		pop/rock
Miles Davis			jazz
Bob Dylan		*Blood on the Tracks* Maggie's Farm	folk
Earth, Wind & Fire	X		R & B
Aretha Franklin	X	Think	R & B
The Fugees		Ready or Not	pop/rock, rap
Marvin Gaye	X	What's Going On	R & B
The Grateful Dead			pop/rock
Howlin' Wolf			blues
The Isley Brothers	X		R & B
Jay-Z		*American Gangster*	rap
Elton John			pop/rock
Yo-Yo Ma			classical
OutKast			rap
Charlie Parker			jazz
Nina Simone		Sinnerman	jazz
Frank Sinatra		You'd Be So Easy to Love	stage & screen
Rolling Stones		Gimme Shelter	pop/rock
Bruce Springsteen	X	I'm on Fire The Rising	pop/rock
The Temptations	X		R & B
U2	X	City of Blinding Lights	pop/rock
Kanye West	X	Touch the Sky	rap
will.i.am	X	Yes We Can	rap, R & B

Table 2—*Continued*

Artist cited in interview	Cited artist also represented on rally playlist	Song or album cited in interview	Genre
Stevie Wonder	X	*Music of My Mind* *Talking Book* *Innervisions* *Fulfillingness' First Finale* *Songs in the Key of Life*	R & B

Table 3. Playlist for a January 2008 Barack Obama rally

Song title	Artist	Date
Ain't No Mountain High Enough	Marvin Gaye and Tammi Terrell	1967
St. Elmo's Fire (Man in Motion)	John Parr	1985
The Best	Tina Turner	1989
Takin' It to the Streets	The Doobie Brothers	1976
Shining Star	Earth, Wind & Fire	1975
Give the People What They Want	The O'Jays	1975
Hold On, I'm Comin'	Sam & Dave	1966
Celebration	Kool & the Gang	1980
Unwritten	Natasha Bedingfield	2004
Shout	The Isley Brothers	1959
Get Ready	The Temptations	1966
There's Hope	India.Arie	2006
Ain't No Stoppin' Us Now	McFadden & Whitehead	1979
I'll Take You There	The Staple Singers	1972
Still the One	Orleans	1976
Everyday People	Sly and the Family Stone	1968
Long Train Runnin'	The Doobie Brothers	1973
Sir Duke	Stevie Wonder	1976
Centerfield	John Fogerty	1985
City of Blinding Lights (Obama Entrance)	U2	2004
Signed, Sealed, Delivered I'm Yours	Stevie Wonder	1970

the candidate, Motown's erstwhile wunderkind, Stevie Wonder, directly referred to Martin Luther King Jr., the legacy of the civil rights movement, and Obama's place in that lineage.

Wonder was a twenty-year-old prodigy when he released "Signed, Sealed, Delivered I'm Yours" on his critically successful album *Signed, Sealed & Delivered* in 1970.[75] Since then, he has received countless accolades for a career spanning six decades. The spirited song was a staple for 2008 rallies, and the artist performed the song on the last night of the Democratic National Convention and in sing-along style at the Neighborhood Inaugural Ball. An article in the *New York Times* revealed that Obama campaign chief strategist David Axelrod even used the song as an exclusive ringtone for incoming calls from the candidate.[76] The song was also included on the campaign's compilation CD, *Yes We Can: Voices of a Grassroots Movement*. In his 2008 *Rolling Stone* interview, Obama, a lifelong Stevie fan, stated, "When I was just at that point where you start getting involved in music, Stevie had that run with *Music of My Mind, Talking Book, Fulfillingness' First Finale*, and *Innervisions*, and then *Songs in the Key of Life*. Those are as brilliant a set of five albums as we've ever seen."[77] The interview leaves no question in the reader's mind as to whether or not Obama truly loves Wonder's music as he demonstrates here his keen knowledge of the artist's history and catalog.

"Signed, Sealed, Delivered I'm Yours," narrated from a first-person perspective, features a man singing of his fierce love for a woman. The song's verses, with musings such as "Seen a lot of things in this old world / when I touched them, they did nothing, girl" and "That's why I know you're my one and only desire," establish the relationship between the man and his female addressee as a monogamous one. Wonder and the backup singers punctuate these verses by singing the refrain "Ooh, baby, here I am, signed, sealed, delivered I'm yours" together in a homorhythmic texture with dense chordal harmonies. The homorhythmic verses give way to call-and-response textures with overlapping entries in the choruses and the outro. As the backup singers chant "signed, sealed, delivered" here, Wonder quips, "You've got my future in your hands" above them, creating a layered effect, but with each line equally emphasized, perhaps suggesting equal footing between the man and woman. At the second bridge, one of the backup singers interrupts Wonder's line, "But here I am / with your future," with a wailing high note before he can sing the word "am," and thus, for a fleeting moment, a woman takes up the vocal lead. The song's call-and-response texture affirms their mutual celebration of shared affection.

At first glance, the hook, "signed, sealed, delivered I'm yours," may be understood as the declaration of a haughty and boastful lover who perceives himself as a "gift" to the addressee, or, in the case of the Obama campaign, the braggadocio of a hubristic politician who thinks he has clinched his party's nomination. However, I would argue the playful interaction between Wonder and the backup singers, the surrounding text, and Wonder's own vocal stylings lessen the presumed arrogance of the hook, which simply states that the man (Wonder) "belongs" to the addressee (represented by the female backup singers). The man's pronouncement, "I'm yours" (rather than "You're mine"), puts the addressee in the dominant position. The organization of voices, most significantly the fact that the female backup singers sing the hook along with Wonder in harmonious accord, suggests that the addressee elatedly accepts his offer. At times, the man appears meek and self-deprecating. He sings, "Like a fool I went and stayed too long" and "I've done a lot of foolish things," thus confessing his own wrongdoings. Although the song never makes clear what has transpired between this couple, the phrase "Now I'm back" could be an indication that some process of growth, self-awareness, or transformation has taken place in the man's life. Additionally, the man frames his happiness and restoration of wholeness as contingent upon her willingness to accept him. The addressee holds the power to accept or refuse what is signed, sealed, and delivered to her. The man, in other words, can only be empowered through her, as she's got his future in her hands. The admission of culpability for some unstated transgression, the confession of brokenness, and an outward display of emotion (he is "not ashamed to cry") weakens—or, one might argue, feminizes—the male protagonist. Text aside, Wonder's vocal style in the song, rooted in the tradition of female gospel singing with its whoops, sighs, and stratospheric range, reinforces the man's subordinate position.

Before addressing how songs like "Signed, Sealed, Delivered I'm Yours" allowed Obama to engage with female voters, then, it is worth briefly exploring the ways in which Wonder's song, and the rally playlists more broadly, mirrored and propagated discourses regarding Obama's own feminine style and its connection with his identity as a Black candidate. In a 2008 editorial, Carol Marin stated, "If Bill Clinton was once considered America's first Black president, Obama may one day be viewed as our first woman president."[78] Her journalistic piece was one of many that dissected the candidate's feminine communication style, rhetoric, and approach to leadership. According to Philippa Roberts and Jane Cunningham, Obama's values were "more collaborative, more human, more feelings-led and people-focused" than Hillary Clinton's.[79] Although the former First Lady's gender strategy morphed over the course of the primary, one labor leader extolled her "testicular fortitude" late in the game, and Governor Mike Easley (D-NC) even claimed she "[made] Rocky Balboa look like a pansy."[80] Indeed, team Clinton played up their candidate's tenacity and framed her as a fighter, and in doing so, they mitigated the image of Hillary Clinton as First Lady and helpmate to Bill Clinton, or even drew attention away from her failure to serve in the traditional ways expected of a politician's wife.[81] Several articles in the mainstream press played up the apparent gender role reversal between the two Democratic frontrunners with titles such as "Leading Like a Girl: For Men Only," "Hillary Is from Mars, Obama Is from Venus," and "¿Quién Es Less Macho?"[82]

Whereas many candidates who preceded Obama primarily tapped into the concept of the "mythic presidency" by emphasizing the virtues of strength and charisma, the Obama campaign humanized the candidate by focusing on idealized intimate relationships.[83] (The "concerned father" narrative that the candidate adopted in response to hip-hop exemplifies this strategy.) The campaign soundtrack followed suit. Like other candidates before him, Obama did use the music of iconic rocker Bruce Springsteen, but rather than relying primarily on his testosterone-driven, rousing 1980s anthems, he featured songs like "The Rising" from the artist's post-9/11 album of the same title, which meditates on the themes of redemption and healing.[84] The Boss himself offered live performances of some of his older melancholy and introspective songs, such as "The Promised Land," "Youngstown," and "Thunder Road," at a few Obama rallies. Although far less subdued, the songs recorded by Stevie Wonder, Jackie Wilson, and Curtis Mayfield are smooth and sentimental, and the general tenor is the power of love as opposed to power chords.[85] It would be somewhat of an overgeneralization to describe this music as "feminine" per se; however, these songs shun the more virulent, aggressive aspects of masculinity in favor of an ethos of nurturing, caring, and responsiveness.[86]

Pre-2008 campaign playlists of unaltered pop songs favored solo male performers or all-male bands; however, the Obama camp embraced music featuring female lead performers or backup singers—perhaps suggesting a harmony between the genders, rather than "One man triumphs over adversity" narratives. In one coffee shop appearance (where the candidate brought along his younger daughter, Sasha), the Indigo Girls' female empowerment anthem "Hammer and a Nail" preceded his speech.[87] Although the Indigo Girls never became standard fare at Obama events, the music of another feminist artist did. Like "Signed, Sealed, Delivered I'm Yours," Aretha Franklin's "Think" offers a spirited refrain. In this song, the singer and her backup vocalists (or the audience) bandy the word "freedom" back and forth (which at least partly explains its appeal as a campaign song). Considering Franklin's iconic status and the song's strong connection with both the civil rights and women's equality movements, the elevation of heterosexual monogamy in the lyrics (as in Wonder's song) may be less significant than its connotations related to racial equality, Black self-determination, and female empowerment. The song's funky style, blaring horn section, and kinetic drive that incrementally increases in both texture and dynamic level, as well as Franklin's raw vocal style, epitomize the "Say it loud, I'm Black and I'm proud" ethos of soul artists in the 1960s and 1970s who refused to bend to more polished, pop-oriented methods of production.

As a Black candidate, Obama could not uncritically embrace the garden-variety "regular guy" tropes deployed by the White male candidates who preceded him, Jackson Katz argues.[88] We see such tropes in the playlist of Obama's Republican opponent, Senator John McCain, who made use of "Gonna Fly Now" and "Eye of the Tiger" (from the *Rocky* films), songs that surely reinforce what Katherine Adam and Charles Derber call the "supermasculinized vision of international politics" that defined the Republican brand in 2008.[89] In selecting nostalgic and sentimental love songs such as Wonder's, and also Wilson's "(Your Love Keeps Lifting Me) Higher and Higher," Obama performed the comforting and assimilationist "Good Black Man" side of what Frank Rudy Cooper calls bipolar black masculinity. A desire to avoid perpetuating stereotypes about Black male sexuality—that is, Cooper's threatening and race-affirming "Bad Black Man" side of Black bipolarity—may have steered the candidate's team away from selecting other artists of the same era such as James Brown or Wilson Pickett.[90] These stereotypes are, of course, another reason why Obama kept hip-hop at a safe distance while skillfully appropriating some of its linguistic and gestural modes of signification.[91] In her study on visual representation and presidential masculinities, Emma Cannen argues that "whilst

Obama transcends mainstream hip-hop's construction and promotion of African American men as hypersexual violent criminals, he retains and embodies its maleness, ghetto-cool and aura of protest masculinity."[92] An "aura of protest" still shaped the rally playlists, but the candidate, on many occasions, chose the safer route of specifically female protest songs (not surprisingly, Franklin's "Respect" also graced the Obama soundtrack, albeit with less frequency).

Whereas Hillary Clinton attempted to downplay her marriage, Obama highlighted his role in the familial sphere and frequently praised his wife. Indeed, songs such as Wonder's, which praises monogamy, and Wilson's, which apotheosizes the saving power of romantic attachment, elevate the domesticated male as a source of inspiration. As I cited earlier in my discussion of Obama's response to hip-hop lyrics, the candidate often alluded to being the father of two young daughters when calling for social change and spoke in relational terms about the importance of nurturing parents. In one instance, he went so far as to criticize absentee Black fathers for failing their children.[93] Indeed, the candidate aligned himself with what Anthony Lemelle calls "dutiful masculinity," in that he emphasized the centrality of family and fatherhood in the life of the Black male.[94]

Obama's soundtrack not only reinforced his image as a sensitive guy and devoted husband, but also served him up as a romantic leading man, and this positioning spilled over into DIY expressions of devotion to the candidate. In the viral video "Crush on Obama," model Amber Lee Ettinger (Obama Girl) boldly positions the candidate as an object of both political and sexual desire.[95] The candidate himself did not respond too fondly to the scantily-clad Ettinger's performance: in an interview, he acknowledged the lighthearted tone of the video, but said he "wish[ed] people would think about what impact their actions have on kids and families"—yet another performance of dutiful masculinity in response to questionable music.[96] The general public's response, however, was quite different: the video received 3.1 million hits on YouTube between June and August 2007.[97] But of course not everyone embraced "Obama mania" with unbridled enthusiasm. One conservative journalist, berating citizens affected by the "Obama crush," claimed the phenomenon only served to prove the mindless ignorance of liberal women:

> Everywhere Obama goes, before he even opens his mouth, Democrat women fall all over themselves in awe. They chant. They swoon. They get so all fired up

and excited that they don't even seem to consider what utter *fools* they are making of themselves. . . . I've actually heard women say they *love* him, though they know nothing about him except that he is running for president.[98]

Like "Crush on Obama," several of the songs featured at rallies—"Signed, Sealed, Delivered I'm Yours," "(Your Love Keeps Lifting Me) Higher and Higher," and "Ain't No Mountain High Enough"—explore the dimensions of romantic relationships. Although the women seem to have the upper hand in the unions represented, and the men show hints of vulnerability, both music and lyrics affirm that it takes two; with these songs, the candidate thus reaffirms the traditional values of family and fidelity, but with a progressive edge. The Obamas themselves exemplify this relationship dynamic: Barack once stated, "It's true my wife is smarter (and better looking)—she's also a little meaner than I am."[99] And as an article titled "Wife Lessons: Why Michelle Obama Is No Hillary Clinton" pointed out, the press embraced Michelle's "Tough Broad" narrative, describing her as "strong-willed," "gutsy," "regal," "steely," "direct," "outspoken," and "military" in bearing.[100] Her stereotypically masculine traits may have feminized the candidate to a certain extent, but like Obama's own deployment of a feminized communication style, such gendered performances on her part allowed him to transcend stereotypes regarding Black masculinity without appearing emasculated.

Within the context of the women-loving-Obama phenomenon, the relationships constructed in these songs can symbolize the desired, ideal relationship between candidate and voter, and a desire for monogamy can become analogous with political loyalty. Figure 2 illustrates how the personal might be mapped onto the political in "Signed, Sealed, Delivered I'm Yours." Like the female addressee in Wonder's song, who is in a position to empower the male protagonist through her love, the women constituents are in a position to empower the candidate—which they accomplish through voting (the ultimate civic responsibility). Man (the candidate) is made (president) through Woman (the voter). Thus, this symbolic exchange establishes a system of reciprocity: women empower the candidate with votes, and in turn the candidate empowers women through his progressive social policies.

In discussing the content of pop songs and their potential to evoke emotional responses, Simon Frith argues, "Pop love songs do not 'reflect' emotions, then, but give people the romantic terms in which to articu-

> Protagonist [Man] (empowered by) →Addressee [Woman] can achieve wholeness
>
> OR
>
> If voters use romantic terms to articulate a "political" relationship:
>
> Presidential Candidate [Man] (empowered by) → Voter [Woman] can become president
>
> AND
>
> Voter [Woman] (empowered by) → President [Man] can gain agency through his
> progressive social program

Fig. 2. Signed, Sealed, Delivered: Obama and the woman voter; the personal becomes political. Figure by author.

late and so experience their emotions."[101] A questionnaire and interviews I conducted with women who attended 2008 Obama rallies suggest that songs employing what Frith calls "romantic terms" can indeed be used by voters to articulate their relationships to a politician. Consider one fifty-year-old woman's response to the question, "What does the phrase 'signed, sealed, delivered I'm yours' mean to you?"

> As a love song (originally), of course it means I give myself to the other totally, completely. In the context of the election, I feel it is meant to convey loyalty, truth, and hope. Upon reflection, I believe it to mean that the action is reciprocal. In taking the gift of my complete commitment to the other, I am also offering trust, which I hope to receive in return. Signed and sealed—a relationship that I would hope to be getting back in the same spirit in which I, my "self," is offered.[102]

The informants were not specifically asked to comment on how their understanding of the song's romantic relationship might be understood as political allegiance or affiliation. However, several responded to the question by drawing an analogy between the two. Here, the informant zones in on loyalty, truth, and reciprocity—three themes touched upon in the song. She also suggests that the song implies "hope," even though the lyrics do not make a direct or even oblique reference to this sentiment. She may be recalling a theme in Wonder's song catalog, or perhaps the idea of hope came to her mind because it served as a central tenet of Obama's campaign platform. As Peter Wicke has posited:

The "content" of rock songs cannot be reduced to what is directly played or even what appears to be expressed in the lyrics. For its listeners these aspects only form the medium of which they themselves make *active* use. They integrate them into their lives and use them as symbols to make public their own experiences, just as, seen from another angle, these aspects give the experience of social reality a cultural form conveyed by the senses and thereby influence that reality.[103]

In other words, just as the informant projects the foundation for a strong romantic relationship onto a possible political one with Obama, Obama's campaign message inflects her reading of the song. The participatory engagement motivated by the song's prominent texture—call-and-response—works to facilitate this exchange on a sonic level. Richard Middleton claims that call-and-response signifies conversation and mutuality, and I would argue that this texture, which pervades Obama's soul-centric playlists, establishes a spirited dialectic between the songs' lead vocalists and backup singers, who may stand in for Obama and his female voters respectively.[104]

Of course, not all women engaged with the music in this way. One twenty-two-year-old rally attendee provided the following response to the "Signed, Sealed, Delivered I'm Yours" inquiry: "[The song has] got a good beat, and [it is] fun to listen to, but I don't really think about anything while listening."[105] Even if the attendees did not engage with the song's lyrics and themes in the manner shown in Figure 2, the act of participating in and of itself reinforced the idea of mutuality for attendees at any level of musical competence. The young informant affirmed this viewpoint: observing the rally attendees' responses to the song, she reported, "Most people clapped or sang along. It was a very charged atmosphere." Music, in this sense, engenders entrainment, what Satinder P. Gill refers to as "the coordinating of the timing of our behaviors and the synchronizing of our attentional resources."[106] In the videos I viewed of Obama rallies, supporters chose to sing either the call or the response portions of songs; such involvement requires them to listen, wait, and respond at the right moment. Although they might not have viewed their participatory gestures as an affirmation of loyalty to the candidate, the physical act of singing and the active engagement requisite to call-and-response were powerful exercises in community building that allowed voters to see and hear the harmonious communities Obama imagines in his speeches.

As Frith suggests, music (in this case, campaign music) can serve as the vehicle through which people voice their emotions. Perhaps the presence of music allows feeling to eclipse fact. As Katz suggests in his study of presidential masculinity, "Presidential elections in the age of media spectacle are won and lost largely in the realm of myth, symbolism, and identity, where *feelings* about a candidate's intangible qualities of character, stature, and gravitas carry much greater weight than *facts* about where they stand on issues or whose economic interests they actually represent."[107] The role music played in the Obama campaign's success cannot be quantified, but clearly the candidate did appeal to female voters: women represented 42.2% of his campaign donors, whereas only 28% of John McCain's came from this group.[108] As Caroline Streeter suggests, the Obama crush was not the exclusive purview of female voters—the media had its own "crush on Obama."[109] *Saturday Night Live* even featured a skit on the Obama crush with impersonators for news reporter Campbell Brown (a self-proclaimed Obamanic), and journalists John King (who recently suffered his third Barack-attack) and Jorge Ramos (an Obama stalker) mooning over Obama while shamelessly sidelining his opponent, Hillary Clinton.[110]

OBAMA: A REAL RESPECTABLE CANDIDATE

Responding to the media hype that surrounded his US senatorial bid and 2004 Democratic National Convention keynote speech invitation, Obama claimed that he was "rooted in the African American community but not limited to it."[111] Indeed, Obama's multiracial background presented his campaign team with formidable challenges. However, the candidate generated a campaign soundscape and established music alliances that allowed him to successfully navigate these challenges and ultimately forge a presidential brand that appealed to the politically disenfranchised hip-hop generation as well as to older constituencies of Black voters and female voters. To use Keli Goff's terms, Obama's music strategy allowed him to speak for hip-hop voters and Huxtable voters alike.[112]

As Gosa argues, "The racialization of Obama as the black (male), hip-hop president was at odds with the image of Obama as the post-racial candidate for all Americans."[113] The candidate's deft musical balancing act mitigated this quandary. Although the circulation of Obama's voice and image in user-generated, hip-hop-styled videos imbued the candidate with street cred and hypermasculine bravado, he deployed various distancing strategies to safeguard his respectable image. The "cool dad" offered effusive praise for hip-hop's genius and creativity while criticizing the conditions that gave rise to its poetic content, and by doing so, he tacitly informed impoverished Black communities that he comprehended the complexity of their social situation, while simultaneously affirming his adherence to mainstream values.

Obama did not always keep it real, but neither did hip-hop. To a certain extent, the tension between authentic artistic expression and corporate interests has defined hip-hop from its inception. And, one can argue, that limits its political economy, at least in the context of electoral politics. However, as I have shown here, hip-hop's internal struggles are what allowed it to represent, or speak for, Obama in nuanced, meaningful ways.[114] Obama's complex biography and hip-hop's internal conflicts, as well as its position within a larger constellation of genres, mirror the broader political and social struggles that have defined racial politics in the post-civil rights era. It is also worth noting that the hip-hop artists Obama elevated as agents of change frequently sample from the hits of their Black music progenitors: Wonder, Mayfield, and Gaye. Through their musical appropriation, they share in the same legacy as Obama, who appropriated the political tropes and rhetorical strategies of his Black political forebears to affirm his own legitimacy and respectability.

Just as Obama used biography to forge an alliance between himself and Selma, and thus the legacy of early civil rights activists, his nostalgic soul playlists culturally aligned him with the soundtrack of this historic struggle. Although these selections offer a universal theme—love—the sonic qualities of the songs that tell the stories not only signify blackness but also, more specifically, embody a style of Black music associated with racial uplift, mainstream tastes, and middle-class respectability. The pairs of lovers who unite in the songs can be understood as symbolic representations of Obama and the female voter, but the duos can also act as placeholders for any two entities coming together—men and women (as suggested by the songs' lyrics); Black and White communities (as implied by the songs' historical position and the Motown label's assimilationist stance); or larger, socially diverse communities divided by race, class, religion, geographic boundaries, or political affiliation (as implied when the songs are read against Obama's universalizing campaign rhetoric). Although the struggles these songs explore are framed as romantic ones, the prevailing narrative of overcoming adversity, which underlies the biographies of artists like Wilson and Wonder, speaks to the Black experience of the 1960s, as well as to the contemporary national struggles the candidate framed as "battles" to be fought by the Joshua generation. That is to say, music encouraged Black voters to envision Obama as a partner in their struggles in both the past and the present. Responding to Obama's inspirational soundtrack at a rally in Pittsburgh, one voter articulated this connection: "We can't wait till it's signed, sealed, and delivered. We like Stevie Wonder because he's an inspiration, just like this man [Obama]. Nothing kept them down."[115] Ultimately, the rally playlists not only contributed to the candidate's identity formation, but also reinscribed a set of values for his constituency—community, human rights, and equality, as well as family, fidelity, and civic-mindedness.

In the United States, Black masculinity, Lemelle argues, "is marked by its social feminization and simultaneously by its stereotyped hypermasculinization."[116] Obama's music strategy allowed him to simultaneously occupy both poles, as well as many positions in between them. Although some hip-hop artists and audiences constructed Obama as the stereotypical Black male, the candidate proclaimed fandom for music more closely aligned with his feminine communication style. As an "old school" candidate, Obama—who, according to Michael Scherer, is "from Venus"—more closely identified with the sentimental protagonists in the songs of Wonder and Wilson. To women swept up by Obama mania, the senator from Illinois was part presidential candidate, part celebrity, part romantic lead, and music allowed their playful objectification to work to the candidate's advantage.

In the 2008 Obama campaign, "Hope" was not only a speech, slogan, and soundbite, but also a soundtrack that catapulted Obama to the status of superbrand. With the boundary between the political and pop cultural fields effaced, a presidential candidate's cultural competence can function as a form of political competence, and his music-aesthetic disposition can offer insight into his political values. Ultimately, a creative music strategy and the discourses it precipitated allowed Barack Obama to embody a safe middle ground between the race-specific and the universal, the masculine and the feminine, the past and the present, and most importantly, the real and the respectable.[117]

CHAPTER 2

Anatomy of a Campaign Launch

Heal, Inspire, Revive, Erase *with Ben Carson*

Ben and Candy Carson terrific. What about a real black President who can properly address the racial divide? And much else.

—RUPERT MURDOCH ON TWITTER, OCTOBER 7, 2015[1]

Heal. (Vote, vote.) Inspire. (Vote, vote.) Revive. (Vote, vote.) Ben Carson 2016. Vote and support Ben Carson for our next president and be awesome.

—RAPPER ASPIRING MOGUL IN BEN CARSON'S AD "FREEDOM," NOVEMBER 6, 2015[2]

"A REAL BLACK PRESIDENT"

On November 6, 2015, Republican presidential candidate Ben Carson's campaign team released a sixty-second radio ad titled "Freedom." For a cost of $150,000, the ad aired for two weeks in urban markets, including Atlanta, Birmingham (AL), Detroit, Houston, Jackson (MS), Little Rock (AR), Miami, and Memphis. Adopting the successful formula of will.i.am's "Yes We Can," the ad pairs soundbites from a Carson speech with the verses of Republican Christian rapper Aspiring Mogul (né Robert Donaldson). The Carson campaign hoped the ad would "[reach] out and [talk] to [urban youth] in a language that they prefer and in a language that, and in a cultural format that they appreciate."[3] According to Carson staffer Doug Watts, the ad addresses "urban youth that feel disenfranchised, not only from the election process but from mainstream America. . . . We're trying to say that we are listening to you, we care about you, we want to have communication and a dialog."[4] The text and lyrics of the ad are as follows:

ASPIRING MOGUL: Heal. (Vote, vote.) Inspire. (Vote, vote.) Revive. (Vote, vote.) Ben Carson 2016. Vote and support Ben Carson for our next president and be awesome.

BEN CARSON: America became a great nation early on, not because it was flooded with politicians, but because it was flooded with people who understood the value of personal responsibility, hard work, creativity, innovation, and that's what will get us on the right track now. I'm very hopeful that I'm not the only one who's willing to pick up the baton of freedom, because freedom is not free, and we must fight for it every day. Every one of us must fight for it because we're fighting for our children and the next generation.

ASPIRING MOGUL: If we want to get America back on track, we gotta vote Ben Carson a matter of fact. Go out and vote.

BEN CARSON: I'm Ben Carson, and I approve this message.[5]

Journalists, and especially Black Twitter, were quick to criticize Carson's efforts to reach urban audiences. One Twitter user likened the ad to a McDonald's commercial,[6] while another described the radio spot as "a political payday loan ad."[7] The low production value, the misguided attempt to invoke old-school rap, and the mismatch between the chipper flute loop and Carson's comatose delivery all became fodder for critique. Most of all, the ad was panned for its "pure condescension"[8] and sheer lack of artistic merit.[9] The hokey lyrics, especially the unfortunate attempt to rhyme "Carson" with "awesome," fell hopelessly flat. Indeed, Aspiring Mogul's verses lack the lyrical dexterity and cleverness that are the hallmarks of the genre. Rapper and activist Talib Kweli even weighed in, stating, "The most effective way for Ben Carson to reach out to young black voters is to actually care about other black people, which Ben Carson has proven to be incapable of."[10]

The parodies were quick to follow. One of the most creative, appropriately titled "Panderdom," puts to music all that is lacking in Carson's efforts to connect with urban youth. In short, the parody targets the original ad's pandering to urban voters and the lack of authenticity it exhibits, both on the part of Carson as candidate and in the articulation of hip-hop—the sounds as well as the values this cultural practice encodes. "Panderdom" features a man with a high-pitched, nasal voice, which sounds distinctly White when he enunciates the Rs as he raps "inspire" and "pander." He opens with a spirited "Hi!" greeting before introducing himself as Carson's campaign manager, possibly an intertextual reference to Eminem's "My Name Is," which Loren Kajikawa has argued parodies various tropes of whiteness.[11] The robotic delivery of the vocals and near rhymes (underlined) mock Aspiring Mogul's lack of flow and a cogent rhyme scheme as the lyrics take on an honest character, revealing the presumed strategy of the ad's creators:

> I know one thing, it's if you're <u>Black</u>,
> you'll like Ben Carson if we put him in a <u>rap</u>.
> . . .
> This hip hop campaign won't likely be playin' up in Portland, Maine.
> So come on, y'all, you voted for <u>Obama</u>
> Ben Carson's Black too, and that's all they have <u>in common</u>.[12]

"Panderdom" substitutes the original ad's speech on personal responsibility and the high price of freedom with some of Carson's more controversial remarks where he compares Obamacare to slavery and argues that the biblical Joseph built the pyramids to store grain.[13] Candidates need to strike a delicate balance when developing a music strategy; music must authentically articulate the candidate's biography and brand while also acknowledging the taste disposition of the target constituency.[14] While many aspects of "Freedom" warrant criticism, a tinge of irony is added to the equation by the fact that just months before its release, Carson had denounced hip-hop culture for bringing on the destruction of Black communities.[15] This musical misfire and its aftermath point to the challenges of Ben Carson's candidacy, both political *and* musical.[16]

BEN WHO?

In many regards, Ben Carson, like Barack Obama before him, was an unconventional candidate. The son of an army veteran who worked in the auto industry, he was raised in southwest Detroit and educated in the public school system. He attended a Seventh Day Adventist church throughout his youth and identifies his faith as the guiding force that allowed him to manage his violent temper. Despite an impoverished beginning, Carson earned a scholarship to Yale University and later enrolled in the University of Michigan Medical School. After graduation, he spent six years in the Johns Hopkins University School of Medicine neurosurgery program, and then returned in 1984 when he was appointed as the director of pediatric neurosurgery. During his successful career as a neurosurgeon, he published several books and was in demand as a public speaker. After a keynote speech at the 2013 National Prayer Breakfast, where he was highly critical of the Obama administration, Carson became a rising star in the eyes of the Republican Party.[17] Registered as an independent since 2001, Carson rejoined the Republican Party in 2014, which fueled speculation over a presidential run.[18] The political newcomer frequently attracted criticism due to his controversial remarks. In an interview with CNN's Wolf Blitzer, Carson clarified statements made in his book titled *A More Perfect Union: What We the People Can Do to Reclaim Our Constitutional Liberties* (2015), claiming that the Nazi Party could not have executed the Holocaust if German Jews were armed.[19] In 2015, he affirmed his belief about the origins of the pyramids of Giza, which he first stated in 1998.[20] Politics aside, journalists and news outlets noted a disconnect between his academic pedigree and his professed beliefs that seemed to reject basic scientific principles and the tenets of evolutionary biology.[21] While his "rags to riches" narrative, emphasis on self-reliance, consistent effort to sidestep race when addressing social issues, and adherence to Christian principles may have appealed to some White evangelicals within the Republican Party, these remarks, combined with his lack of foreign policy experience, presented distinct challenges as he set his sights on a political career.[22]

Moreover, Carson entered the political fray during a time when blackness, or more specifically, the social and political meanings attached to race and racial identity, had shifted in the wake of the Obama presidency. The ascendency of Obama inspired optimism, but persistent employment inequities, healthcare disparities, and the state of the criminal justice system suggest that a truly postracial world has yet to be realized.[23] Before 2008, Black presidential candidates Shirley Chisholm (1972), Reverend Jesse Jackson (1984, 1988), and Reverend Al Sharpton (2004) foregrounded policies relevant to Black communities in their respective campaigns.[24] Eschewing the traditional platforms of his Black Democratic predecessors, Obama ran a deracialized campaign, avoiding direct engagement with race-specific issues in favor of those perceived as racially transcendent.[25] This strategy led some to question whether or not he was "Black enough" and reinvigorated debates over the status of race and race relations in the twenty-first-century United States. Journalists and pundits mapped these conversations onto analyses of Obama's musical tastes and alliances. As Michael P. Jeffries, H. Samy Alim and Geneva Smitherman, Murray Forman, and I (in chapter 1) have shown, Obama situated himself in relation to the hip-hop community through the deployment of linguistic and cultural markers of blackness.[26] For Carson, a Black Republican, there was no obvious political (or musical) road map to success. Yet six months before his rap ad rustled the urban airwaves, Ben Carson did try to invent such a road map, and he did so right from the start.

READY TO LAUNCH

As a formal declaration of a politician's candidacy, the campaign launch event endorses the candidate both professionally and personally, assuring the voting public of his qualifications, moral character, and vision for the nation's future. These events are somewhat formulaic in their aesthetic and practical dimensions. Aside from the candidate himself, the roster of speakers typically includes a fellow politician who speaks of the candidate's impressive record and a close friend or family member who offers intimate insight into the candidate's character. A warm-up playlist of prerecorded music rouses the crowd, walk-on songs herald the entrance of each speaker, and a local group or two (think high school marching band) might offer a brief performance. Disregarding this formula, Carson announced his candidacy on May 4, 2015, with what Ryan Teague Beckwith called "one of the most unusual campaign launches in recent memory."[27] Carson forwent the traditional use of anecdotes and prerecorded pop songs in favor of a lineup of live musical performances at Detroit's historic Music Hall Center for the Performing Arts.[28] For Carson, music did not merely enhance or embellish the storytelling of the event. Rather, music both *told* the story and *was* the story. Using the slogan "Heal, Inspire, Revive" as a starting point, Carson strategically harnessed music to crystallize his presidential brand as well as sonically reinforce an alliance with his party's core demographic— working and middle-class White men. This chapter offers a close reading of Ben Carson's "most unusual campaign launch," revealing how his campaign team recontextualized and reworked music and musical traditions in order to elevate the heroism of his forefathers, the Christian faith, and a postracial worldview while at the same time suppressing less politically expedient narratives.

Carson's campaign launch opened with the presentation of the colors, a performance of the National Anthem (with his wife Candy playing violin), and a benediction (Table 4).[29] In his aim for stylistic, geographic, and racial diversity, Carson selected two performing groups for his event. Selected of God—which gained national recognition through their appearance in an extended-length Chrysler 200 commercial for the 2011 Super Bowl— regularly performs in their native Detroit and across the United States, "bridging the gap of hopelessness, unemployment and economic downturn with the love of God and song."[30] Under the direction of Pastor Larry Callahan, the gospel choir not only performs contemporary gospel tunes, but also crosses over into pop, with covers of Destiny's Child's "Survivor" and Shontelle's "Impossible." In 2015 they even brought this crossover repertoire to the television juggernaut *America's Got Talent*. The second group, Veritas, is a five-voice, all-male, contemporary-classical crossover group with southern roots. Veritas's performances typically include covers of contemporary Christian songs such as "I Can Only Imagine" (MercyMe) and "Dare You to Move" (Switchfoot), standards from the American songbook such as "You'll Never Walk Alone," and traditional sacred music such as Albert Hay Malotte's "The Lord's Prayer."[31]

Selected of God's gospel-inflected cover of Eminem's "Lose Yourself," a chart-topper from the 2002 semiautobiographical film *8 Mile* (2002), generated the most buzz in the press following Carson's campaign launch.[32] The *Washington Post*'s Hunter Schwarz even gave the performance the top spot in his "The 9 Best Moments from Ben Carson's *Bizarre and Glorious* Campaign Launch/Concert" list.[33] While the group has a history of pop covers, it is perhaps perplexing (or ironic) that Carson's team would choose to feature the music of a White hip-hop artist with a history of lampooning conservatives in his verses. Despite Carson's well-publicized criticism of hip-hop, he may have had a calculated reason for establishing a connection between his own campaign and *8 Mile*. In the film, fellow Detroit native Eminem (né Marshall Bruce Mathers III) plays Jimmy "B-Rabbit" Smith Jr., a poor White kid trying to make his way in a cultural field dominated by Black artists; similarly, Carson is a Black man, trying to make it in the Republican political arena, a field dominated by White politicians, as an antiestablishment candidate.[34] Before seeking political office, Carson

Table 4. Lineup of performers for Ben Carson's campaign launch event

Event	Personnel	Composer/lyricist
Opening Announcement		
Presentation of the Colors	Myron H. Beals American Legion Post 32, Livonia Michigan	
National Anthem	Selected of God Candy Carson (violin)	Francis Scott Key John Stafford Smith
Benediction		
Lose Yourself	Selected of God	Marshall Mathers (Eminem), Jeff Bass, Luis Resto
Total Praise	Selected of God Candy Carson (voice)	Richard Smallwood
You'll Never Walk Alone from *Carousel*	Veritas	Richard Rodgers and Oscar Hammerstein II
America the Beautiful	Veritas	Katharine Lee Bates Samuel A. Ward
God Bless America		Irving Berlin
Battle Hymn of the Republic		Julia Ward Howe William Steffe, ed.
Ben Carson Campaign Video		
Ben Carson Speech		
Battle Hymn of the Republic (reprise)	Selected of God, Veritas, Carson family	Julia Ward Howe William Steffe, ed.

practiced as a surgeon in a subspecialty of medicine that reports only 2% of practitioners identifying as African American.[35] That is to say, both Carson *and* Eminem's Rabbit are racial outsiders in their respective fields. In voicing the triumphant anthem of a White artist through a Black choir, Carson offers a sonically constituted allusion to his own biography and highlights the universality of the underclass struggle, reinforcing the belief that perseverance breeds success, regardless of racial identity.

This ethos carries over into Carson's platform. In his launch speech (and elsewhere on the trail), Carson de-emphasized race, denying the existence of structural racism and systematic prejudice in favor of a reliance on self-sufficiency and hard work—themes that also underscore the narrative trajectory of the fictive Rabbit as well as the biography of Eminem himself. While candidates like Obama were cautious in their associations with hip-hop, by 2016, the antics of Eminem's early career—be it bravado, misogyny, or contempt for the office of the presidency—had been neutralized through the lens of nostalgia in the minds of much of the public, a process facilitated by the effects of mass commercialism and hip-hop's general acceptance within the mainstream market. An autobiographical song from a semiautobiographical film provides a good counterpoint to Carson's kick-off speech, which leans heavily on the candidate's own biography. Moreover, the mixing of subtle and pronounced racially coded gestures, textual alterations to the original song, and the fluid constellation of associations surrounding it play a significant role in shaping the launch event's narrative of spiritual and societal renewal, themes also explored in Carson's books.[36]

Selected of God's cover of "Lose Yourself" attempts to neutralize the racial signifiers of the original song even as it emphasizes other aspects of racialized performativity. After an initial impassioned wordless opening, the choir sings lyrics only on the song's choruses, omitting the verses, one of which would potentially highlight Carson's lack of oratory skills: "He keeps on forgetting what he wrote down, the whole crowd goes so loud / He opens his mouth, but the words won't come out."[37] But the performance also features a less notable, yet significant omission from the chorus. In the fourth line, Eminem shouts "Yo!" at the end of the lyric "This opportunity comes once in a lifetime" so that the phrase matches the rhyme scheme of the second and third lines (go/blow). Selected of God omits the "Yo!" exclamation, likely because they were cognizant of the class-based, secular connotations of Black street slang.[38]

> You better lose yourself in the music
> The moment, you own it, you better never let it go
> You only get one shot, do not miss your chance to blow
> This opportunity comes once in a lifetime, yo.[39]

In the absence of the chorus's slang and the verses that showcase Eminem's lyrical virtuosity and biographical specificity, what remains is an ode to self-affirmation, universalized and depleted of its class-based signifiers as well as its tonal semantics. Instead, the choir substitutes Eminem's rapping with clichéd gestures of gospel performativity—emotive hypervocalization, glissandi, and swoops, for example. Such "wails and cries," Jerma Jackson argues, "made the pain of daily living an integral component of the good news supplied by religious faith."[40] The singers also make use of registral accenting on the words "one shot," which gives the song a more idiomatically gospel flavor. In addition to highlighting "one shot" as the thematically salient moment of the song (and Carson's event), they also communicate strength and jubilation by raising their hands and pointing upward each time this utterance occurs, perhaps gesturing toward heaven as gospel choirs frequently do in more sacred settings. Thus, Eminem's powerful articulation of underclass subjectivity and secular testifyin' becomes *testifying* in the religious sense, sacralized to appeal to Carson's predominantly White, evangelical base. The sonic markers of the gospel style situate the song's aspirational message as a spiritual and communal one, rather than an individual one rooted in monetary reward and fame. The song's signature riff and energy remain intact, but gospel's adjacency to respectability politics makes the performance palatable to Whites.

While Eminem's bootstraps narrative and the shared biographical and geographical touchpoints between rapper and politician may have struck a chord among multiple demographics, his artistry and storytelling connect with a more specific audience—the disenfranchised, young White men who felt excluded from the American dream in the wake of the Obama years. Indeed, Eminem's relationship to politics is complicated. Like many other artists, he openly criticized George W. Bush for his interventionist policies toward Iraq. In "Mosh" and its accompanying video, released shortly before the 2004 presidential election, he imagines a racially diverse coalition targeting the Oval Office.[41] More recently, in 2017, Eminem offered trenchant criticism of Donald Trump in a freestyle at the BET Hip Hop Awards, claiming later in a *Billboard* interview that he did not care if the rant cost him half his fan base.[42] But far from a liberal worldview, Eminem frequently expresses homophobic and misogynist attitudes on and off stage. In the words of critic Kurt Loder, Eminem's success marked "the decline of the whole p.c. [political correctness] regime of the early '90s."[43] While his personal politics do not align with the Republican establishment, Eminem has thus deftly cultivated various personas and adopted antithetical stances throughout his career. As Simon Stow has argued, "The juxtaposition of such contradictory viewpoints is a persistent trope in the artist's work."[44] Marcia Alesan Dawkins has similarly stated, "Eminem seemingly becomes 'the only one that matters' through the tactics of mirroring the identity desired by his audiences and by denying a singularity and certainty."[45]

But although Eminem may perform multiple subjectivities, he has consistently assumed an antiestablishment stance, rejected the status quo, and, at least in the early part of his career, steered clear of corporate America. Thus, Eminem functions as a broad signifier of rebellion—a trickster who playfully disrupts the social order and then remakes it on his own terms. Loren Kajikawa notes that "Eminem's violent, cartoonish, and misogynistic humor consciously distances him from conventional representations of whiteness, positioning him as a social rebel on par with, but clearly not the same as, his African American counterparts."[46] This same style of juvenile humor—sometimes accompanied by the cartoon image of Pepe the Frog—emerged as the lingua franca of far-right-leaning men on social media platforms such as 4chan and Reddit in 2015 and 2016.[47] The disenfranchised may also see themselves in Eminem's performance of abjection.[48] Stow notes how the rapper frequently alludes to his own tears, misery, and victimhood, challenging the traditional machismo posturing adopted by hip-hop artists.[49] In short, Eminem's rejection of political correctness, his sophomoric humor, and his performance of abjection allow his music and image to speak to the disenfranchised across ideological, racial, and political lines.

But Carson may have had another reason for aligning himself with "Lose Yourself," its artist, and the gospel group. Selected of God and Eminem came together four years earlier to create a Chrysler commercial, "Born of Fire" (or "Imported from Detroit"), that aired on Fox during the February 2011 Super Bowl.[50] While Eminem had previously refused to lease the song for commercial use, he green-lighted Chrysler's project and even volunteered to appear in the spot (in a nonsinging role) promoting the Chrysler 200, an affordable luxury model.[51] With cinematic flair and epic proportions, Wieden+Kennedy's commercial offers an alternative narrative of Detroit's demise and renewal, one told through the authentic voices of Michigan's residents (Kevin Yon, the choir, and Eminem). The narrator within the ad summarily rejects the story written by other folks in the papers, and instead positions the art of building cars as a form of embodied knowledge uniquely situated in Detroit.

KEVIN YON (NARRATOR): I got a question for ya.

What does this city know about luxury, huh?

What does a town that's been to hell and back know about the finer things in life?

Well, I'll tell ya: more than most.

Ya see, it's the hottest fires that make the hardest steel.

Add hard work and conviction and the know-how that runs generations deep in every last one of us.

That's who we are. That's our story.

Now, it's probably not the one you've been reading in papers.

The one being written by folks who've never even been here and don't know what we're capable of.

Because when it comes to luxury, it's as much about where it's from as who it's for.

Now, we're from America, but this isn't New York City, or the Windy City, or Sin City, and we're certainly no one's Emerald City.

EMINEM: This is the Motor City, and this is what we do.

The commercial's visuals trace the car's path from bleakness (urban blight) to grandeur (urban renewal), from street space (Interstate 75) to cultural space (the Fox Theatre), from chaos to order—a trajectory that is underscored by the choir's performance, which transitions from its opening primal cry to a rousing wordless chorus as the rapper enters the theater's luxurious surroundings. The commercial's chronicle and gospel soundtrack project this narrative trajectory of revival onto the auto industry postbailout as well as onto the city and its inhabitants (Selected of God and Eminem).

Five months later, Selected of God partnered with Chrysler and 8 Mile Style to release a music video in support of various Detroit charities, including the Abayomi Community Development Corporation, the Yunion, and the Robert S. Shumake Foundation.[52] Like the "Born of Fire" ad, the music video offers "Lose Yourself" as an anthem for the promotion of revitalization in Detroit and follows a similar narrative. The video opens with a foggy skyline blurred by rising smoke and desolate streets and parking lots. These bleak images are juxtaposed with landmarks of civic pride: (1) the *Spirit of Detroit* statue, which holds a gold sphere representing the divine in one hand and a family group depicting humanity in the other; (2) the Monument to Joe Louis, a bronze fist celebrating the boxer's fight inside and outside the ring; (3) a statue of former Detroit mayor and businessman Hazen S. Pingree, commemorating him as "The Idol of the People"; and (4) a carving of a stone angel on the side of an edifice. The camera circles each in motion with an angle that suggests a pair of eyes are looking up at them, perhaps as material testaments to Detroit's proud history and future potential. Two figures play a central role: a ballet dancer *en pointe* who represents grace, elegance, and refinement, and a boxer, who represents toughness, grit, and strength. The video connects the stories of the two by showing each in their respective spaces—the studio and the gym—but enacting similar gestures. As the ballet dancer laces the ribbons on her pointe shoes, the boxer wraps his hands in tape. As the dancer moves into a spirited performance, the boxer meets his opponent in the ring. The choir also gets ready for the performance: individual singers step into their cars, apply makeup, rehearse, pray, and don their robes before they finally appear onstage. Leisure and labor each play a role, with footage of girls jumping rope and men playing basketball as well as firefighters and police officers in uniform, and this is mirrored in the signage: "Enjoy Detroit," "Hitsville USA," and "Motor City." Success is shown in the form of the boxer holding prizewinning belts, murals of people making cars in harmony, and the choir fully robed and singing on stage. In short, the music video introduces a diverse group of people—men and women, Black and White, young and old, artists and laborers—and a city, getting their "one shot" and succeeding. The Cass Technical High School marching band, demonstrating both athleticism and precision, appears in the second half, offering a powerful visual representation of a community coming together. Musically and visually, the video communicates an uplifting message regarding urban rebirth and renewal, as well as a working-class solidarity that transcends racial and socioeconomic divides.[53]

Viewers familiar with the Emmy Award–winning ad and music video would likely see Carson's own narrative through this lens, which effectively interweaves the city's cultural (gospel) and industrial (automotive) legacies into a compelling narrative of revival. With two words that hold significance in both religious and medical parlance, Carson's campaign slogan "Heal, Inspire, Revive" effectively encapsulates both his Christian faith and his status as a medical pioneer. "Lose Yourself," with its connection to Eminem's biography, the Chrysler 200 ad, and the music video, offers multiple visual and sonic articulations of revival that afford legitimacy to Carson's slogan and root his narrative in a shared urban space. The ad's embrace of working-class identity (as articulated through the dramatization of the automotive industry's rebirth) and competitiveness and athleticism (as implied by the Super Bowl connection and the depiction of boxing) allow Carson to align himself with signifiers of traditional masculinity, working-class identity, and the values of Republicanism. Indeed, the racialized (and respectable) sounds in the Chrysler ad, the music video, and the campaign launch performance center blackness, but through the universality of the narratives therein and the revoicing of a White artist, Eminem, through Black gospel, Carson asserts political solidarity with his White Republican counterparts, by extension making the claim that blackness can represent whiteness.

While Selected of God afforded the campaign launch event a certain contemporary urban sensibility, Veritas offered music with a more traditional, rural vibe as a counterpoint, including songs that exuded optimism, faith in God, and love of country. The all-male quintet performed an arrangement of "You'll Never Walk Alone" from the musical *Carousel*, and a medley of patriotic favorites titled *An American Anthology*. According to their website, the group chose the name "Veritas" because of its "ties to the message [they] share about God's simple truth," but I would argue that the association of its name with Harvard University is not inconsequential. Even though the group's biography states that Veritas evolved from an original collective of singers at the University of Mobile (not Harvard), their cultural indebtedness to White Ivy League glee clubs sends clear messages about racial identity and privilege that, as I will argue later on, manifest themselves in the racialized power dynamics that shape the event finale.[54]

The first two songs in the medley, "God Bless America" and "America the Beautiful," might readily be considered unofficial US anthems. The songs' emphases on landscapes—mountains, prairies, oceans—foreground spaces that are supposedly untouched by urbanization and industrialization, and such imagery therefore acts as an effective foil to the Detroit narratives. "Battle Hymn of the Republic" concludes the medley and in some ways diverges from the first two songs. Rather than pondering American landscapes, "Battle Hymn of the Republic" turns to war, positioning battle as a God-sanctioned mission. Julia Ward Howe's 1861 text is set to "John Brown's Body," which finds its roots in the camp meeting tune "Say Brothers."[55] As the quintet breaks out into "Glory, glory, hallelujah," the audience raises their hands, making the event seem more akin to religious revival than the "American revival" of which Carson speaks. (Considering the candidate's political leanings and spiritual orientation, however, as well as the song's religious roots and textual references, the leap from the spiritual battle depicted in the song to Carson's political battle does not seem like too much of a stretch.) The use of older patriotic songs aligns with Carson's focus on a return to the America of the past as well as the ethos of American exceptionalism, a point that is driven home in the campaign film that follows the performance of the song medley. The film's narrator states, "If America is to survive the challenges of the modern world, we need to heal, we need to be inspired, and we need to revive the exceptional spirit that built America."[56]

In the speech that follows the performances by Selected of God and Veritas, Carson muses over the American values that shaped his personal history as well as his vision for the nation. These words resonate with his musical selections. He opens the speech by acknowledging his wife Candy, who, like Carson, is from Detroit. He states, "Even though we are both from Detroit, we had to go to New Haven to meet each other." To folks from New England, "New Haven" is *not* simply a town in Connecticut; it is the location of Yale University. From the outset of the speech, Carson assures the elite class that although his roots are in Detroit, he possesses the right institutional pedigree and shares their same intellectual background. Carson traces his parents' roots back to rural Tennessee, their home state before they moved to Detroit where his father got a factory job at GM. He also recalls a memory of the Music Hall Center for the Performing Arts: "I remember one Christmas being right here in this auditorium, sitting right over there with [*sic*], for GM employees they had a Christmas program for the kids." Thus, Carson connects his biography to urban (Detroit) and rural ([Chattanooga], Tennessee) spaces and once again asserts that while he comes from a working-class background as the son of a factory worker, he also feels at home in bastions of high culture (Music Hall Center). The dual narratives of high culture and working-class identity are mirrored in the figures of the ballerina and boxer in the Selected of God "Lose Yourself" music video. Carson centers his own mother in his narrative, praising her desire to push her children to succeed while working herself to the bone in order to stay off public assistance. He also lauds her thriftiness, which allowed her to purchase a new car. In the "Born of Fire" ad and Selected of God's "Lose Yourself" music video, the car becomes a symbol, not only of Detroit's rebirth, but also of personal freedom and upward mobility. Carson similarly positions the car, Detroit's main export, as such a symbol in his mother's own story.[57]

When Carson turns to policy, other ideals come into play: intellectual curiosity, self-reliance, and the foundational principles of the Constitution. The can-do attitude that Carson praises in his mother makes a comeback when he delves into the mythos surrounding the country's earliest settlers: "You've got to remember it was the can-do attitude that allowed this nation to rise so quickly. Because we had people who didn't stop when there was an obstacle." Veritas' patriotic medley, with tunes such as "God Bless America" and "America the Beautiful," taps into the same mythos surrounding the formation of the nation and its identity as a specifically Christian nation. Like Carson's speech, these traditional patriotic songs center the role of God as a guiding force. To use Carson's words, it was his mother's prayers that lifted him as a child, and should he end up in the White House, his journey will be God-ordained.[58]

After Carson's speech concludes, the two singing groups enter the stage once again, this time joining together in song behind the candidate for a reprise of "Battle Hymn of the Republic." An oversized American flag slowly cascades downward from the proscenium. Carson stands center stage, flanked by his progeny, and sings along. The two formerly separate groups of singers, now united, represent discrete music genres, spiritual traditions, age groups, and most importantly races. Under Carson's paternal gaze they gather in solidarity to remind voters that Christ "died to make men holy / Let us live to make men free," again providing a Christian mandate for the country's fight for freedom. Presenting the two musical traditions separately *before* his speech allows Carson to be positioned as the facilitator of transracial harmony at its conclusion. In other words, Carson occupies a position as a unifier, as someone who reaches across color lines and speaks for both Black and White communities in a way that is musically and visually constituted in this emblematic moment (Fig. 3).[59]

But while on the surface the event asserts a message of unity, it simultaneously perpetuates racial stereotypes, undermines less politically expedient narratives, and ultimately erases certain aspects of the Black experience. The song medley clearly blurs the line between the civic and the sacred, and Veritas's performance places patriotism and American exceptionalism in a specifically White context. Veritas's signature classical-crossover sound—a melding of pop and quasi-operatic singing—contains sonic markers of whiteness, not to mention the fact that White performers dominate the genre, and White middle-class audiences are its primary consumers. In other words, as much as gospel musically encodes blackness, classical crossover strongly connotes whiteness. Visually, the groups come together in the reprise of the medley's final song; musically, however, not everyone is created equal. In the finale, one simply cannot hear the

Fig. 3. Veritas, Selected of God, Ben Carson, and Carson's family at the end of the candidate's launch event. Still from Ben Carson Presidential Campaign Announcement, C-SPAN, May 4, 2015.

Black singers; White male voices overpower and ultimately silence them. Moreover, the "cultivated" White, "poperatic" style dominates while the stylistic markers of Black vocality present in "Lose Yourself" are erased. Musically disempowered, the Black performers appear to sing in the voices of their White counterparts as they are denied their musical idiom and vocal authority. In their sonic absence, the White performers are left to voice the battle tune (connected to an earlier text that apotheosizes a White savior, abolitionist John Brown).[60] The silencing of Black narratives in this musical context serves as a reminder of the actual silencing that spills into the streets outside of the music hall's walls. The finale reiterates the racial ideologies and social hierarchies previously established by reaffirming the following binaries:

Black	White
Selected of God	Veritas
city	country
North	South
Detroit	Nashville
gritty	cultivated
church	concert hall
Black religious traditions	White religious traditions
present	past

Carson's campaign launch constructs a bipolar representation of the nation: a gritty, urban America of the present and a folksy, simpler America of the past. At the same time, it manages borders and establishes a hierarchy between the two sides through erasure strategies that extend from Carson's platform to the event's musical performances. Ultimately, the music undermines the visually constituted racial harmony of the launch's final moments.

The architects of Carson's launch event worked to make race visible in ways that were palatable to the White mainstream—a gospel choir performs a traditional gospel tune and the national anthem. However, in their "vernacular" moment, Selected of God assumes the voice and adopts the subject position of a White male rapper, and as they sing a sanitized version of his iconic song, they erase the linguistic markers of "low-brow" Black culture and the narrative of urban street life. In their place, the choir pours the tropes of the gospel style, connoting a specifically Christian worldview, and raises their voices in refrains that laud self-sufficiency as a universal value that transcends class, race, time, and space. In 2008, hip-hop alliances and a soul soundtrack allowed Barack Obama to respond to the question, "Is he Black enough?" Going in the other musical direction, Carson worked to sonically cultivate a universalist, postracial, Christian vision of the United States in order to appease the White Republican establishment. His musical choices beg the question, "Is he White enough?" Ultimately, Carson's launch demonstrates how the political can be mapped onto the musical and vice versa in mass-mediated spectacles. But as my analysis here shows, the semantic openness of popular songs, with their complex and convoluted histories, and the multivalence of genre, complicates readings of how they might signify in political contexts.

CHAPTER 3

Kamala Harris, Rap Genius?

I'm so glad this generation is seeing through the bs. I needed y'all when Bill Clinton ran and went on *Arsenio* playing the sax and locked up the black vote and had folks talking about he was the 1st black president smh. Kamala just be yourself girl!

—MODED_CORRODED, TWITTER POST, FEBRUARY 13, 2019.[1]

A *STARRK* REALITY

YouTuber Cameron J achieved internet celebrity in 2013 with the birth of his blue-haired lady alter ego named "Starrkeisha." In one of his popular videos, "The Starrkeisha Cheer Squad" (2016), J relies on video magic to "clone" himself into a posse of five cheerleaders. With their snappy beats, infectious chant, and quirky dance moves, J's squad spawned the "Petty Dance Challenge," a viral dance craze that inspired viewers to remix the song and/or post videos of themselves performing the dance. Two years later, another YouTuber superimposed the faces of Hillary Clinton, Kamala Harris, Elizabeth Warren, Nancy Pelosi, and Maxine Waters onto J's cheerleaders, with Al Green (D-TX) serving in the role of coach (Fig. 4). In early 2019, a Twitter user reposted the video in response to Kamala Harris's mixtape, released shortly before she officially declared her candidacy for the 2020 Democratic presidential nomination.[2]

In this reinvention of J's original, left-leaning women politicians of formidable stature are relegated to the status of dancing girls who sing an anthem to profess their pettiness—a tongue-in-cheek feminine display, not so much to appeal to the male gaze but rather to elicit male laughter. The video reduces each woman, bearing an angry and distorted facial expression, to a novelty, the visual backdrop for a viral trend that will be here today and gone tomorrow. While the figure of the cheerleader is a White girl archetype, the linguistic markers and gesture carried over

Fig. 4. Nancy Pelosi, Maxine Waters, Hillary Clinton, Kamala Harris, and Elizabeth Warren join in on "The Petty Challenge." Still from "Petty," posted on YouTube on May 30, 2018.

from the original "Starrkeisha Cheer Squad" video point toward the figure of the "sassy Black woman," a remixed and recirculated stereotype that illustrates what Lauren Michele Jackson calls "our cultural propensity to see Black people as walking hyperbole."[3] While one can only speculate on the intentions of the maker, the negative stereotypes therein, familiar yet grotesque in their constitution, point toward the challenges women—especially women of color—face when engaging in the political sphere. As Negin Ghavami and Letitia Anne Peplau have argued, such stereotypes can "set up biased expectations, reinforce prejudiced attitudes, and foster discrimination—even if we personally do not endorse these beliefs."[4]

"THE MOST HIP-HOP MINDED OF ALL THE CANDIDATES"

Kamala Harris, the daughter of an Indian scientist and a Jamaican economist, began her career as a prosecutor and then later served as San Francisco district attorney (2004–2011) and attorney general of California (2011–2017).[5] From the early 2000s, Harris enacted "tough on crime" policies that were draconian, although very much in tune with the social climate of a time, when lawmakers and politicians across the ideological spectrum were similarly unrelenting. She supported a 2011 law that criminalized the parents of youth who were chronically truant from school, a policy that disproportionately impacted people of color.[6] Her critics pointed toward her failure to root out police and prosecutorial misconduct during her tenure in San Francisco. In early 2019, Lara Bazelon even went so far as to say Harris was "on the wrong side of history" during her time as attorney general.[7]

Harris entered the presidential race on January 21, 2019 (Martin Luther King Day), selecting "For the People" as her campaign slogan. While Harris described herself as a "progressive prosecutor" in her memoir, *The Truths We Hold: An American Journey* (2019), and on the campaign trail, the contradictions between her espousal of high-minded ideals and her actual record dominated discussions surrounding her suitability as a presidential candidate.[8] Therefore, Harris needed to mitigate her past and her public-facing image as "top cop"—an identity she once embraced—in order to earn the trust and respect of her Black constituents.[9] (This moniker even inspired a popular meme—"Kamala is a cop"—that made the rounds on social media.) In short, Harris needed to remind voters of her years in the Senate (2017–2021), where her policy positions aligned with the values of most mainstream progressives—she supported efforts to ensure women's reproductive health care, environmental regulations proposed by Representative Alexandria Ocasio-Cortez (D-NY), the elimination of barriers that prevent DREAMers from securing citizenship, the expansion of gun control measures, criminal justice reforms, and the passage of Medicare for All.[10] While Black women achieved historic gains in the 2018 election,[11] Harris's record, not to mention the significant hurdles Black women candidates regularly face—a higher level of scrutiny, lack of party support due to the perception that they are "less electable," and the racial wealth disparity that impedes fundraising—all posed significant challenges.[12] More broadly, intersectionally situated candidates (like Harris) face obstacles that White women and male candidates do not when it comes to achieving and sustaining leadership roles.[13]

In the first few weeks of her eleven-month campaign, Harris notably engaged with music on three occasions: (1) a mixtape produced by *The Late Show with Stephen Colbert*; (2) a Twitter video in which she dances to Cardi B's "I Like It"; and (3) an interview on *The Breakfast Club*, a popular radio show focusing on Black culture, where she discusses both her candidacy and her tastes in music. In these moments of musical engagement, we see Harris attempt to transform her image from that of tough prosecutor / top cop to that of progressive reformer, to establish relatability, and to invent a narrative that aligns her own coming-of-age with the Black experience.[14] Although her music strategy mirrored that of Obama in 2008 in many respects, her engagement unleashed an unduly harsh firestorm of criticism. This response is no surprise, as women politicians (more so than their male counterparts) frequently are accused of managing their image and must grapple with issues surrounding authenticity. As was the case for Obama in 2008, Harris's multiracial background created an additional minefield with regard to representation, and colorism (discrimination based on skin tone) inflected the language of both her supporters and her detractors. In the case of Harris, a critical look at music is especially vital, as video clips of her music engagement emerged and were received in the early stages of her campaign, where her identity as presidential candidate was crystallizing. In the analysis that follows, it is not my intention to downplay Harris's South Asian identity, its role in her presentation, or her reception within this community during her campaign, but as her appeals to the South Asian community were not music based, I do not directly address them here.[15]

While the public weighed in on Harris's musical engagement across various forums, some of the most robust and sustained discussions occurred on Twitter. In her work on communication styles and "Black Twitter,"[16] Sarah Florini notes that in the absence of "corporeal signifiers of racial difference," users render their identities "visible" online by engaging with Black oral traditions (signifyin') in order "to index Black cultural practices, to enact Black subjectivities, and to communicate shared knowledge and experiences."[17] Such exchanges allow users to cultivate individual and collective identities and racial solidarity in virtual spaces.[18] Using conversations on Twitter as a point of departure, this chapter analyzes the media discourses surrounding Harris's musicking and the communication strategies therein against the backdrop of recent scholarship on the intersection of sound, race, and gender. While engagement with music may confer cultural capital on male candidates, women, and especially Black women, must navigate countless obstacles as they attempt to construct a coherent presidential identity through the medium of sound.

IN THE MOOD

On January 14, 2019, just a week before formally declaring her candidacy, Harris participated in a "Mood Mix" segment on *The Late Show with*

Fig. 5. Kamala Harris participates in a "Mood Mix" on *The Late Show with Stephen Colbert*. Still from *The Late Show with Stephen Colbert*, posted on YouTube on January 14, 2019.

Stephen Colbert (Fig. 5).[19] This popular segment customarily features musicians, but a handful of politicians have created them as well, so Harris's appearance isn't unusual per se. Neither is the release of a candidate-curated playlist or mixtape, which, as we saw with Bill Clinton in 1992 and Barack Obama in 2008, is generally "*not* a hodgepodge of uplifting tunes but rather a thoughtfully organized cluster of songs intended to establish a presidential persona or brand . . . and appeal to a specific demographic."[20] In 2016, Hillary Clinton included tracks by artists such as Kelly Clarkson, Demi Lovato, and Katy Perry on her Spotify playlist in hopes of appealing to millennial female voters.[21] Harris's choice to share her mixtape via video interview afforded possibilities that a simple Spotify release announced via Twitter (such as Hillary Clinton's) could not.

The interview format of the "Mood Mix" segment allows Harris to contextualize her music choices and connect them to specific life experiences. She discloses her personal history through references to the aural backdrop that complemented periods in her life (childhood, college), memorable events (cookout, dance), or places (California, her home state; Howard University, her alma mater). The guided tour through Harris's mix appropriately ends with a "presidential song," Funkadelic's "One Nation Under a Groove," signaling a transition from her past to her desired future. After singing the title lyric of Funkadelic's song, she pauses and calls out to the off-screen interviewer, "Can I get it on the . . ." (presumably she is asking the interviewer to play the actual song).[22] After her request trails off, she says, "I hope you guys enjoyed my 'Mood Mix.' More to come. Thank you." Her soundtrack ends for now, but more will be added, as there is more to Harris's story. Although the "Mood Mix" takes a more overtly political turn at the end, Harris reminds the listener that although she was serving as a prosecutor during the 1990s, she shares the same soundtrack, and by extension, the same life experiences and milestones as the voters she wishes to attract.

The "Mood Mix" represents Harris's attempt at being relational. Intimacy is equally forged through the style of the video, which features a single close-up shot of Harris speaking directly to the camera. Since we never see and only briefly hear the offstage voice, we the viewers are put in the subject position of the interviewer. Harris appears to be speaking directly to us, the mediation almost invisible.[23] The confessional style of her responses allows her to establish intimacy with the voter, a necessary component of campaigns in the postmodern political landscape where "voters [are] accustomed to a televisual diet of intimacy and personal display."[24]

Harris's casualness and the informality of the segment become the most apparent in moments where she laughs at herself, which she does after singing a verse from Bob Marley's "Sun Is Shining," a song that, according to Harris, "must be played loud because you have to hear the bass." One could argue that Harris's enthusiastic-but-awkward grooves and subpar singing are endearing and humanize her in a way. Or not. Obama burst into Al Green's "Let's Stay Together" at a speech at the Apollo just as his 2012 re-election campaign moved into full swing, and the crowd heartily approved. Ted Cruz's "Amazing Grace" and Mitt Romney's "America the Beautiful," by contrast, fell horribly flat.[25] Harris's performance in this music confessional relies on rhetorical strategies that Karlyn Kohrs Campbell aligns with a feminine style of rhetoric: personal experience (in the form of her own singing), personal tone (she makes eye contact with the camera, and deploys a conversational demeanor), and audience participation (we see her respond to the questions of the hypothetical viewer).[26] This form of discourse is effective in instances where the speaker and the audience share common values and experiences.[27]

The softer, relational temperament displayed here is a part of Harris's strategy, but it also extends to the music she chose to foreground, at least with regards to some parts of the artists' histories (Table 5). Kendrick Lamar and A Tribe Called Quest are recognized as socially conscious artists. Aretha

Table. 5. Tracks included on Kamala Harris's "Mood Mix"

Occasion	Track	Artist	Release	Genre
A song that has always made me dance	Check the Rhime	A Tribe Called Quest	1997	rap
A song from my favorite movie	Purple Rain	Prince	1984	R & B
	Shallow	Lady Gaga (and Bradley Cooper)	2018	pop/rock
Favorite song at a cookout	*Lemonade* (album)	Beyoncé	2016	R & B
A song that lifts my spirits always	O Happy Day	The Edwin Hawkins Singers	1967	religious
A song that has to be played loud because you have to hear the bass	Sun Is Shining	Bob Marley and the Wailers	1971	reggae
A song that reminds me of my alma mater, Howard University	Push It	Salt-N-Pepa	1986	rap
Favorite song from my childhood	Young, Gifted and Black	Aretha Franklin	1972	R & B
A song that makes me think of my birthplace, Oakland	anything	Too Short	1983–	rap
A song by one of my favorite rappers from California	Humble	Kendrick Lamar	2017	rap
A presidential song for anyone	One Nation Under a Groove	Funkadelic	1978	R & B

Franklin, Beyoncé, and Lady Gaga are unabashedly feminist. A strong advocate for LGBTQ+ rights and an activist onstage and off, Lady Gaga is an iconic figure within the gay community. The theme of overcoming connects "Shallow," "Young, Gifted and Black," and *Lemonade*. Collectively, the "Mood Mix" gives a musical voice to Harris's progressive reformer persona by positioning her as woke in terms of race and gender equality. As Katherine Adam and Charles Derber have argued, voters invested in *feminized values* (support for a strong welfare state, social justice, education, and environmental protection, to name a few) became the majority by September 2007; therefore, candidates developed strategies to connect with voters (women *and* men) who adhered to these values.[28] Just as the trajectory of songs delineates Harris's personal history, the songs catalog Black artists' engagement with social issues, and in creating the mix, Harris crafts a connection to this history. Moreover, she uses the mix as an opportunity to assert her connection to Oakland (Too Short) and her alma mater Howard University (Salt-N-Pepa). Indeed, Harris may have hoped that careful attention to music and its accompanying experiences might promote the image of her as a down-to-earth, thoughtful listening subject, thus posing a challenge to the cop persona that she needed to combat.

But did she accomplish this goal? Four out of the eleven tracks included are hip-hop, and to many, this seemed an inauthentic choice for Harris, just as much as the pop strains of Katy Perry and Kelly Clarkson seemed a mismatch for Hillary Clinton in 2016. In both cases, the playlists reflected the music tastes of the desired demographics (millennial female voters in the case of Clinton in 2016, and Black men who came of age in the 1980s and 1990s for Harris in 2020) but had very little connection to the perceived musical tastes of the candidates themselves. Some could hardly manage to pair the image of "Kamala is a cop" with a hip-hop soundtrack. And Twitter posters gleefully pointed to specific moments in the segment that bespoke her lack of cultural knowledge. For example, she appears to say, "Salt and Pepper" rather than "Salt-N-Pepa."[29] After she adds A Tribe Called Quest's song to the mix, she gives a shout out to one group member with "You know what I'm talkin' about, Phife." One poster schooled her on the fact that Phife Dawg (né Malik Taylor) was dead.[30] Others who questioned her authenticity recalled missteps by other female candidates, namely Clinton's "hot sauce" remarks and Elizabeth Warren's beer-drinking video.[31] Various memes were posted to drive these points home, including the Steve Buscemi "How Do You Do, Fellow Kids?" reaction image, which is intended to berate someone who unsuccessfully tries to appeal to a specific subculture.[32] A much-derided image of former vice presidential candidate (and P90X devotee) Paul Ryan lifting a dumbbell and sporting a backward red baseball cap and muscle shirt also made the rounds, once with the caption "You are the Paul Ryan of 2019," a clear dig at Harris's attempts to seem hip.[33] Harris's embrace of "loud music" appears to fall into a hackneyed stereotype regarding racial identity and noise. Journalists and scholars alike have documented the fear and scrutiny surrounding Black noise and its presence as justification for surveillance and sometimes violence against Black bodies.[34] (Consider for example the case of Jordan Davis, a seventeen-year-old high school student who was fatally shot by a man for refusing to turn down rap music in his friend's car.)[35] While authenticity, a core aesthetic value in hip-hop culture, is a fluid and continually shifting concept, personal authenticity (or being true to oneself) is its nuts and bolts, and to Harris's detractors, she missed the mark.[36]

Harris's identity came under fire as well, with claims that she was "not Black" and "almost as Canadian as Senator [Ted] Cruz."[37] In several instances, posters relied on music as a springboard to comment on Harris as cop. (For example, several posters referred to the group the Police;[38] another posted a GIF of dancing cops with the caption "And the precinct be . . .")[39] Other aspects of Harris's history and competency came in to play as well, with some users pointing to her past relationship with a married politician to call the legitimacy of her career into question.[40] Posters also directly questioned the veracity of her proclaimed music tastes. Can Harris *really* love Bob Marley considering that her policies as prosecutor would have put him in jail?[41] While some posters recognized (and applauded) Harris's mix as evidence of her relatability with remarks such as "Love it! Nice to know she is hip and human," the majority used it as a springboard for criticizing her record and, more significantly, her character.[42] In short, Harris's laughter, lack of musical knowledge, and embrace of musical traditions connected to the communities oppressed by her policies as prosecutor made audiences perceive her assertions of music taste as inauthentic.

I LIKE IT

Just over a week later, Harris similarly attempted to bring pop culture into the political sphere once again, and her efforts were met with sim-

Fig. 6. Kamala Harris grooves to Cardi B. Still from a video posted on Twitter by Lily Adams on January 22, 2019. "When we get tired of speech prep there's only one thing to do."

ilar criticism. On January 22, 2019, her communications director, Lily Adams, posted a video on Twitter of Harris taking a break from speech prep to dance to Cardi B's "I Like It" (Fig. 6).[43] Adams tried to frame her candidate's moment as spontaneous and unscripted, but Harris's actions and choice of soundtrack seem to quite deliberately engage with two widely circulated videos that pundits had feasted on a few weeks prior. (Not to mention that Obama also showed off his dance moves early in his 2008 campaign.)[44] The first video, posted by an anonymous

Twitter user on January 2, 2019, features edited footage of Alexandria Ocasio-Cortez dancing in 2010, back in her college days. The poster embraced the opportunity to dismiss the freshman representative from New York as "America's favorite commie know-it-all acting like the clueless nitwit she is," but the smear campaign actually backfired, with many coming out in support of Ocasio-Cortez.[45] Two days later she fired back with her own Twitter post: "I hear the GOP thinks women dancing are scandalous. Wait till they find out Congresswomen dance too!"[46] The second video, an expletive-laden Instagram post by Cardi B, excoriates then-president Trump for demanding that federal employees return to work without pay during the government shutdown.[47] Democratic politicians praised the January 16 rant, but openly pondered whether or not they should retweet it, as it features the raw, unfiltered, confrontational style that the artist is known for.[48] Just days later, Ocasio-Cortez tweeted out her support for Cardi B in the wake of her feud with conservative commentator Tomi Lahren, who had roasted the rapper-entrepreneur for her anti-Trump rant.[49]

Cardi B (née Belcalis Marlenis Almánzar) was a stripper, Instagram model, and reality television star (*Love & Hip Hop: New York*) before becoming the first solo female rap artist to achieve the top spot on Billboard's Hot 100 list since Lauryn Hill (1998).[50] She is also a self-proclaimed feminist, although her brand of feminism is a much criticized and contested one.[51] As Sherri Williams, who calls the Bronx native an "unlikely feminist hero," argues, "Cardi B's very presence is an act of resistance to oppressive and restrictive ideologies. She does feminist work through pop culture but it is not validated because her path to feminism is not traditional and, most importantly, she is a sex-positive woman of color from a working class background who challenges some of the traditional views that even feminists possess."[52] Harris describes herself as both tough and fearless, and in this sense, the two women would seem to be of similar dispositions. However, Cardi B's brand of feminism, what Gwendolyn Pough might call "bringing wreck" (to the institutional structures that enable sexism and misogyny to proliferate), seems to go against the grain of the respectability demanded of Black female candidates.[53] But Harris herself has a complicated relationship with feminism, and the genuineness of her feminism was even called into question during the presidential campaign. As senator, Harris voted to approve spending bills that included the Hyde

Amendment, which prohibits federal funding for abortion (except for the most extreme cases), and as attorney general of the state of California, she dismissed a suit that would have decriminalized sex work and afforded protections to sex workers. As her presidential run approached, Harris flip-flopped on the Hyde Amendment, softened her stance on Black mothers who were impacted by her antitruancy policy, and positioned herself as an advocate for sex worker safety.[54] But a disconnect remained, as Harris appeared to reinforce the very elements of the system Cardi B's feminism works to disrupt.

At almost forty million followers on Twitter, Cardi B is a cultural force that wields a lot of influence. Using the phrase "Cardi B Effect," NPR editor Sidney Madden describes the performer as possessing "a branding power rooted in specific authenticity."[55] Harris could have been seeking an endorsement, but she may have also wanted to appeal to Cardi B's fan base. Because of her light skin and Afro-Latina heritage, Cardi B has faced accusations of "not being Black enough," and, as described earlier, Harris has been subjected to similar identity policing. While proximity to whiteness *does* afford certain privileges, as I discussed in chapter 1 with Obama, strategic performances of blackness can offer cultural currency as well. As Amanda Matos posits, "Cardi rejects respectability politics by challenging the mainstream embodiment of womanhood with her fashion, cadence, and expression of her sexuality."[56] With the "I Like It" dance, Harris attempts to perform "edginess" by aligning with a Black rap artist. But many posters saw through the act, and they were critical of Harris for opportunistically "performing blackness" to appeal to the Black vote.[57] This idea of blackness as a "masquerade" of sorts found kinship with the "Kamala is a cop" trope in tweets such as "Pretty sure the technical cop term for this is 'going undercover'"[58] and "Why does kamala harris dance like a police officer."[59] In both instances, the posters align Harris with the White male oppressor rather than positioning her dance video as an authentic expression of Black womanhood.

The timing of the "I Like It" video, just three weeks after the resurfacing of Ocasio-Cortez's "scandalous" dancing and her subsequent defense of Cardi B, suggests that Harris wanted to show solidarity with the freshman House member, another trailblazing and popular female politician. The video could also be a subtle jab directed at Ocasio-Cortez's detractors for implying that women cannot both enjoy themselves and be competent politicians. In other words, Harris uses music and dancing to demonstrate her solidarity with other progressive women, while asserting that she, like Cardi B, is tough and refuses to confine herself to traditional conceptions of womanhood.[60] But there was also a downside, as many posters turned to stereotypes regarding criminality and Black female hypersexuality, framing both Cardi B and Harris in this light: "Promoting a gang affiliated pole dancer . . . I'm not surprised."[61] And others saw the video as Harris's failed attempt to cast herself as a bona fide progressive: "Letting people sniff their traffic was totally worth it to try to capitalize @AOC's fame",[62] and "Epic fail. Trying to copy AOC. Now watch while I pretend to be a Progressive."[63]

The criticism that followed Harris's dancing on Twitter drew on many of the same tropes embedded in discussions of her "Mood Mix," but with the majority of the focus on Harris's attempt to appeal, or some might say, pander, to Black voters. However misplaced, we see Harris's attempt to be relational in her online engagement, countering the cop persona detractors wished to pin on her. As Regina Lawrence and Melody Rose have argued, acting as a leader yet simultaneously appearing feminine presents difficulties for the female politician. Therefore, female presidential hopefuls must adopt a *gender strategy* to counter deeply ingrained cultural attitudes, as "Gender stereotypes and masculinized images of the presidency shape women's paths to power."[64] In this instance, the public again questioned Harris's authenticity by alluding to the gaffes of other female politicians, including Hillary Clinton's "hot sauce," "just chillin' in Cedar Rapids," and "Pokemon Go to the polls" remarks.[65] These allusions rely on totalizing rhetoric that paints all women as false and fundamentally untruthful, willing to awkwardly dabble in pop culture in order to indulge certain audiences. Several posters even issued warnings that such activity could compromise the campaign: "Please rethink your campaign strategy when it comes to the African American vote. Right now it's becoming insulting. All we want to hear from her is a relevant and specific agenda. We don't care what music she likes or how well she can dance! Democratic Party has to step it up."[66]

HOW DO YOU DO, FELLOW KIDS?

Harris again professed her admiration for Cardi B during a February 11, 2019, interview on an episode of *The Breakfast Club*. During the interview, cohosts DJ Envy and Charlamagne Tha God explore Harris's personal and political history through topics ranging from her time as prosecutor to her agenda for the Black community, from her experimentation with marijuana to her Bolognese sauce. The topic of whether she is "Black enough" comes into focus at several points in the interview when she responds to questions about her career, her marriage, her parents' background as civil rights activists, her superlative collard greens, and the reception of her candidacy within the Black community. Toward the end of the interview, when the questions turn to music, film, and hobbies, the following exchange ensues:

DJ ENVY: What does Kamala Harris listen to?
CHARLAMAGNE THA GOD: What were you listening to when you was high? What was on . . . What song was . . .
KAMALA HARRIS: [laughing]
DJ ENVY: Was it Snoop?
HARRIS: Oh my goodness. Oh yeah, definitely Snoop, uh huh, uh, Tupac for sure, for sure.[67]

Before Harris can answer DJ Envy's question, "What does Kamala Harris listen to?" Charlamagne Tha God interjects and asks her what music she was listening to when she smoked marijuana, a disclosure she made earlier in the segment when discussing her college years. Harris disregards Charlamagne's question and replies to DJ Envy's with "Oh yeah, definitely Snoop. Tupac for sure." One Twitter user heard Harris's Tupac/Snoop remark as a response to Charlamagne's question about the music she listened to while smoking in college rather than DJ Envy's more general question about what she listens to now. He pointed out that Tupac's first album (*2Pacalypse Now*) dropped in 1991, and Snoop's first album (*Doggystyle*) in 1993, whereas Harris graduated from college in 1986.[68] While her campaign tried to manage the backlash that followed the interview, media outlets already began reporting on the alleged gaffe, questioning Harris's credibility.

Within a day, the hashtag #KamalaHarrisRapGenius was born and the criticism across social media moved into full swing. Some brought humor into the mix, ventriloquizing Harris to call her hip-hop cred into question:

I Love A Tribe Called Quest! My favorite member has to be Questlove.[69]

My favorite rap song from the Fresh Prince was Purple Rain.[70]

I gotta tell you that Kross Kris just had to be one of the greatest rap groups ever. Those four fellas really knew how turn it up![71]

That whole East Coast/West Coast beef which led to the tragic loss of Boosie and 2 Chainz is what made me wanna become a cop.[72]

I remember The Miseducation of Lauryn Hill being such a defining album for me in my late teens. So powerful. A black woman I could identify with in the late 70s. Amazing.[73]

I'll tell ya, Champagneman The God. MCLyte's song "You Cannot Touch This" was my jammy jam back in the day.[74]

In the posters' imagined Kamala Harris tweets, the "candidate" attempts to demonstrate her knowledge of hip-hop, but it backfires quite horribly. *Quest*love is a record producer, disc jockey, and drummer for the Roots, the house band for *The Tonight Show Starring Jimmy Fallon*. A Tribe Called *Quest* was a 1990s hip-hop group with Q-Tip, Phife Dawg, Ali Shaheed Muhammad, and Jarobi White. The Fresh *Prince* (Will Smith) was one-half of the duo DJ Jazzy Jeff & The Fresh Prince, whereas *Prince* was a singer-songwriter, multi-instrumentalist, producer, and composer of the song "Purple Rain." Kris Kross (not *Kross Kris*) was a rap duo, not a four-man band. 2 Chainz and Boosie are from the South and still alive and well. *The Miseducation of Lauryn Hill* dropped in 1998, not the 1970s, and "U Can't Touch This" was cowritten and performed by *MC* Hammer, not *MC* Lyte.

Displays of wit and humor are central to signifyin', and a means of signaling racial identity on Twitter.[75] To locate the humor in the posters' musings as Kamala Harris, one needs to possess the requisite cultural knowledge. In this instance, the tweets became a way for the folks on Black Twitter to diss Harris, thereby affirming *their* status as insiders and *Harris's* as outsider. Some posters altered the stylized language in songs to emphasize Harris's linguistic distance. For example, one reads, "You Cannot Touch This" instead of "U Can't Touch This," the slang "U" replaced with the more formal "You." Charlamagne Tha God becomes "Champagneman The God," the slang "tha" replaced by "the" and the cohost's name transformed into a material signifier of upper-class identity (champagne). Acoustic identity, Alice Ashton Filmer notes, is "negotiated and defined within a complex set of historical/sociopolitical/cultural relations and expectations that ultimately conflate the use of (Standard) English(es) with Whiteness and Western imperialism."[76] Here, posters imagine Harris's voice imposing Standard English on slang, thus aligning her with the oppressor and positioning themselves on the linguistic margins.[77]

Geneva Smitherman situates the diss as a "verbal game" that can be carried out in jest or as a form of social critique.[78] I would argue that the above posts, which rely on cultural knowledge, take on a more lighthearted tone, whereas others appear to be more serious critiques. For example, several posters criticized Harris for reducing blackness to rap and weed, implying that she lacks an authentic appreciation of the values, histories, and embodied life experiences of Black Americans: "Kamala Harris had her Howard Dean Scream moment. She thinks getting the Black vote is all about rap and getting high. When she was AG she sent thousands to prison for the same offense. . . . She's cancelled!"[79] and "I'm offended that she thought #smokingweed and #hiphop was going to get my vote more then the actual lie."[80] On *Jamaica Global Online*, Harris's own father, Donald Harris, expressed his disdain over some of her remarks in the interview: "My dear departed grandmothers . . . as well as my deceased parents, must be turning in their grave right now to see their family's name, reputation and proud Jamaican identity being connected, in any way, jokingly or not with the fraudulent stereotype of a pot-smoking joy seeker and in the pursuit of identity politics."[81]

Wordplay, also central to signifyin', came into play with several posts: "I will never forget when I first heard Rapture's Delight,"[82] and "I'm down with O.P.P. (Oppressive Private Prisons)."[83] In the first post, the substitution of "rapture" for "rapper's" recalls a track from the Sugarhill Gang, hip-hop's earliest commercial success. The poster plays with the doubleness of the word "rapture"—do we hear "rapture" as in intense pleasure, or "Rapture" as in the transportation of believers with the second coming of Christ? In the second post, Naughty by Nature's "O.P.P." (other people's pussy) becomes "Oppressive Private Prisons," another allusion to Harris's record as prosecutor. Ultimately, these perceived missteps, as critiqued through verbal games, revealed the public's mistrust and skepticism directed at Harris.

On December 3, 2019, Kamala Harris suspended her campaign. Pundits were quick to explain why Harris was unsuccessful. The *Atlantic*'s Peter Beinart blamed progressives for failing to acknowledge the fact that *both* parties took a hard-line stance on crime in the 1990s and 2000s and that Harris was but a product of that environment where women and Black officeholders were under pressure to "prove" that they could be tough on crime.[84] Amanda Marcotte blamed the "Kamala is a cop" meme for "wiping out a nuanced discussion of her history in favor of a gross generalization" and pegged "a bunch of douchey white guys" as the culprits for appropriating legitimate issues raised by people of color.[85] Camille Squires, pushing back against Marcotte's contention that toxic internet culture could be blamed, pointed toward the labor of Black folks, especially women, who offered legitimate critiques of Harris's policy stances and criminal justice record.[86] Early in the Harris campaign, journalist Jill Filipovic had criticized public scrutiny over Harris's history and simplistic critiques of her record, pointing toward the challenges Black women face in comparison to their White male counterparts who "get to be complicated, have imperfect records, and be treated like individuals."[87] But perhaps the media's framing of Harris hurt her as well. After her Tupac and Snoop remarks caught fire, the *New York Times* published a piece called "Kamala Harris Is Accused of Lying about Listening to Tupac." Several commenters who weighed in on this article noted gender and racial biases in such framing: "When it's Trump, you gingerly call them 'possible falsehoods.' When it's a female person of color, the word 'lying' magically appears."[88] Others called out the Right for blowing the incident out of proportion and trying to instigate "Reefergate" in response to an innocent act of misremembering.[89]

But was it really policy and the facts of her record that brought down the Harris campaign? In the age of media spectacle, Jackson Katz argues, feeling often trumps fact, with presidential elections "won and lost largely in the realm of myth, symbolism, and identity."[90] Popular music, with its semiotic flexibility and tangled histories, operates within this realm, so it is not surprising that Harris relied on the mixtape and the assertion of music tastes to establish herself as a Black candidate and to connect with Black voters. Aimee Allison, the founder of She the People, a national network of women of color (voters, organizers, movement builders, elected leaders), encourages Black women running for office "to lean into the fact that fellow Black women are the most powerful Democrats."[91] And Tasha Philpot and Hanes Walton's research has shown that Black women voters are the greatest supporters of Black women candidates.[92] Johnnie Cordero, chair of the South Carolina Democratic Black Caucus, argued that Harris (and fellow candidate Cory Booker) did not spend sufficient time seeking Black support.[93] While this point may be true when it comes to Harris's overarching political strategy, Harris (and her team) *did* center Black voters when it came to music. So why did her *music* strategy misfire? In the words of one Twitter poster responding to the Tupac/Snoop kerfuffle:

> Well, she was trying to run the Obama playbook. She thought she could just use us as a backdrop and get our votes without any policies or tangibles. Apparently, she hasn't noticed that we aren't falling for it.[94]

Key to the success of Obama's strategy (or "playbook," to use the poster's words) was his adeptness in code-switching / style switching, which Michael Jeffries argues allowed him "to manage and perform his racial identity."[95] Harris struggled in this regard, and music was one area where her attempts were scrutinized.

To begin, there was a presumed *misalignment* between Harris's personal history, her policymaking, her professed identity as a progressive, and the genre of hip-hop. This disconnect becomes all the more apparent when comparing Harris's hip-hop engagement to that of Obama, who, like Harris, is multiracial and spent some of his early years outside of the United States. Obama was strategic and tempered in the way he established his relationship to the genre. He was adept enough in hip-hop culture to suggest political alignment with a pro-Black agenda, but distant enough to skirt the unsavory stereotypes and connotations pinned to the genre, its artists, and its audiences. He maintained an awareness of what Tricia Rose calls the "hip hop wars" (critics who position hip-hop as signaling the decline of civilization vs. defenders who overlook sexism and violence and embrace Black authenticity) but knew how to occupy neutral ground and mobilize the community on his behalf.[96] He openly spoke of his admiration for Kanye West and Jay-Z in his 2008 interview with Jeff Johnson, but at the same time, he underscored the generational distance between himself and the rappers (Obama is an Earth, Wind & Fire, Stevie Wonder, and Isley Brothers kind of guy).[97] On several occasions, including a *Rolling Stone* interview, he expressed concern over the genre's sometimes offensive lyrical content, but used words such as "genius" and "art," praising hip-hop's potential to promote desegregation.[98] In such contexts, Obama assumed the role of the concerned father, focusing on the potential for Black uplift and rejecting the notion of Black authenticity being rooted in street life, thuggery, and sexism.[99] Journalist Gabe Meline described Obama as hip-hop's "really, really cool dad," and this "old-school" dad character even extended to his rally playlist, which he stacked with R & B chart-toppers from the 1960s and 1970s.[100] In short, Obama cautiously positioned himself as a role model, father figure, and admirer of hip-hop, *not* as an insider.

Harris offered no such distance. Her remarks about Phife Dawg and her uncritical embrace of gangsta artists such as Snoop Dogg and Too Short made her seem an uninformed interloper, rather than a cautious onlooker or thoughtfully engaged fan. The mispronunciation of Salt-N-Pepa and the presumed gaffe about her college soundtrack made her appear inauthentic and unschooled in hip-hop culture, which further reinforced her interloper status. One Facebook poster remarked, "This nice white lady sure loves our black hippity hop rap music."[101] By flippantly calling Harris's racial identity *and* cultural knowledge into question, the poster implies that Harris is not just an interloper but also a threat, an accusation that is explicitly stated in posts that allude to her record as prosecutor. To cite one, "No one cares that [Kamala Harris] smoked some cannabis. The issue is that she locked people up for it."[102] In the year preceding Harris's presidential bid, there were numerous highly publicized instances of White women calling the police on people of color for trivial or nonexistent offenses. Barbecue Becky, Permit Patty, Golfcart Gail, Cornerstore Caroline—monikers for privileged White women who feel entitled to surveil spaces they perceive as for Whites only and needlessly endanger Black lives.[103] That is to say, a former prosecutor turned presidential candidate was similarly threatening to Black men. In a scathing *Miami New Times* column, rapper Luther Campbell of 2 Live Crew fame echoed these sentiments, though it should be noted that he later changed his tune. These discourses damaged Harris's credibility and reinforced the negative "Kamala is a cop" narrative that she was trying to neutralize in order to appeal to Black voters.[104]

And there was a second issue: Harris's professed love for gangsta rap was out of sync with the relatable, more feminine-gendered communication style she cultivated in her "Mood Mix" and "I Like It" videos. To some who could not reconcile her past as prosecutor with her record in the Senate, it might seem like Harris professes love for Black culture yet shows no empathy for Black suffering, especially that of Black men. It is interesting to note that two Black women—Aretha Franklin and Beyoncé—were represented on the "Mood Mix," and her launch walk-on song was Mary J. Blige's "Work That," yet in all the recrimination on social media, there was seldom any mention of these artists or songs. This may be because iconic Black feminists *do* seem an appropriate fit for Harris, who describes herself as tough, principled, and fearless. Perhaps Harris's racial identification was not the issue, but rather her gender was. While Harris was "permitted" the music of Black feminists, the associations of gangsta as hypermasculine, misogynist, non-White, and antiestablishment were a mismatch with her platform and communication style. In other words, the problem wasn't Harris's presence in Black spaces, but rather her intrusion into male-gendered Black spaces. To return to Aimee Allison's remarks, Black women candidates *need* the support of Black women voters, and the majority of Harris's soundtrack and tastes did not find resonance with this voting bloc. But because of colorism, the deck may have already been stacked against Harris in this regard. Danielle Casarez Lemi and Nadia E. Brown have shown that "dark-skinned candidates are believed to have a stronger tie to racialized communities, whereas light-skinned candidates are rated closer to Whites on trait measures."[105] Similarly, Byron D'Andra Orey and Yu Zhang's research has shown that millennials (specifically, their student interviewees at a historically Black university) perceive female African American candidates with phenotypes that mirror the typical African American to be more supportive of progressive policies than their lighter-skinned counterparts.[106]

While the "Mood Mix" segment, the Cardi B "I Like It" dance video, and the *Breakfast Club* interview were early instances of Harris's musical engagement, they were not the only ones. Harris made some less controversial choices as well. "My Shot" from *Hamilton* made the rotation at her rallies, which also included some of Obama's 1960s and 1970s classics (Stevie Wonder, the Staple Singers, and Aretha Franklin) and girl power anthems by Black artists (Andra Day's "Rise Up," Beyoncé's "Rule the World," Alicia Keys's "Girl on Fire," and Janelle Monáe's "Tightrope").[107] Local acts sometimes made appearances at her live events. (A drumline welcomed her to the South Carolina Democratic Party Convention.)[108] In June 2019, she released a summer playlist, which received high praise from *Rolling Stone* with the title "If Playlists Won Elections, Kamala Harris Would Be an Easy Frontrunner."[109] But while Obama quite thoughtfully weighed in on music culture and his music tastes on multiple occasions, Harris never offered a coherent, plausible narrative to position herself as a similarly thoughtful listening subject or music fan, and this added fuel to the critics' fire.

Even after her presidential campaign ended, Harris's musical choices followed the broad appeal trajectory. On the day that Harris removed herself from the race, Lily Adams posted a video of the former candidate leading her staff in a dance routine to Beyoncé's "Before I Let Go," with the following tweet: "As Kamala says, being a leader is not about who you beat down. It's about who you lift up. Here she is lifting up our Baltimore staff tonight. Cheers to our leader."[110] In spring 2019, Beyoncé's cover of the R & B song, which critic Jeneé Osterheldt called "a staple at family reunions, weddings, and the last dance of a good black party since 1981," appeared at the end of her concert film, *Homecoming*.[111] The Netflix film features the artist's historic 2018 Coachella performances, which were praised as a tribute to historically Black colleges and universities, Black Greek life, and Black intellectual and artistic traditions. Within days of the concert film release and live album drop, the "Before I Let Go" dance challenge launched.[112] The song choice is a strategic one for Harris in that its constellation of associations incorporates touchpoints of Harris's biography much like the "Mood Mix": she is an HBCU graduate and a member of the Alpha Kappa Alpha sorority. The song simultaneously looks backward and forward. While the original R & B version of the song may resonate with Gen-Xers raised with *The Cosby Show*, Beyoncé's cover, which Osterheldt describes as "equal parts New Orleans bounce, soul, and Cameo 'Candy' funk," speaks to the stylistic dexterity of Beyoncé and the omnivorous music consumption practices of millennials.[113] And while Harris's grooves in Adams's tweet may remind the viewer of her other dance moves on the trail, including the Cardi B video, the TikTok dance challenge phenomenon speaks to the participatory culture of today's digital natives and their impulse to create and recreate dance trends circulated online. Moreover, the song's association with the film memorializing Beyoncé's Coachella appearance—a historic performance in a space that has historically excluded Black artists and female headliners—reminds the listener that Harris too is a trailblazer succeeding in an arena (politics) where Black women have been subjected to exclusion.

On August 19, 2020, Harris officially accepted the vice presidential nomination at the Democratic National Convention in a speech that was flanked by the affirming words of her niece, stepdaughter, and younger sister and a projected screen of clapping female supporters, as Mary J. Blige's spirited ode to female empowerment, "Work That," swelled in the background. Although Harris's musical signaling early in the primary may have seemed all over the map and devoid of clear messaging, indeed she found her stride in this moment. Yet just five weeks later, Harris made perhaps her most damning musical misfire. In an interview with Angela Rye during the NAACP virtual convention on September 25, 2020, Harris cited Tupac as the "best rapper alive." Rye reminded her that the rapper died in 1996.[114] President Trump's campaign even trolled Harris by reserving Tupac a ticket for the vice-presidential debate.[115] But we might consider another explanation for this presumed gaffe. For as much as the "Mood Mix" was about Harris affirming that she was "in the know" when it came to hip-hop culture, the Tupac gaffe could be an assertion of the reverse—a distancing strategy by a vice-presidential candidate who wanted to appear less "hip-hop minded" and prove her broad appeal within the party. Unfortunately, Harris's detractors were more apt to scrutinize her questionable choices than to applaud her good ones. If, as Lisa Lerer and Jennifer Medina argue, Black female candidates are subjected to a greater level of scrutiny, it is no surprise that music choices would be treated in the same manner.[116]

Political scientists and sociologists argue that women's participation in the political field is circumscribed by double binds, defined as "psychological impasse[s] created when contradictory demands are made of an individual . . . so that no matter which directive is followed, the response will be construed as incorrect."[117] This certainly rings true for Harris in that assertions of racial identity and affiliation were complicated by her gender, and vice versa, her performance of gender complicated her assertions of racial identity and affiliation. These "contradictory demands" impeded Harris's cultivation of a coherent musical identity.[118] For voters, Harris's musical engagement offered a blank space in which they could deploy allusion, humor, and intertextual references as a means of making sense of her identity as a Black female candidate. While indeed Harris's musical misfires and the ensuing conversations brought these "psychological impasses" into sharp relief, research addressing the impact of intersectional stereotyping on political decision-making shows that "double jeopardy and double disadvantage are not an inevitable obstacle for intersectionally situated candidates."[119] Therefore, a cogent and nuanced music strategy might ultimately work to negotiate these impasses for future Black female candidates.

CHAPTER 4

Girls "Keep America Great"

Singing the White *Stuff for Donald Trump*

Suburban women, will you please like me? I saved your damn neighborhood, OK?

—DONALD TRUMP AT A CAMPAIGN RALLY IN JOHNSTOWN,
PENNSYLVANIA, OCTOBER 13, 2020[1]

Kind of like going to a family reunion, but you've just never met the people yet.

—SINGER CAMILLE HARRIS, DESCRIBING THE ATMOSPHERE AT A
TRUMP RALLY TO A *FOX NEWS* INTERVIEWER, OCTOBER 31, 2020[2]

THE FEMININE *MISTAKE*

A tween song-and-dance act known as the USA Freedom Kids performed "Freedom's Call," a kitschy parody of George M. Cohan's World War I patriotic song "Over There" (1917), at a Donald Trump rally in January 2016.[3] The fresh-faced trio, bedecked in 1950s-style cheerleader attire, delivered a message that perfectly aligned with the candidate's campaign platform and rhetorical style (Fig. 7):[4]

> Enemies of freedom. Face the music, come on boys, take 'em down! President Donald Trump knows how to make America great. Deal from strength or get crushed every time.

The belt-style vocals, underscored by robotic synthesized beats, made lyrics such as "Deal from strength or get crushed every time" take on the character of a schoolyard bully's threat.[5] While the early twentieth-century tune and distinctly feminine throwback attire may have potentially invoked nostalgic sentiments among the predominantly White crowd, the

Fig. 7. The USA Freedom Kids perform at a Donald Trump rally in Pensacola, Florida, on January 13, 2016. Still from "Freedom's Call," posted on YouTube on January 13, 2016.

disconnect between the song's jingoist message and the trio's girly cuteness unsettled others. *Time* magazine included the USA Freedom Kids on its list of "45 Americans Who Defined the Election," and their star turn for Trump was perhaps one of the most viral musical moments of the 2016 presidential campaign.[6] Jimmy Kimmel and Stephen Colbert parodied the performance, and major news outlets weighed in on the tween act.[7] Some journalists described the girls' patriotic spectacle as "horrifying," "creepy," and "tortuous," while folks on Twitter made analogies between the USA Freedom Kids and the youth movements of Nazi Germany and North Korea.[8] Others focused on the trio's *musical* talents. Colbert, for example, likened the music to the sound of "a bald eagle marching on a Casio keyboard."[9] Accusations of child exploitation were thrown into the critical mix as well. The group's leader and the father of one of the singers, Jeff Popick, deflected the flak, stating, "It just shows this country needs more of what we're doing. It was somebody maybe smarter than me who said 'a child shall lead them.'"[10] Many conservatives agreed with the scripture-quoting dad, with one claiming, "This [performance] is reminiscent of what America once was." Another commenter praised the performance for evoking "WWII era America," while yet another applauded the girls for their modest vintage attire, which was "Not like Miley Cyrus, Madonna, or any of today's TRULY TARTED UP youngsters or adult female 'stars.'"[11] (Both Cyrus and Madonna engage with Black performance styles, so there may be a trace of racial stereotyping here as well, with modesty positioned as the distinct purview of White womanhood.) Overall, supporters on right-leaning websites applauded the performance's evocation of nostalgia and praised the Kids' palpable love of country and traditional values, which they elevated as a model worthy of emulation.[12]

Left-leaning critics latched onto this performance for two reasons: one, the children's role in proliferating what some deemed a purely propagandistic message, and two, the act's lack of artistic and musical substance. However, I would like to point to a third aspect of the performance that made it a unicorn of sorts in 2016. The official Trump campaign playlist and even "unofficial" songs and videos inspired by his candidacy were primarily authored and performed by men; in official contexts, songs by the Shangri-Las, Betty Buckley, and Adele were a few of the notable exceptions. The incumbent candidate's 2020 list was similarly lacking in female voices.[13] To a certain extent, this lacuna in the Trump soundtrack has been replicated in scholarly work on music and campaigns. As chapter 1 illustrates, the Obama candidacy inspired many thoughtful essays on the articulation of race and music on the trail; however, only a scant amount of work has addressed how the intersecting categories of whiteness and femininity operate in campaign music.[14] As Ruth Frankenberg has argued, "Whiteness makes itself invisible precisely by asserting its normalcy, its transparency, in contrast with the marking of others on which its transparency depends."[15] Girl groups for Trump, such as the USA Freedom Kids, provide an opportunity to investigate the meanings attached to the girl's voice on the campaign trail.[16] Focusing on the sister act Camille & Haley in 2020, I analyze how American identity, Christian values, and White middle-class girlhood coalesce in their pro-Trump performances. I situate these musical offerings against the backdrop of broader research theorizing conceptions of gender and race in the age of Donald Trump and consider how such performances appealed to the political Right while also serving as a target for those who wished to critique veiled assertions of White supremacy.

SETTING THE STAGE FOR THE RAGE

In the aftermath of the 2016 election, pundits posited theories that would account for the surprising win of a corrupt businessman and reality television star with no political experience or expertise. Trump's campaign platform, which fueled fear over unrestricted immigration and limitations to gun rights, played into the anxieties of White men who were profoundly impacted by deindustrialization and outsourcing. This disenfranchised demographic harbored resentment toward the outgoing Obama administration, with many perceiving the attendant rise of identity politics, ethos of multiculturalism, and political correctness as the cultural shifts that threatened their traditional values, rights, and economic self-determination.[17] Historically, political parties have exerted a broad influence over election outcomes, but in 2016, voters with authoritarian leanings—a group that eschews diversity and values uniformity, obedience, and order—greatly contributed to Trump's victory.[18] Matthew MacWilliams describes authoritarians as rigid thinkers who think exclusively in terms of black and white. Trump frequently aligned with this perspective, espousing an "us vs. them," "good guys vs. bad guys" mentality.[19] Threat and fear played a role in stimulating authoritarian behavior and attitudes, and Trump was able to capitalize on these anxieties by stoking the public's real and imagined fears over undocumented immigrants and refugees and the economic dominance of countries such as China, Japan, and Mexico.

Although evangelical Christians would presumably find Trump's personal (and even professional) history to be morally suspect and in discord with basic biblical principles, his policy positions, strongman rhetoric, and authoritarian leanings appealed to believers. John Fea points to Trump's "win back" and "restore the culture" language as strongly appealing to this demographic. That is to say, evangelicals—many of whom view the world through an authoritarian lens—have historically been motivated by fear, and "have built their understanding of political engagement around the anxiety they have felt amid times of social and cultural change."[20] Obama, a multiracial man raised by a single parent and educated abroad, became the embodiment of these anxieties, seen as a troubling symbol of the demographic changes that were sweeping the country.[21] Fear that the nation's moral fiber became weaker in the wake of the Obama presidency, with legislation legalizing same-sex marriage and health care that required employers to cover contraceptive care, made Trump's promise to "Make America Great Again" a desirable vision. As the "law and order candidate," Trump cleverly situated himself as the antidote to both the inefficacy of traditional conservativism and the hypocrisy of liberal elitism.[22] In coded language and sometimes in a direct manner, Trump painted the God-fearing White man as imperiled by dark forces from the outside and policies from within. While this victimization narrative is questionable, many think pieces in 2015–2016 pondered the plight of this demographic. In a survey on the attitudes and perceptions of White US citizens, Justin Gest, Tyler Reny, and Jeremy Mayer found a correlation between a psychological phenomenon they call "nostalgic deprivation—the discrepancy between individuals' understandings of their current status and their perceptions about their past"—and support for the radical Right.[23]

By time the 2020 election was underway, the same rhetoric persisted, but additional "threats" amassed: to those on the right, "caravans of migrants" were bringing crime and chaos to towns across America, and protests and violence carried out by Black Lives Matter rioters and Antifa posed a risk to law enforcement officers and threatened the public's safety. In the announcement of his candidacy in 2015, Trump included Mexican immigrants in his litany of entities to fear, asserting that Mexicans crossing the border were rapists.[24] In associating criminality with brown-skinned foreigners, he animates long-standing White supremacist discourses that justify the subjugation of minorities in service of protecting White womanhood. C. J. Pascoe argues that Trump "mobilizes rape" as a means of "distancing himself from his own sexually predatory behavior by projecting it on to other, less masculine men." Thus, "The label of 'rapist' is transferred to poor men and men of color, symbolically purifying white, middle class or educated men of this sort of undesirable behavior."[25] This pattern of stoking fear and then displaying a protectionist stance was par for the course at Trump's 2020 rallies, and he emphasized threats from within the nation's borders as well. At one Johnstown, Pennsylvania, rally in October 2020, Trump spoke of his desire to keep low-income housing out of suburban neighborhoods, saying, "Suburban women should like me more than anyone here tonight because I ended the regulation that destroyed your neighborhood."[26] The term "suburban women," which Trump has used in a racialized manner, generally refers to middle- and upper-class White women.[27] In harmony with his MAGA (Make America Great Again) ethos, Trump's imagining of homogeneous White suburbs is more aligned with the past than the present. As political scientists have noted, the suburbs have diversified over the past three decades and are home to people of various racial, ethnic, and economic backgrounds.[28]

In many respects, these professed protective impulses directed toward women would appear to run counter to Trump's history of relationships with romantic partners, subordinates, and others who have crossed his path. In October 2016, shortly before the second presidential debate, the *Washington Post* circulated a 2005 recording of Trump making lewd remarks about women to *Access Hollywood* host Billy Bush and a few others.[29] The candidate dismissed the remarks, claiming that they were merely "locker-room banter" and instead deflected the criticism to Bill Clinton, whom he just a week earlier called "the single greatest abuser of women in the history of politics."[30] Republicans who supported Trump were quick to distance themselves from his remarks despite his apologies. After the tape of the *Access Hollywood* exchange went public, numerous women came forward with stories of Trump's sexual misconduct over the past thirty years. Some journalists and talking heads assumed his record of misogynist and sexist remarks and allegations of misconduct would signal the demise of his campaign, yet toxic masculinity only seemed to heighten his appeal among certain swaths of the electorate. As Deborah Cameron notes, the *Access Hollywood* remarks affirmed Trump's alpha male status and "reinforced the impression that he possessed several qualities traditionally associated with strong male leaders, such as authority, aggressiveness, competitiveness, and high libido."[31] Moreover, the transgressive nature of the decade-old verbal exchange affirmed his status as a political outsider who did not concern himself with offending the establishment.[32]

Nicholas A. Valentino, Carly Wayne, and Marzia Oceno argue that the "angry emotional climate" of the election enhanced the impact of sexism in 2016. People who felt threated by immigrants, minorities, and feminists responded with anger, and that same emotion stoked sexist attitudes.[33] In their work on ambivalent sexism theory, Peter Glick and Susan Fiske view sexism as possessing two dimensions: hostile and benevolent.[34] While hostile sexism might see men and women in competition for dominance, benevolent sexism endorses positive but patronizing attitudes toward women. Women who serve in traditionally feminine roles such as wife, mother, and romantic partner are rewarded with protection, whereas women who transgress these roles are considered unworthy of such care.[35] This dualism played out during the 2016 and 2020 campaigns as the Republican contender displayed both hostile and benevolent sexism by turns.

Discourses surrounding nativism and imperiled White womanhood set the stage for the reception of the girl groups that came out in support of Trump in 2016 and 2020. Tulsa natives Camille and Haley Harris, who describe themselves as "singers, songwriters, and sisters," started singing when they were teenagers, leading worship in their church. They first received mainstream attention in 2012 when they composed a campaign song for Republican primary candidate Rick Santorum. The music video for "Game On" received over one million views in two weeks.[36] The story was covered by several news channels, and the duo began traveling with Santorum and singing their original country music, the national anthem, and his new theme song at campaign stops in five different states over the five-week period preceding the suspension of his campaign in April 2012.[37] Over the following decade, the duo performed at countless churches and civic events, released a handful of CDs featuring their hybrid country-pop/contemporary Christian sound, and maintained a robust presence on YouTube. According to their website, they "are committed to the cause of American freedom, raising patriotism among millennials & spreading the Gospel through music & media." This commitment is reflected in their oeuvre—which boasts a large corpus of cover songs, including contemporary Christian music, patriotic fare, and show tunes, as well as original pro-police and pro–Donald Trump songs and videos. Camille is the duo's soprano and songwriter, while Haley, an alto, assists with song editing.[38]

The home page of their website features an image of the duo wearing jeans and T-shirts emblazoned with the phrase "USA: Made in America" in red, white, and blue. Camille holds a guitar, and both girls accessorize with red, white, and blue jewelry (Fig. 8).[39] The short description of the girls' act mentions their viral hit for Trump, "Keep America Great." Also featured on the home page is the video for "Back the Blue." The opening frame shows both girls, hands on their hearts, flanked by law enforcement officers. A banner with the words "Pro Police Song" sits at the bottom. Visitors can purchase songs from the C&H music collection by clicking on a collage showing their album covers. Each image shows the girls' flowing blond locks and perfect skin with minimal makeup. Although the attire changes from leather boots, cowboy hats, and denim, to boho skirts and flowery blouses, to crisp sundresses, the color white—a symbol of purity and chastity—appears in each image. Natural elements take up the background in each cover: a field, trees, and wood paneling, with the exception of one image, which includes snowflakes and white lace.[40] These images capture the values the girls espouse under the tab titled "Causes"—patriotism, prayer and sharing the Christian faith, and purity and modesty. These professed values align with what Barbara Welter identifies as the attributes of so-called True Womanhood: piety, purity, submissiveness, and domesticity.[41]

In many ways, Camille & Haley's presentation on social media resembles the style of other fringe conservative Christian media personalities, such as the girls in the Duggar and Bates families, both of which have had successful television series and maintain an active social media presence. While Camille and Haley were in their mid-to-late twenties in the summer of 2020, I am intentionally using the term "girl" here as I believe juvenation strategies were at play in their presentation and performance; both sisters were unmarried at the time, a status that positions them as a commodity, whether it be as sister, best friend, or role model.[42] In their music and media, assertions of patriotism go hand in hand with proclamations of faith. Such messaging conforms to the tenets of Christian nationalism—"the belief that the United States was founded as, and continues to be, a Christian nation."[43] On their website, they state,

> We are Christian Conservatives and we believe in being active in politics. For a Christian to abdicate their civic responsibility is unwise and short sighted. Our politicians affect the freedoms of the church and the future of our country. We can't just let our voice be silenced by other's [sic] who do not honor God and His law in our land.[44]

For Camille & Haley, their identities as political conservatives and Christians are intertwined; faith commands political activism. In the words of Welter, a true woman under this ideology must "uphold the pillars of the temple with her frail white hand."[45] It is the sisters' moral responsibility to ensure protection for the church as it is tied to the destiny of the nation. The last part of the sisters' statement resonates with the rhetoric of fear Fea associates with evangelicals and MacWilliams sees in those possessing an authoritarian worldview: Camille & Haley will honor God's law and will not be silenced by those who disobey his authority.[46]

Under the "Patriotism" header on the "Causes" page of their website, Camille & Haley include the music video and live versions of "Keep America

Fig. 8. Camille & Haley don patriotic garb on the home page of their official website.

Great" (2020), the music video for their Rick Santorum song "Game On" (2012), and a live patriotic concert (2018).[47] This patriotic concert features the duo singing and playing guitar and banjo at a retirement center in Tulsa where they have performed on other occasions. They open the event by reminding the audience that it is Flag Day *and* President Trump's birthday before performing "Hail to the Chief" as the concert opener. The song is performed with Albert Gamse's text only on rare occasions—military band instrumentation is the standard. Rather than present the energetic march style that one would expect, the duo transforms the presidential salute into a distinctly feminine, lyrical ballad. Dulcet vocal harmonies and gently plucked arpeggios on guitar replace the assertive fanfare of brass and percussion, thus depleting the musical signifiers that connote strength and fortitude. In the song's final phrase, Camille sustains the tonic E♭, while Haley gracefully sings a third above, briefly moving to the upper neighbor tone on A♭ before resolving back to the tonic triad. In this moment, the duo manages to transform "Hail to the Chief," a song that heralds the very public arrival of presidents to events of national and civic importance, into a solemn prayer for one president in particular.

The remainder of the event features standard patriotic fare, with a few pop songs and originals added in. Lesser-known verses of patriotic songs are performed in several instances, often with content that aligns with a Christian nationalist worldview. For example, "Stars and Stripes Forever" and "America (My Country, 'Tis of Thee)" allude to fathers (heavenly or earthly) and position these patriarchs as the figures with both the "might" and the "right" to "proclaim" and "protect" the nation. "America (My Country, 'Tis of Thee)" refers to God as the "author of liberty," who, like the nation, is worthy of praise. Camille & Haley's remarks prime this reading. Before singing "Stars and Stripes Forever," they opine on the interconnectivity of their religious beliefs and their love of country: "We believe in praying for every president we have, standing behind them because the Lord, the Bible, says that God puts leadership in power, right, and so sometimes the reflection of our nation is who we get, sometimes we get blessed, so here we go."

America (My Country, 'Tis of Thee) (fourth verse)

Our Fathers' God to Thee,
Author of liberty
To Thee we sing.
Long may our land be bright
With freedom's holy light,
Protect us by Thy might,
Great God, our King.[48]

The Stars and Stripes Forever (second verse of the Trio)

Let despots remember the day
When our fathers with mighty endeavor
Proclaim'd as they march'd to the fray
That by their might, and by their right
It waves forever![49]

Although he only makes a brief appearance, the figure of Camille and Haley's father looms over the event, as they regularly engage him in banter between songs and express their gratitude for his musical and spiritual guidance. When Camille brings out the banjo, she tells a story about her father leading worship on the instrument, which she later learned to play. When the duo sings one of their originals, "Rocky Road," a story about a father and daughter, Haley acknowledges their uncle, who provided the chords to the song, as well as their father. Toward the middle of the program, the duo sings a cover of "Leader of the Band" and praises their father, who "taught us how to play guitar . . . [and] encouraged us in our musical giftings." In the words of Dan Fogelberg, "My life has been a poor attempt / To imitate the man / I'm just a living legacy / To the leader of the band."[50] The father's presence serves as a constant reminder that the girls' public performance is sanctioned by a male authority who provides both protection and surveillance. By elevating their father as teacher, protector, and provider, Camille & Haley position themselves as passive vessels through which his religious teachings, patriotic ideals, and musical talents can flow.

KEEP AMERICA GREAT

In June 2020, Camille & Haley recorded "Keep America Great," a pro-Trump music video, outside of the venue where the incumbent candidate would hold his first "post-Covid" rally. On June 17, MSNBC's Cal Perry posted a brief clip of the duo and their family singing the spirited anthem live in Tulsa. His video garnered over twenty-nine million views by the end of October 2020 (Fig. 9).[51] The music video, released on June 20, the same day as Trump's rally, received over one million YouTube hits and spawned covers, parodies, and TikToks. Countless users weighed in on social media, alternatively praising and mocking the performance.

The music video for "Keep America Great" showcases footage of Camille & Haley and their entourage in four different locations: the studio (where the recording of the song is taking place), an unidentified space with Tulsa County Republican Party signage, a sidewalk and street, and the steps of the BOK Center (where Perry's Twitter clip was recorded). At first glance, the video's visual imagery, dominated by Trump signs and regalia and no shortage of American flags, would appear to be standard patriotic fare with a pro-candidate message. But closer analysis of the video reveals a more circumscribed definition of patriotism, one rooted in the cultural framework of Christian nationalism. The video begins and ends with slow motion footage of a twenty-something, KAG-hat-wearing man waving an oversized American flag (Fig. 10a). His T-shirt shows a sketch of a man rid-

← **Tweet**

Cal Perry ✔
@CalNBC

· · ·

Welcome to #Tulsa. People are already in line. Also, re-election songs. #MSNBC

▶ 30M views   0:06 / 0:45 🔊 ⤢

8:45 PM · Jun 17, 2020 · Twitter for iPhone

13.5K Retweets   **80.9K** Quote Tweets   **57K** Likes

Fig. 9. Video of Camille, Haley, their father, and other friends and family singing outside the BOK Center. Still from a video posted on Twitter by Cal Perry on June 17, 2020.

ing a dinosaur skeleton, quite possibly a nod to creationism, which postulates that both humans and dinosaurs mingled on earth as of the sixth day of creation. The video's second image is a large canvas of President Trump with outstretched arms, a posture reminiscent of Christ in Christian iconography (Fig. 10b). Brief shots of a street banner proclaiming "Tulsa does it better" and the Declaration of Independence quickly follow (Figs. 10c and 10d). This opening is underscored by a pulsating, distinctly masculine bass riff. Thus, in its first moments, the video melds America's heritage, the Christian faith, and patriotic duty, positioning President Trump as both political and spiritual authority.

Camille & Haley are front and center in the studio and on the street, but they never stand alone. As they break into cheerleader poses, using their arms to motion a V(ote) and T(rump), we can see older men in the background surveilling their activity (Fig. 10e). In the BOK Center segments where the multigenerational family unit joins in (including siblings and possibly grandparents), the girls' father hovers behind with the portable speaker in his hand (Fig. 10f). It is he who controls the amplification of their voices. The same holds true in the studio, where the men control the soundboard through which the girls' voices are channeled (Fig. 10g). After all, the girls are there to be looked at, especially in moments when the video shifts to slow motion. Haley seductively shakes her head side to side, her long blond wavy locks cascading down as she exudes what feminist film critic Laura Mulvey calls "to-be-looked-at-ness" (Fig. 10h).[52] These actions are shown within the confines of the studio, a semiprivate space into which the viewer (or should I say voyeur) is invited. While the girls' presumed innocence and vulnerability may indeed elicit protective instincts, they are not necessarily free from sexualization. At the same time, we are also reminded of Camille & Haley's purity and their status as helpmates. Early in the video, the camera flashes to a plastic cup imprinted with the words "Praying for Trump." The web address given below the slogan is for the National Women's Prayer and Voting Army. Its mission: "to pray that the base of public policy would adhere to Biblical and Constitutional principles that our founding fathers established."[53]

The visual and music-stylistic aesthetic in the video further reinforces narratives of moral rectitude and feminine beauty, which are tied to ideas regarding nation. Viewers picked up these signals, even in the duo's "live" performances, and their observations are noted in the comments that follow a clip of the song posted on YouTube by Breitbart News:

Fig. 10. Camille & Haley's "Keep America Great" video in support of Donald Trump. Stills from "Keep America Great," Wallace Productions, 2020.

Very catchy song sung with fun, enthusiasm and smiles. Pretty Patriotic Princesses with great American talent.—TubeFrog

No pink hair, no purple lipstick, conservative womens are so beautiful.—DS

No black fingernails color. No, one inch thick & long fake eyelashes.—TrumpIsn'tDoneYet

I love Keep America Great song so much with all my heart, Welldone Beautiful Blonde American Ladies, Trump 2020, usususususususus.—Anıl Uner

Ahhh the image of what America should be and was intended to be.—986C

Patriotic, smiling, happy looking, enthusiastic ladies—the miserable looting left are gonna hate them (but who cares what they think:))—PalmVegas

Leftist women shriek with hate. Conservative women sing with love.—Lynx

These girls have really nice voices and an infectious positive energy. It's very refreshing to see young women with no visible tattoos. God bless them.—lincbond442

*Gee . . . Happy smiling faces. That's refreshing. I'm not a fan of cheesy political songs . . . but what a contrast to the ugly, mean, bitter left.
—Paul Schuster[54]*

Posters embraced the girls' unadorned simplicity and authenticity, and in many instances, they used the performance as an opportunity to opine on some of the differences between the Left and the Right: women of the Right are patriotic, smiling, happy, enthusiastic princesses, whereas women of the Left "shriek with hate" and are ugly, mean, miserable, and bitter. While there is very little discussion about the specific attributes of their voices, the naturalness of their appearance does come into play in drawing attention to what is absent (tattoos, colorful hair, black fingernails, lipstick, and fake eyelashes). For the posters, the girls represent "the image of what America should be and was intended to be." Camille & Haley offer an appealing vision of femininity and patriotic zeal, and the commitment to purity and virtue they espouse in their online media finds its analogue in the way they present themselves in performance.

Richard Dyer claims that "when whiteness *qua* whiteness does come into focus, it is often revealed as emptiness, absence, denial or even a kind of death."[55] However, I would argue that some of the girls' performance strategies make what is invisible visible. The articulation of White femininity is indeed present in their appearance, but also noticeable in their voices. Both girls sing with a forward-placed, clear, focused tone that is fluid and even throughout the vocal range. Completely absent are the registral breaks, intonation, and placement issues often heard in young female voices.[56] They sing the melody with clarity and precision, without any embellishment in the form of slides, swoops, or melismas, and without quirks in the form of vowel distortion or vocal fry, signifiers of vocal "excess" that are frequently racialized. Vocally the girls demonstrate both modesty and restraint. Many posters praised the positivity and wholesomeness of their activism and positioned it as antithetical to the violence, rioting, and chaos through which the other side (the Democratic side) supposedly asserts its point of view. Indeed, there are racial undertones here, as the posters are likely referring to Black Lives Matter or possibly Antifa activists.

I know, you'd have more respect for them if they were destroying things! Maybe you should worry about the horrible crime rates in the Democrat run areas!![57]

Weird to see people expressing their political opinion without all the looting/robbing/beating.[58]

To fans, the squeaky-clean, family-oriented duo came to represent the civility the Left was presumed to lack. And supporters did not hesitate to call out what they saw as other posters bullying Camille & Haley—the male desire to protect White womanhood on full display.[59]

To Laurie Stras, the girl singer is "an object of desire, and an icon of possibility, be it sexual, aspirational, or even nostalgic in nature."[60] Camille & Haley served as such objects of desire for Trump's base, as they reinscribed a vision of whiteness, traditional femininity, and patriotic ardor that perfectly aligned with the nostalgic messaging of Trump's "Make America Great Again" mantra and the spiritual orientation of his base. Svetlana

Boym describes nostalgia as a "sentiment of loss and displacement" that "inevitably reappears as a defense mechanism in a time of accelerated rhythms of life and historical upheavals."[61] Such upheavals in the wake of the Obama years, as well as the declining population of White Christians due in part to demographic shifts, stoked fear among conservatives, so it is not surprising that presentations of traditional femininity would appeal to Trump supporters.[62] Indeed Camille & Haley channel their music for a cause: to elevate the gospel and Donald Trump, or should we say, Donald Trump's gospel? At a time when conservatives felt the weight of the loss of Christian values in a rapidly changing world, the blond, blue-eyed girl next door, who embodies heteronormativity, feminine frailty, Christian charity, and patriotic fervor, served as the perfect symbol of potential amid the chaos.

WHITE FRIGHT

While many praised Camille & Haley's energy, vocal prowess, and message, the duo had their detractors as well, many of whom weighed in on Cal Perry's video clip. In some instances, social media users teased out what they believed to be propagandistic messaging within the performance, much in the way they did with the USA Freedom Kids in 2016. The posts tend to parody the act's whiteness, drawing allusions to White supremacist movements as well as to religious cults in real life and on film. In her work on Taylor Swift and fan cultures, Annelot Prins investigates alt-right engagement with the artist's music and self-presentation. Prins argues that "Swift is not merely the object of these activities" but rather "offers ample hooks for them in her music," and that her "star text courts and facilitates a white-supremacist reading."[63] Camille & Haley, who coincidentally bear quite a bit of physical resemblance to Swift and align with the brand of traditional femininity she embodied in the early part of her career, court the same kinds of readings. (One Twitter user even made note of this: "I don't know if @taylorswift13 supports or endorses Trump, but she's at least partially responsible for this aesthetic.")[64] Detractors recognized the duo's amenability for such readings and critiqued these aspects of their performance:

When Did Klan rallies get so festive?[65]

They forgot to wear their matching white robes and hoods. I guess the @ realDonaldTrump t-shirts were the best alternative clothing they had available.[66]

Kinda reminds me of this display 80 years ago.[67]
[Includes YouTube video of German Youth in 1940]

They're very talented. The Third Reich had many talented singers and artist as well. Adorable. Dangerous.[68]

The Nazis had music at their rallies too[69]
[Includes image of German Youth]

The von Trapps couldn't escape the Nazis in Austria and were forced to sing for them. Renamed by Nazis to von Krapp Family.[70]

In several instances, posters included archival footage of Hitlerjugend events and Klan meetings, pointing out affinities between 1940s Germany and the present-day United States. One post that includes footage of Hitlerjugend activities shows young women singing and marching with flags through a gate emblazoned with the phrase "Flink wie Windhunde, zäh wie Leder, hart wie Kruppstahl!" ("Swift as greyhounds, tough as leather, hard as Krupp steel"), words Hitler used to describe the ideal youth in a 1935 speech. The footage also features images of the girls in uniforms performing calisthenics and coming together for a folk dance accompanied by accordion. Whether dancing, marching, or exercising, conformity is the overriding ethos.[71] Another post compares Camille & Haley's act to the Hitlerjugend scene and song "Tomorrow Belongs to Me" from the film *Cabaret*, which is set in the final days of the Weimar Republic.[72] The number begins with an attractive, blond-haired, blue-eyed young man singing a cappella. At the end of the first verse, there is a slow pan downward that reveals an armband with the swastika and Hitlerjugend regalia. The crowd looks disinterested at first, but eventually people of all ages stand and join in the boy's song. Cymbal crashes, thicker and more marchlike orchestration, a more emphatic tempo, and aggressive singing from the boy and others transform what first seemed a lyrical folk ditty into a propaganda song.

The archival footage of circa 1940 Germany and the scene from *Cabaret* set in 1931 communicate similar messages: the presumed innocence of youth masks, or at least makes palatable, violent ideologies. The youths' mellifluous singing voices and the songs' folkish signifiers play a role in this deception. This masking becomes even more apparent in a DIY video where a YouTube user combines Camille & Haley's song "Keep America Great" with remixed footage of protests. "KEEP AMERICA GREAT (2020 Police Brutality Edition)" features short clips that show acts of violence, including a police officer kicking a man who is sitting down with his hands covering his face, three police officers surrounding a man in prone position with one kneeing him, police cars plowing into crowds of protesters, two police officers using their shields to knock over an old man with a cane as he is walking away, and a group of police officers casually walking around a man whom officers had pushed down minutes earlier. Donald Trump's voice serves as a framing device. The opening of the video shows footage of Trump giving a speech where he affirms his support for police: "We support the overwhelming majority of police officers who are incredible in every way and devoted public servants." His second appearance occurs as a voiceover with footage of Colin Kaepernick kneeling on a football field: "Wouldn't you love to see one of these NFL owners, when somebody disrespects our flag, to say, 'Get that son of a bitch off the field right now. Out! He's fired, he's fired'?" The misalignment of cheerful, upbeat music with violent images reveals the consequences of Trump's policies and takes on an almost grotesque dimension.[73]

More than a few posters leveled accusations of cultism at the duo. With nods to Jim Jones, the leader of the Peoples Temple who led 912 people to mass suicide (1978), and David Koresh, leader of the Branch Davidians, a sect that perished after a controversial fifty-one-day standoff with the FBI (1993), they suggest that Trump, like Jones and Koresh, is a false messiah.

I think only members of the PLO [Palestine Liberation Organization] or Branch Davidians are more cultish in their behavior. MAGA folks are as shameless as Let's Make a Deal audience members. Oh, white people![74]

They look like cult members ready to pass out the Kool-Aid.[75]

Most disturbing line: "There will never be another USA
if we don't vote Trump"

What? This is a very warped thing to say & believe. The USA is not owned
or defined by Donald Trump. To even suggest it would cease to exist if he
doesn't win the election is pure cultism.[76]

One post alludes to Kool-Aid (a reference to the Peoples Temple mass suicide),[77] but includes a GIF of *Midsommar* (2019), a horror film where a group of unsuspecting students are ritualistically killed by a lily-white Scandinavian cult, which at first glance appears peaceful and welcoming. With these images and narratives, posters challenged the assumption that youth and whiteness connote innocence.

Other posters turned to White stereotypes as a means of generating humor, drawing on class and racial assumptions. One GIF shows a "redneck" couple, the woman in a red paisley shirt with bare midriff, and the man bare-chested in overalls, both with their blond hair askew and missing teeth on display.[78] Another poster claimed that the sisters' act "looks like a bunch of Kent State gun girl clones were adopted by the dad from Chrisley Knows Best."[79] (*Chrisley Knows Best* is a reality TV show that follows the lives of a domineering and flamboyant father and his family. The "Kent State gun girl" is Kaitlin Bennett, a gun rights activist best known for a 2018 photo where she posed open-carrying an AR-10 rifle at Kent State University following her graduation.)[80] With this description, the poster opined on the protections afforded by both class and White privilege. In both posts, whiteness as articulated by Camille & Haley became a springboard for critiquing White identity, whether it is "poor Whites" or "basic White girls."

"JESUS IS MY SAVIOR. TRUMP IS MY PRESIDENT."

Journalists who covered the storming of the US Capitol in January 2021 reported that the conflation of President Trump and Jesus was a common theme.[81] This is evidenced by slogans such as "Jesus 2020" and "Jesus is my savior. Trump is my president." Brandi Miller, host of the podcast *Reclaiming My Theology*, has argued that "the image of Jesus in a lot of white evangelical conservative Christianity has been conformed to the image of Donald Trump himself: full of violence, power, hoarding, name calling, violently taking what you want and engaging with power and privilege."[82] Camille & Haley did not espouse the more explicit strain of Christian nationalist rhetoric that was on display at the Capitol, but through their interviews, media, and music, they appealed to White evangelicals who shared this worldview without alienating more conventional Republicans. The wholesome middle-America nostalgia and traditionalism on display in their act surely resonated with those that harbored fear over issues such as immigration, the rise of liberal secularism, and social and demographic change, and who longed for a return to the fictional past that resides in President Trump's imagination. In the girls' act, these nostalgic sentiments go hand in hand with paternalism, which Mary Jackman refers to as "the sweetest persuasion" in that it masks systemic inequality.[83] Male authority—religious, political, civic, and parental—stands as the central force that makes all things possible, whether in the duo's repertoire praising police officers, soldiers, and Trump; deference to the God who bestowed their musical gifts; or acknowledgments of the gentle pedagogy of their father who molded them into fine musicians. Camille & Haley's presentation of traditional femininity and the invisibility afforded by their whiteness made the seemingly innocuous message both palatable and marketable to the mainstream. And perhaps this is where the power in such girl groups for Trump lies. To paraphrase one poster, dangerous ideology is hidden beneath the veil of adorable packaging.

However, I would argue that there is something inherently problematic about rhetoric that reduces Camille & Haley to mindless cogs for the conservative movement or unwitting pawns of the patriarchy. Beneath the musical hagiography they have created around their father, the girl-next-door presentation, and the religious rhetoric, there are signs that the women (*not* girls) actually possess more agency than their performances might suggest. After all, Camille and Haley were in their mid-to-late twenties in 2020 and neither was married; they have served as worship leaders and have asserted their knowledge of electoral politics in interviews and on news shows.[84] But their demonstration of competence and authority does not end there. In a July 4, 2021, Facebook post, they quote a line from "Keep America Great"—"Gotta stick to our guns, keep the freedom we've won"—and include an image of themselves in Trump regalia packing Beretta 9mm pistols. The pose evokes the images typically found on buddy cop movie posters and promotional stills, but with their blond locks and subtle smiles reminding us that even though they are striking a masculine pose, they are, after all, girls.

Or are they? Offering up the function of the masquerade, Joan Rivière claims that women may intentionally mask their cognitive abilities by performing traditional femininity as a defense "to avert anxiety and the retribution feared from men."[85] While most of their country-pop oeuvre revolves around themes of God, country, and heterosexual romance, the two have also penned songs in solidarity with groups working to end abortion and human trafficking. Indeed, activism is an important piece of their brand identity, a point that comes across in an unaired *Fox News* interview where they discuss their informal performances outside Trump rallies as well as their support for Republican policies and law enforcement officers. According to Camille:

> It's fun to be young people that are involved politically, 'cause a lot of people, a lot of young people, aren't involved politically, and they don't really know. . . . They see headlines, or they see what their friends are saying, or they see what celebrities are saying, but they don't do a lot of study themselves. And so a lot of people think Republicans are, you know, old White men or something, rich men. And we're like, well, we're young, we're girls, and we're not rich, but we like President Trump, and we like what the Republican Party stands for, and so we think it's important to be a new face, you know, of the Republican Party, a younger face. And there's so many Republicans out there right now that are really fighting for freedom and saying, "You know what, like, we want lower taxes, we want things that make sense, we want commonsense policies, foreign policy, veterans, health care," you know, all the different things that President Trump is working on. So it's really fun, and so we go around and we sing outside the campaigns. We wanna give a song that's exciting for the Trumpers because we need encouragement. Everyone needs encouragement, too, you know, and so sometimes it's a long road and we're just like, hey, we want to be a bright spot, you know, for the people . . . and for President Trump, if he sees it.[86]

In interviews such as this one, on their website, and in their banter with audiences during performances, Camille & Haley place a lot of emphasis on finding one's voice and using that voice to initiate social change and to be a positive force in the world. These affirmations are typically embellished with giggles, descriptions of politics as "fun," or brief dialogue with their father, who readily provides guidance on what to say, even as he stands just outside the camera's view. Could professed allegiance to God and father and stereotypically feminine presentation, manifest in their mode of speech and dress, merely be the masquerade of two talented musicians who must work within the confines of evangelical culture in order to establish a career in music? There is perhaps no way to answer this question; however, I believe it is worth considering the possibility of Camille & Haley's agency here, lest we as scholars replicate the very structures that we presume work to silence them.

CHAPTER 5

Settling the Score

Pop Songs, Protest, and Punishment

Is there anything more fun than a Trump rally?
  —DONALD TRUMP AT A RALLY IN MOON TOWNSHIP,
  PENNSYLVANIA, MARCH 10, 2018[1]

Even in great *punishment* there is so much which is festive.
  —FRIEDRICH NIETZSCHE, *THE GENEALOGY OF MORALS*[2]

DEPLORABLE HUMOR

At a September 2016 fundraiser held at the posh restaurant Cipriani
Wall Street, Democratic contender Hillary Clinton made the following
remark: "You could put half of Trump's supporters into what I call the
basket of deplorables. Right? The racist, sexist, homophobic, xenophobic,
Islamophobic—you name it. And unfortunately, there are people like that.
And he has lifted them up."[3] A week after she unleashed her memorable
"basket of deplorables" soundbite to an audience that boasted liberal luminaries such as Barbra Streisand and Rufus Wainwright, Donald Trump
plotted a new musical course. At a Miami rally, he responded to his com-
petitor's quirky turn of phrase with a visual mashup featuring a Trump
campaign banner and an American flag remixed with the iconic barricade
scene from *Les Misérables* (now, Les Deplorables), courtesy of the subreddit r/The_Donald (Fig. 11).[4] "Do You Hear the People Sing?," the rousing
call to arms passionately sung by the student revolutionaries in the Tony
Award–winning megamusical, heralded his arrival to the podium.[5] With
the subreddit image and walk-on music, Trump fashioned himself as an
everyman and an underdog, a self-proclaimed "deplorable." And as he

Fig. 11. From *Misérables* to deplorables. Still from Donald Trump's September 2016 Miami rally, posted on YouTube on September 17, 2016.

reclaimed Clinton's insult, his band of deplorables—the oppressed, White victims whom Clinton mocked in the presence of her liberal elite coterie— were cast in a noble and heroic light. In iterations both comedic and dramatic, Clinton's meme-worthy phrase only snowballed in unofficial contexts where "deplorable" merchandise, mashups, and remixes blanketed the internet in the days that followed Trump's rallying cry.[6]

The "basket of deplorables" gaffe and the ripple effects of its afterlife among Trump supporters in various forms—musical, visual, and commercial—illustrate the transformative impact of social media on both creator and consumer as their roles become interchangeable and intertwined. Moreover, the dissolution of boundaries between public and private life, power and entertainment, politics and celebrity, television and viral video in the twenty-first century has shaped the public's engagement with electoral politics, as evidenced by the proliferation of comedic offerings, such as spoofs and parodies, that have trumped "official" campaign discourses and become the news.[7] With his deplorables rejoinder at the rally, Trump made "unofficial" content (the visual mashup) "official," with full awareness that this type of media attracts significant attention during political events.[8] Such "purposeful play" may model new civic possibilities, as the accessibility of personal digital devices with social media apps transfers power from traditional media powerbrokers to the public.[9] At the same time, the social media platforms that facilitate such play rely on artificial intelligence algorithms that amass information about user engagement and recommend and rank content based on popularity rather than quality; they therefore assume an active role in amplifying the spread of misinformation and fanning the flames of partisan discord.[10]

Indeed, the rise of the internet and interoperable media platforms has expanded the public's engagement when it comes to generating political humor in the form of music. As "Crush on Obama" in 2008 and Camille & Haley's "Keep America Great" in 2020 attest, the widespread availability of video-sharing sites combined with the accessibility of software that facilitates a DIY approach to video production has created a virtual marketplace where "unofficial" musical gems can find a rapt audience that in turn becomes a group of participatory actors, fashioning their own responses whether through commenting, sharing, "liking," or reinventing.[11] And such activity is not limited to music videos with newly composed, candidate-themed songs. As discussed in chapter 1 with Barack Obama's shoulder-brushing gesture, or here with Clinton's deplorables barb, video clips of candidates' speeches, memorable quips, and quirky turns of phrases are uploaded on YouTube or social media sites such as Twitter, where they are remixed, songified, and recreated with both speed and ingenuity. Each richly intertextual creation offers images and/or music that perpetually reflect back on content created by other users. Whitney Phillips and Ryan M. Milner use the term "ambivalent" in their study of internet communication, arguing that online utterances such as these are polysemic by nature and can be interpreted in multiple ways, thus complicating "authorial intent, social consequence, and cultural worth."[12]

Back when Bill Clinton was conjuring up a classic rock playlist in 1992, campaign songs were generally directed from the campaign to the people, but as Justin Patch has noted in his work on 2016 candidate tribute videos, pop songs can also pass horizontally between citizens, thus becoming "a democratic tool for the cultivation and articulation of new, complex political subjectivities."[13] One such instance of this lateral exchange began on September 5, 2020, with a Black Lives Matter protest in Portland, Oregon. Bystanders with iPhones captured the horrifying moment when a Molotov cocktail set a protester's feet aflame. Dan Scavino, White House deputy chief of staff and director of social media, tweeted a version of the footage set to Kenny Loggins's "Footloose" (henceforth called the "Footloose" video) and the strange pairing was subsequently retweeted by President Donald Trump and viewed 3.4 million times within forty-eight hours of its posting. This scene enthralled virtual spectators in the Twitterverse, where posters felt compelled to create their own substitute "soundtracks" for the clip, transforming one man's moment of terror on film into a click-worthy meme.[14]

A meme can be thought of as "a piece of media that is repurposed to deliver a cultural, social or political expression, mainly through humor."[15] Some memes enjoy longevity—consider "Grumpy Cat," "Success Kid," or even "How Do You Do, Fellow Kids?" from chapter 3—but others are tied to specific cultural moments and typically fade from memory by the end of the twenty-four-hour news cycle. While memetic content may not seem worthy of sustained inquiry, when it comes to presidential campaigns, music/image pairings like the "Footloose" video can offer another vantage point for analyzing the role of viral media in presidential branding and communication; the meanings attached to spectator engagement and its community-building function in virtual spaces; and, more broadly, the complex intersections of music, political humor, and (in this particular instance) race. Such "digital antiphony," Braxton Shelley notes, "simultaneously materializes and refigures social categories and concepts like race and gender, belief and authorship."[16] In this chapter, research on internet troll culture and political communication provides a framework for analyzing how rhetorics of online humor are constituted in the realm of sound as Twitter users repurpose pop songs in service of political expression. Additionally, this chapter turns to theories on punishment and the more recent phenomenon of digital lynching to reveal how sound can be harnessed as a tool for political polarization.

RACIAL POLITICS IN THE TRUMP ERA

During the Trump administration, the United States witnessed increasing social and political discord over police violence directed toward people of color, which resulted in widespread protests in cities large and small. This disruptive activity reached fever pitch during the summer of 2020 in the wake of several high-profile incidences of police violence. On March 13, 2020, Breonna Taylor, an emergency room technician, was shot to death in her Louisville home when narcotics officers improperly executed a search warrant. On May 25, 2020, George Floyd was arrested for allegedly using a counterfeit bill at a grocery store in Minneapolis. One of the four officers on the scene handcuffed Floyd and another knelt on his neck for over nine minutes, causing death by asphyxiation. On August 23, 2020, Jacob Blake was critically injured when he was shot seven times by an officer executing an arrest warrant in Kenosha. While racial tensions brewed unrest and sparked global protests, the flames of racial animus were further fanned across the nation by the unrestrained spread of Covid-19, which disproportionately impacted communities of color; anxieties over illegal immigration; and even public debates over the removal of Confederate statues.[17] And the reactions to this upheaval revealed deep divisions among the US citizenry. According to a Pew poll, 78% of Democrats (up from 66% in 2019) felt the country had not gone far enough in securing equal rights for Black people, whereas just 17% of Republicans (down from 18% the previous year) expressed the same sentiment. Such a divide persisted even when considering the racial composition of each political party.[18] Rising anxiety and fear among Black Americans marked a sharp turn from the optimism that characterized the Obama years despite the recession and the dwindling job market's impact on this demographic during his presidency.[19]

Following the death of George Floyd at the end of May 2020, the city of Portland witnessed a spate of protests to combat racism and police violence. Each night, protesters gathered around the Multnomah County Justice Center. The Portland police relied on tear gas and impact munitions to disperse nonviolent attendees, but one week into the protests a judge issued a temporary restraining order that limited the use of such tactics to situations where police or public lives or safety were at risk.[20] By July, federal officers were maintaining a presence in Portland, which only served to escalate tensions between protesters and law enforcement. In several instances, agents from Customs and Border Protection detained protesters without explanation.[21] Research by the Armed Conflict Location & Event Data Project has shown that 83% of demonstrations in Oregon *prior* to the deployment of federal authorities were nonviolent. *After* the deployment, the percentage of violent demonstrations rose from under 17% to over 42%.[22] By the end of July, Oregon State Police troopers replaced federal officers; Governor Kate Brown argued that federal officers were acting as an "occupying force" that only exacerbated the violence. But this solution was short lived, as the state police pulled out only two weeks later. The situation turned more violent in August when several pro-Trump and right-wing groups entered the fray and Aaron J. Danielson, a supporter of the Patriot Prayer group, was shot and killed.[23]

The September 5 incident occurred shortly after 9 p.m. With his feet in flames, the protester ran frantically for about twenty-five seconds before fellow protesters and law enforcement officers extinguished the flames.[24] The phone cameras were rolling. Tayler Hansen posted a video of the incident on Twitter with the caption "ANTIFA lights themselves on fire—5 minutes into the March, officers attempted to put him out" (Fig. 12).[25] Just over thirty minutes later, another Twitter user, Just a Humanist, tweeted, "I can't wait for someone to put a music track on this video," and the Twitterverse was quick to reply.[26] Scavino tweeted a clip of Hansen's burning man footage with Kenny Loggins's "Footloose" as underscore, and a second video from Steve Inman with mixed-martial-arts-style commentary (henceforth called the Announcer video) with the caption "Peaceful protestors in SE Portland this evening . . ."[27] While President Trump did not explicitly mention Antifa, he retweeted Scavino's videos, replicating his facetious "peaceful protesters" retort with "These are the Democrats 'peaceful protests.' Sick!"[28] It is not surprising that the president would tweet out evidence of unrest in American cities to his 88.7 million Twitter followers,[29] as his reelection strategy revolved around convincing Americans that their cities were dissolving into uncontrollable chaos, overrun by riotous Black Lives Matter activists and Antifa. While this was a departure from his 2016 narrative focusing on the threats of Islamic terrorism, the circulation of images depicting protests, political unrest, and clashes between police and BLM activists allowed Trump to continue to stoke the fear of his base as well as to position himself as the strongman who has what it takes to quell the violence.[30] Various media reported on Trump's tweet, with some right-leaning news outlets adding fuel to the Antifa-on-fire narrative.[31]

While the MMA-style announcer's commentary in Scavino's second video primarily works to transform the protester's horror into a moment of comedy and to spectacularize the sight of the burning body, some tweeters digressed from this narrative and instead offered racialized perspectives on the event. The commentary in the Announcer video is as follows:

> Aw, what the hell, let's take a look. Let's take a look at another angle here. Look at a man doing some kind of Fortnite weird dance, and man, he looks like a freakin' human Hot Pocket rolling around. Got this, like, hamburger char-

Tweet

Tayler Hansen
@TaylerUSA

···

ANTIFA lights themselves on fire—

5 minutes into the March, officers attempted to put him out.

▶ 2.9M views   0:05 / 1:03 🔊 ⤢

12:20 AM · Sep 6, 2020 · Twitter for iPhone

2,201 Retweets   **1,365** Quote Tweets   **7,588** Likes

Fig. 12. Portland protest, September 5, 2020. Still from a video posted on Twitter by Tayler Hansen on September 6, 2020.

broiled smell goin' on right now. I don't know if that's cheese on his feet and now just rolling around. Like I said, his feet have become Hot Pockets. And they're trying to put him out with a shield. You can see Antifa is crying like a little bitch, cryin' for mama Karen tonight.[32]

The announcer's allusion to a "hamburger smell" and "human Hot Pocket" description dehumanize the subject and reduce him to an object to be consumed. There is also a tinge of misogyny here as the announcer feminizes the man's suffering by characterizing him as "crying like a little bitch."

Ultimately, this remix of the footage depicts human suffering as a spectator sport, the event no longer a protest to draw attention to the loss of Black lives, but rather a gamified, competitive street fight between law enforcement and the man the announcer identifies as "Antifa."

Footage of the Portland incident in its unaltered form may evoke a visceral response in some viewers; however, in the altered version substituting a pop soundtrack ("Footloose") for the more realistic (and authentic) soundtrack of frantic outcries, the moment is depleted of its realism. This is partly due to the incongruity between the video's images and the grooves of the dance track, which entered the popular imagination through the film of the same title (1984). The upbeat quality of the tune and Kenny Loggins's exuberant lyrics would, on the surface, seem to be misaligned with the violent nature of the image on display. But this grotesque counterpoint plays into the messaging, as the creator seeks to mock the act of protesting and trivialize the protester's suffering by equating his frantic footwork with a bad song-and-dance move.

The sound/image misalignment in the "Footloose" video shares some affinities with iconic moments in film where popular music serves as the underscore for violent acts. Consider, for example, Stanley Kubrick's film *A Clockwork Orange* (1971), based on Anthony Burgess's 1962 novel of the same title, which imagines a crime-infested, nightmarish dystopia in the near future. Charismatic gang leader Alex sexually assaults a woman while singing one of the most cheerful (and recognizable) melodies of Hollywood's golden era, "Singin' in the Rain." The jaunty tune, with its carefree lyrics, offers a jarring contrast to the acts of assault on the woman and the beating of her husband. But Alex is not just singing to himself. His gang ("droogs," as they are called in the novel) bears witness to his act of "ultra-violence," which is less about Alex's own gratification than it is a performance for other men—a twisted and depraved homosocial bonding ritual of sorts.

Just as Alex's song turns the ritualized sexual violence of *A Clockwork Orange* into a spectacle for the amusement of his gang, the addition of "Footloose" to the Portland video lends the same effect to the corporeal violence inflicted on the unknown protester, who becomes a source of entertainment for men in the Twittersphere. In her work on internet trolling culture, Whitney Phillips examines the online use of "lulz," which she describes as a darker version of "LOL" (laughing out loud). Lulz, she argues, "celebrates the anguish of the 'laughed-at victim.'" Lulz is "amusement at other people's distress."[33] It is the addition of music—or, in the case of the Announcer's video, the commentary—that elicits the lulz. But there is a more inconspicuous power dynamic at play here that is brought to the surface by the "Footloose" video's soundtrack. *Footloose* is a film about White people in Middle America. The song's White artist, Kenny Loggins, is associated with the genre retroactively called "yacht rock," a term coined in the early aughts to refer to soft rock from the 1970s and 1980s with a specific vibe. Lyrics that give voice to the heartbreak of foolish men are a hallmark of the style.[34] Recent reevaluations position yacht rock as a form of escapism in the 1970s, a means of distraction for those who wanted to banish Watergate and Vietnam from their psyches.[35] A dance track with the repeated word "footloose" and the genre's association with escapism may generate a reaction of LOL, but the use of music that is strongly coded White as the soundtrack for the anguish of a White man protesting at an event that centers Black suffering indeed aligns with the much darker lulz. The spectators' laughter was directed toward not only the White protester on display, but also the Black victims for whom the BLM movement demands justice.

"FOOTLOOSE" AND ITS OFFSPRING

Twitter users were eager to respond to Hansen's footage, Scavino's tweet with the "Footloose" and Announcer videos, and Trump's retweet of Scavino with their own GIFs, images, and remixed videos. Posters relied on such media as a springboard for expressing their ire toward Democrats, Joe Biden, protesters, and Antifa, and for showing their support for law enforcement and Donald Trump. In their rejoinders, they mirrored not only Trump's worldview, but also his rhetorical style. Three key features define Twitter as a mode of communication: simplicity, impulsivity, and incivility.[36] Thus, as Brian L. Ott and Greg Dickinson have argued, there is a cogent homology between President Trump's communication style and the logic of Twitter as a communication technology.[37] We see evidence of these features in the pithy remarks posted in response to Scavino's tweet:

> *The best part of this is, guess who shows up with an actual fire extin-*
> *guisher . . . thats right, the police!*[38]

The idiots set one of their own on fire and were too stupid to figure out how to extinguish the flames, so the "evil" police officers had to save them! Good stuff![39]

And look who put out of the flames, the police of whom they are protesting should be defunded. Without them you would be a BBQ briquette.[40]

This is great . . . would like to see more of them critters on fire.[41]

Hahahahahahahahaha. The riot is like Biden: Stupid.[42]

I'm laughing so hard I'm crying. These fucking idiots.[43]

This is fucking brilliant and awesome! Love you President Trump.[44]

Lololololol should've stayed in mommy's basement.[45]

Moving from social justice to social Darwinism in a flash.[46]

Fixing . . . "This stupid is on fire . . ."[47] [Posted with a GIF of Alicia Keys singing "Girl on Fire."]

All of those hoodies that would have put out the bilateral drumsticks that were burning. Instead he decides to increase flame with moves. We call them crispie critters.[48]

Mostly flame retardant.[49]

Lives saved / Antifa-0 Police-17 Gazillion.[50]

The incivility on display in the tweets accrued racialized dimensions as the chatter moved across the Twitterverse and beyond. Although the man on fire presents as White, the language used to describe his disposition is similar to language sometimes employed to describe people of color. In their work theorizing the social and political factors that complicate racial categorization post-Obama, Daniel Martinez HoSang and Joseph E. Lowndes use the term "racial transposition"—a useful framework for contextualizing the "Footloose" video against the backdrop of Trump's reelection campaign and the uptick in Black Lives Matter protests. Racial transposition is the "process through which the meaning, valence, and signification of race can be transferred from one context, group, or setting to another, shaping the ways in which racial categories structure broad fields of social meaning."[51] Conservative scholars and pundits, they note, "describe the white poor in language once reserved for people of color—depicting them as socially disorganized, culturally deficient, and even genetically compromised."[52] The chain of responses to the "Footloose" video shows this process in action. According to Trump's supporters, the inept protesters spark disorganized chaos, so the police must therefore restore order. The feminization of suffering as narrativized in the Announcer video also emerges here with the poster's admonishment of the protester who should have "stayed in Mommy's basement." As HoSang and Lowndes write, "Claims about dependency, autonomy, and freedom have always been constructed through racialized and gendered meanings and references."[53] That is to say, the language feminizing the protester positions him as weak and in need of parental intervention; therefore, his subordination is justified.

The theme of cultural deficiency runs through the tweets as well. As in the Announcer video, the tweeters dehumanize the burning protester by calling him a "BBQ briquette" and "crispy critter." He is akin to a slaughtered animal on a spit rather than an actualized human being. Hinting toward eugenicist ideology, the reference to Darwinism roots the degeneracy of the protester in some sort of genetic deficiency—suggesting that his actions are the natural outcome of his defective DNA. The "mostly flame retardant" tweet similarly implies that the protester's behavior is evidence of poor genetic stock.[54] But the racialized language does not end there. Some of the responses are laced with racist stereotypes: one Twitter user questioned why fellow protesters did not use their "hoodies" to extinguish their comrade's "bilateral drumsticks." The hoodie, a "racist stereotype of criminality," has come to be recognized as a "statement of racial pride and defiance" in the wake of Black teenager Trayvon Martin's death at the hands of George Zimmerman, a neighborhood watch vigilante.[55] Fried chicken was central to racist depictions of Black people in the early twentieth century, hence the reference to "drumsticks." Collectively, the users' tweets, GIFs, and images uphold tropes purportedly associated with blackness, and they also animate narratives cultivated by President Trump that stress the looming threat of Antifa and Black Lives Matter protesters, whom he once referred to as a "beehive of terrorists."[56]

At the same time, offshoots of the "Footloose" video, with the addition of music, transcend these racialized narratives and offer a primer for how spectators should *feel* about what they are witnessing and how they should *react*. The Twitterverse became a space where Trump supporters (in this instance, primarily men) could enjoy the spectacle of violence set to merry song and weigh in with their own commentary and cuts of the footage with inserted soundtracks (Table 6).[57] This process of user-generated variation—in this case, changes in soundtrack—commonly occurs as memes spread across virtual spaces. Dance tracks ("Billie Jean"), songs that reference heat in a metaphorical sense (Usher's "Burn," Billy Joel's "We Didn't Start the Fire," and Ini Kamoze's "Here Comes the Hotstepper"), and songs that celebrate a carefree attitude ("Walking on Sunshine") dominate the musical responses. It is also notable that many of these songs refer to sexual or criminal activity, or degeneracy in general. One of the hallmarks of the lulz, according to Phillips, is its generativity. Content that is particularly amusing compels others to recreate it, thus affirming a sense of community among those involved in the creation.[58] But community is forged not only through recreating and sharing content, but also through shared *feelings*. Karin Fierke argues that emotion, while expressed individually, "is inherently social and relational," and, as such, it is a form of world-making that allows subjects to find meaning and a sense of belonging.[59] In this regard, the participating tweeters are akin to what Emma Hutchison calls an "affective community," an entity "constituted through, and distinguished by, social, collective forms of feeling."[60] The participants' collective anger finds release and turns into amusement over the strange humor generated by the musical substitutions.

The creators of these videos intentionally mismatch music and image, likely to establish distance between the spectator and the protester, replacing what might normally be feelings of repulsion and disgust with laughter.[61] Lulz fetishism, Phillips argues, "obscures the social conditions and interpersonal strife that animate a particular story."[62] The substitution of the actual sound from the footage with upbeat popular tracks (a commodity) plays a central role in this erasure, allowing the spectator to disassociate from the object of his gaze, who becomes a stand-in for communities that Trump treats with contempt—Antifa, protesters, Democrats. Ultimately, the body on display is disconnected from the context of Black injustice and protest and instead serves as a locus for the expression of White rage, which is sublimated through the rhetoric of humor.[63] Just as the spectators of horror films rejoice in watching the villain receive his comeuppance, there is joy, even a visceral pleasure in watching retribution be meted out to the alleged perpetrator—in this case, "Antifa," if we are to believe Hansen. Indeed, the body needs discipline, and in this instance, the music tells the viewer that it is okay to take pleasure and to be a voyeur to such acts.

The Trump campaign had set a precedent for feeling pleasure and responding with laughter as one ponders, or bears witness to, violent acts. At a February 1, 2016, Trump rally in Cedar Rapids, the candidate told attendees that there might be someone in the audience throwing tomatoes, and offered the following directive: "If you see somebody getting ready to throw a tomato, knock the crap out of them, would you? Seriously. Okay? Just knock the hell . . . I promise you, I will pay for the legal fees. I promise. I promise."[64] The crowd responded with cheering and laughter. Trump elicited a similar response at a rally in Las Vegas a few weeks later when he told his audience that he longed for the "old days" when those who disrupted a political rally would "be carried out on a stretcher."[65] During his reelection campaign, Trump spoke to a Florida audience and lamented the fact that border security could not take violent actions to deter migrants from attempting to cross the border. When he asked, "How do you stop these people?" one woman called out "Shoot them," and in response, Trump joked, "That's only in the Panhandle you can get away with that statement." Uproarious laughter followed his retort.[66] While such inflammatory rhetoric appealed to those with authoritarian leanings, as I addressed in chapter 4, it also solidified social affiliation within the "in-group" as they shared a laugh over the plight of the "out-group."[67] As Hartley argues, irreverence in online communication can offer an opening to groups and persons that have historically been disempowered.[68]

Although detractors attempted to pathologize the gleeful reactions to violence expressed by Trump and his supporters and bemoaned the demise of respectful and dignified political discourse, the act of feeling pleasure while witnessing punishment has a long history. In his transhistorical study on pleasure and punishment, Magnus Hörnqvist argues that the desire for punishment, primarily through the criminal justice system, has been politicized since the 1960s.[69] Although the act of revenge is executed by the state, spectators perceive the revenge to be their own, and through bearing witness to punishment, they are morally elevated.[70] This moral transformation is paradoxical: spectators harbor feelings of bitterness

Table 6. The Portland incident set to pop songs

Song title	Artist	Genre	Date/time of Twitter post
Here Comes the Hotstepper	Ini Kamoze	reggae	9/6/2020 1:37 a.m. https://twitter.com/thatjerkme/status/1302481066968653824
unidentified			9/6/2020 1:44 a.m. https://twitter.com/CalebJHull/status/1302482835564122112
Walking on Sunshine	Katrina & the Waves	pop/rock	9/6/2020 2:01 a.m. https://twitter.com/thatjerkme/status/1302487043449249794
Here Comes the Hotstepper	Ini Kamoze	reggae	9/6/2020 2:09 a.m. https://twitter.com/PainefulMemes/status/1302489089061654528
Summer in the City	The Lovin' Spoonful	pop/rock	9/6/2020 2:27 a.m. https://twitter.com/Thatoneguy_55/status/1302493578871013376
Footloose	Kenny Loggins	pop/rock	9/6/2020 2:29 a.m. https://twitter.com/DanScavino/status/1302494021617680384
Here Comes the Hotstepper	Ini Kamoze	reggae	9/6/2020 2:30 a.m. https://twitter.com/PainefulMemes/status/1302494399738322944
Here Comes the Hotstepper	Ini Kamoze	reggae	9/6/2020 2:37 a.m. https://twitter.com/PainefulMemes/status/1302496148075294722
Girl on Fire	Alicia Keys	R & B	9/6/2020 2:43 a.m. https://twitter.com/ERINJEAN84/status/1302497642577047552
Motherfucker	Faster & Monny	electronic	9/6/2020 2:49 a.m. https://twitter.com/Americanlll/status/1302499068694863873
Skip It		children's	9/6/2020 3:38 a.m. https://twitter.com/BluesClown/status/1302511553460068352
Billie Jean	Michael Jackson	electronic, pop/rock, R & B	9/6/2020 4:47 a.m. https://twitter.com/SirWilliamScot5/status/1302528856184758272
Ring of Fire	Johnny Cash	country, pop/rock	9/6/2020 6:04 a.m. https://twitter.com/inam_dre/status/1302548276445577216

Table 6—*Continued*

Song title	Artist	Genre	Date/time of Twitter post
The Heat Is On	Glenn Frey	pop/rock	9/6/2020 9:25 a.m. https://twitter.com/RonDuncan7/status/1302598802897907712
Scatman (Ski-Ba-Bop-Ba-Dop-Bop)	Scatman John	electronic	9/6/2020 2:10 p.m. https://twitter.com/thefoggiato/status/1302670547944308736
Footloose	Kenny Loggins	pop/rock	9/6/2020 2:32 p.m. https://twitter.com/realDonaldTrump/status/1302675943241199618
Scatman (Ski-Ba-Bop-Ba-Dop-Bop)	Scatman John	electronic	9/6/2020 3:40 p.m. https://twitter.com/brooklyns_us/status/1302693178877849605
We Didn't Start the Fire	Billy Joel	pop/rock	9/6/2021 3:51 p.m. https://twitter.com/DoomerMars/status/1302695861793689600
Cotton Eye Joe	Rednex	electronic	9/6/2020 8:05 p.m. https://twitter.com/JDManly18/status/1302759764405952512
Festa De Rodeio	Leandro and Leonardo	Latin, international	9/6/2020 9:36 p.m. https://twitter.com/rodrigoloope/status/1302782786076643329
Motherfucker	Faster & Monny	electronic	9/6/2020 10:02 p.m. https://twitter.com/JoshuaSwanson15/status/1302789400464629760
We Didn't Start the Fire	Billy Joel	pop/rock, electronic	9/7/2020 12:40 a.m. https://twitter.com/oldnickels/status/1302829095001104391
Burn	Usher	R & B	9/7/2020 7:13 p.m. https://twitter.com/JeremyLucius/status/1303109094606352390

and powerlessness within their deteriorating world, while they feel relief as they witness the restoration of order and believe themselves to be of upstanding moral character.[71] Such "angry spectator[s]," to use Nietzsche's words, are "impotent against that which has been."[72] The spectators are preoccupied with the injustices of the past yet feel torn between their longing for a certain life and the inability to satisfy that desire.[73] To Nietzsche, punishment is a mechanism capable of transforming spectators' pain into pleasure.[74] This process of transformation is characterized by the transferal of the pain associated with one's own inferiority to a proxy or scapegoat.[75] Trump's strategy included assigning blame to various out-groups while empathizing with his supporters' perceived victimhood; therefore, a punished rally protester or Antifa rabble-rouser (an outsider) became a powerful scapegoat (and symbol) for the disenfranchised and disempowered witnesses in the streets, in the stands, and online. Note that in identifying those responsible for the Black Lives Matter "chaos," Hansen, Scavino, and Trump made use of colorblind terms such as "Antifa," "protesters," and "Democrats." In tweeting the "Footloose" video, Trump offered the burning protester as a scapegoat, but a safe scapegoat, as his (and his supporters') animosity toward Black people was transposed onto an unruly body that is marked White, yet displays traits historically projected onto people of color.[76]

But are these spectators *really* disempowered? Drawing on the work of Elisabeth R. Anker, Paul Elliott Johnson argues that Trump constitutes his audience around "felt powerlessness." In other words, his supporters see themselves as possessing agency and control over their own destinies while perceiving encounters with otherness (in the form of alien ideas, institutions, or people) as indicative of their "personal failure to achieve freedom."[77] One may possess privilege, but this does not offer immunity from feeling excluded. For Trump, precarity encompasses those who may only *feel* powerless; thus economically and socially advantaged subjects can see themselves as occupying the same position as the marginalized and disadvantaged.[78]

Through tweets, GIFs, and soundtracks, the online participants—the truly disempowered and those who just felt that way—became a digital lynch mob of sorts. There was a "crime" (rioting), a punishment (the fire), and spectators who acted as witnesses (Trump's followers on Twitter). Digital lynch mobs, to use Alicia Scott's words, "are directly responsible for fueling the current climate of black anger and white hostility; because they literally leap out of cyberspace an[d] into . . . the real world."[79] In December 2020, Michigan state representative Cynthia A. Johnson was the target of accusations and threats after an edited version of one of her Facebook Live videos circulated via the right-wing mediasphere with the caption "a message from a domestic terrorist." Johnson referred to these attacks as a "digital lynching."[80] Although the "Footloose" video has very different roots and was intended for a different purpose than Johnson's, the Twitter response to the burning protester—a barrage of "off-color commentary and nasty social trolling"—similarly constitutes a digital lynching.[81] I am by no means suggesting that digital lynching bears the same weight as the actual act of lynching or the subsequent intergenerational trauma experienced by people of color as a result of extrajudicial violence; however, the same social factors and cultural anxieties that impelled lynching in the post-Reconstruction South animated acts of digital lynching in 2020. While the victim of digital lynching, in this instance the Portland protester, is *not* Black, Trump and his supporters relied on the same language HoSang and Lowndes argue was "once reserved for people of color."[82]

For both participants and witnesses alike, the act of lynching stood as a visual reminder of White supremacist beliefs in an era when White supremacy and White solidarity were far from entrenched, and therefore required both ritual and repetition to ensure the continuation of the White patriarchy.[83] Anxieties about moral purity and racial purity went hand in hand, often centering the need to protect the minds and bodies of women and children from "the threat of black enfranchisement and autonomy."[84] In 2020, concerns about racial purity came under the guise of anti-immigration rhetoric and Islamophobia. Fears regarding criminality came in the form of the alleged gang activity of migrants south of the border, terrorism when it came to Middle Easterners, and social unrest on the part of Antifa and BLM protesters; these misplaced fears served as justification for policymaking that would supposedly ensure the stability and moral fiber of the nation. More recently, the formerly fringe "replacement theory"—a far-right conspiracy embraced by White supremacists that sees a threat to White power and culture in the migratory patterns of non-White immigrants and a declining birthrate—moved into the mainstream, with Republican politicians and talking heads such as Tucker Carlson and Newt Gingrich airing their views on mainstream news.[85]

President Trump similarly expressed views that aligned with White supremacist beliefs, but he relied on coded language that allowed him to appeal to his base while maintaining some semblance of plausible deni-ability.[86] In a September 2020 speech delivered to an all-White crowd in Bemidji, Minnesota, he quipped, "You have good genes. A lot of it is about the genes, isn't it, don't you believe? The racehorse theory. You think we're so different? You have good genes in Minnesota." In that same speech, he warned supporters that Joe Biden would flood the state with refugees from Somalia.[87] Without directly referring to "race science," Trump's allusion to "good genes" resonates with eugenicist theories that root racial superiority in genetic composition.[88] Elsewhere he alluded to the protection of women as justification for his hard-line stance on issues such as housing and immi-gration. In an October 2020 speech in Pennsylvania, he called on "suburban women" (read: White women) to vote for him because he would keep low-income housing (read: Black people) out of their neighborhoods.[89] In several speeches where he touted his hard-line immigration stance, he invoked the names of Kathryn Steinle and Mollie Tibbetts, two young White women killed by alleged illegal immigrants. Moreover, he regularly stoked fear of Black and Latinx people by describing anti-racism activists as "terrorists" and migrants crossing the border as "invaders."[90] Just as Black men "came to personify the moral corruption that [White southerners] believed to be the root cause of social disorder" in the post-Reconstruction period, the Antifa protester and his ilk came to personify the moral corruption that Republicans considered the root cause of social disorder in 2020.[91]

Reportage on lynching during the post-Reconstruction period relied on dehumanizing language and grotesque descriptions of the victims' bodies. As Amy Louise Wood notes, newspapers often described the person to be lynched "as the inhuman 'prey' or 'fiend.'"[92] In 2020, the Twitter respondents weighing in on the "Footloose" video constructed similar rhetoric in their characterization of the burning protester. He is "barbecue," a "critter," or a "drumstick," merely burning animal parts to be consumed, rather than an actualized person. Repulsion over bodies and their biological functions frequently emerged in Trump speeches, and these remarks were often gendered and racialized.[93] Think, for example, of the instances where Trump expressed disgust over Hillary Clinton's bathroom habits, Megyn Kelly's menstruation, and Marco Rubio's sweat—or even his bodily reenactment of disabled reporter Serge Kovaleski. Through word or gesture, Trump characterizes his opponents' bodies as grotesque, thus reducing them to their most base functions, devoid of ideas and intellect.[94]

Spectators who attended lynchings were not passive consumers, but rather an actively engaged community of witnesses who could testify to the neutralization of the perceived threat and the subsequent reestablishment of moral and social order in its wake.[95] Lynchings, Wood argues, "offered white southerners a vision of themselves as morally pure and spiritually redeemed."[96] In addition to ensuring the continuation of White supremacy in a politically and socially tumultuous time, the act of lynching brought White southerners together through a shared set of values and purpose, forging an idealized community and a sense of White solidarity.[97] It would be hard to make a case that the "Footloose" video spectators were morally elevated by the acts of liking, sharing, commenting, and musical substitution, but their responses to the violent act were similar to the cheering and clapping among those who witnessed a lynching.[98] While the insertion and substitution of musical soundtracks brought levity and cheerfulness to the "disciplinary process," ultimately law enforcement officers subdued the protester's threat and restored order. Bearing witness to "a drama of retribution against sin and criminality" drew the "Footloose" video spectators into a community that reasserts its distance from the disciplined body through its racialized language and collective lulz.[99] As Raúl Pérez notes, collective laughter increases the social distance between the in-group and the target of their insults, in this case, the disruptive protester.[100]

Although there are similarities in spectator engagement that can be teased out when comparing lynching to its digital analogue—ritualistic reenactment of White supremacy, dehumanizing language, cheerful gratification in beholding the act of punishment—the limits (and lack thereof) in the virtual space shape the process of community building in unique ways. In the post-Reconstruction period, photographs, ballads, songs, popular stories, and newspaper accounts circulated after a lynching, reminding southerners of their place in the racial hierarchy, but such artifacts existed alongside other ephemera positing opposing viewpoints on the extrajudicial killings.[101] The Afro-American League, the National Equal Rights Council, and later the NAACP actively spoke out against such violence and sought to establish antilynching legislation. Journalist Ida B. Wells documented lynchings and published pamphlets where she condemned extrajudicial violence and the false narratives that contributed to racial animus. Poet and playwright Angelina Weld Grimké wrote several plays and stories that stood in protest of racial violence. In other words, the marketplace offered a diversity of viewpoints on the act of lynching.

On the surface, it may seem like social media platforms—Facebook, Instagram, Twitter, and TikTok—can facilitate a free exchange of ideas and offer a space where political dialogue can take on various guises, whether in the form of memes, videos, remixes, GIFs, or songs. However, working behind the scenes, AI algorithms determine the content revealed to the user. Platform algorithms track the content users engage with in the forms of liking, sharing, and commenting, and then maximize the users' engagement by placing more of the same kind of content at the top of their feed. But content deemed the most engaging is *not* necessarily of high quality. If low-quality content receives enough engagement, it will continue to be amplified.[102] Thus, the algorithms that ensure steady user engagement can easily be exploited by bad actors, as the United States witnessed during the 2020 presidential election, where disinformation campaigns based out of Eastern Europe reached almost half of all Americans via Facebook.[103] Misinformation and politically divisive content receive higher engagement; therefore, troll farms (groups that make coordinated attempts to post provocative content to social media platforms) continue to post it.[104] Users see this content because Facebook's content-recommendation system places it in their news feeds.

Social media platforms hold the power to control what information is provided to the user, fostering homophily and confirmation bias. In other words, social media shape *how* virtual communities are formed. As users gravitate toward others who share their viewpoints, they are only exposed to information that aligns with their existing beliefs. The result is increasing polarization, where echo chambers develop in the absence of diverse ideas.[105] Several of the examples of media on the trail that I have analyzed in this book—the Barack Obama "Dirt off Your Shoulder" remixes, the Petty Dance feat. Kamala Harris, Camille & Haley's "Keep America Great," and the "Footloose" video—received tens of thousands of likes, shares, and comments. As with other popular content, these media may rise to the top of users' feeds. With their integration of image and sound, they resonate on a different level than text or image alone, and as I have shown here, they are frequently repurposed and reinvented to embody the narratives of those who embrace them. Even seemingly innocuous music media can convey a distorted version of reality or bear a propagandistic or polarizing message. The "Footloose" video and its offshoots, for example, worked to normalize the violence and discord that enveloped the country in 2020 by identifying a scapegoat for perceived injustices and social ills and by deploying sound to establish moral distance. While more overt forms of racism have receded from public spaces since the civil rights period, the jocular repartee surrounding the "Footloose" video only proves that racist discourses stubbornly persist, albeit in their more covert and coded guises.[106] History has shown that dehumanizing language can set the stage for outright violence, and in the case of the "Footloose" video, sound was, if not the catalyst for such discourses, at least a facilitator.[107] For this reason, it is perhaps all the more important that we—not only academics but also the public at large—recognize the roles of sound in shaping the narratives we create, the emotional tenor of the electorate, and ultimately the vote.

NOTES

INTRODUCTION

1. YouTube, "Bill Clinton Playing Saxophone on Arsenio Hall Show (HD)," Video, 1:42, posted by JR85, April 23, 2016, https://www.youtube.com/watch?v=a_WuGDY awFQ

2. Greil Marcus, *Double Trouble: Bill Clinton and Elvis Presley in a Land of No Alternatives* (New York: Picador, 2000), 47–48.

3. Jonathan Freedland, "Hum Along with Bush; Country Music Sweeps the Campaign," *Washington Post*, August 21, 1992, B1. See also Elizabeth Kolbert, "The 1992 Campaign: Media; Whistle-Stops a la 1992: Arsenio, Larry and Phil," *New York Times*, June 5, 1992, http://www.nytimes.com/1992/06/05/us/the-1992-campaign-me dia-whistle-stops-a-la-1992-arsenio-larry-and-phil.html

4. Freya Jarman-Ivens, "'Don't Cry, Daddy': The Degeneration of Elvis Presley's Musical Masculinity," in *Oh Boy! Masculinities and Popular Music*, ed. Freya Jarman-Ivens (New York: Routledge, 2007), 163, 167–69. "Arsenio: What do you like, the old Elvis or the um [unintelligible due to applause.] I know you're an Elvis fan. Clinton: I led a national crusade for the young Elvis. Arsenio: Really? Clinton: Yeah. You know, when you get old, you . . . I mean, he got fat like me. I mean, you know, I think it has to be the young Elvis. That's when he had all his energy and and, and real raw, new, fresh power. I mean, you know, it would be, it would have been a shame to do the old sound, it had to be the new one." YouTube, "American President—Clinton Part 1 in the Arsenio Hall—1992," Video, 7:16, posted by Brian Lee, July 9, 2009, http://www.youtu be.com/watch?v=itKPWt2RklI

5. Christopher Small, *Musicking: The Meanings of Performing and Listening* (Middletown, CT: Wesleyan University Press, 1998), 1–18. To Small, "The act of musicking establishes in the place where it is happening a set of relationships, and it is in those relationships that the meaning of the act lies" (13).

6. Clinton, Toni Morrison writes, "displays almost every trope of blackness: single-parent household, born poor, working-class, saxophone-playing, McDonald's-and-junk-food-loving boy from Arkansas." Toni Morrison, "Comment," *New Yorker*, September 27, 1998, https://www.newyorker.com/magazine/1998/10/05/comment -6543

7. Jackson Katz, *Leading Men: Presidential Campaigns and the Politics of Manhood* (Northampton, MA: Interlink, 2013), 14. See also *Man Enough? Donald Trump, Hillary Clinton, and the Politics of Presidential Masculinity* (Northampton, MA: Interlink, 2016).

8. Irwin Silber's *Songs America Voted By* gives a brief historical survey of the campaign song complete with music from each campaign. William Miles and Danny Crew have done a considerable amount of bibliographic work on the topic: Miles on songsters and Crew on both presidential sheet music and political music. See Irwin Silber, *Songs America Voted By: With the Words and Music That Won and Lost Elections and Influenced the Democratic Process* (Harrisburg, PA: Stackpole Books, 1971); William Miles, *Songs, Odes, Glees and Ballads: A Bibliography of American Presidential Campaign Songsters* (New York: Greenwood Press, 1990); Danny O. Crew, *Presidential Sheet Music: An Illustrated Catalogue of Published Music Associated with the American Presidency and Those Who Sought the Office* (Jefferson, NC: McFarland, 2001); and *American Political Music: A State-by-State Catalog of Printed and Recorded Music Related to Local, State and National Politics, 1756–2004*, 2 vols. (Jefferson, NC: McFarland, 2006). For more on print culture and campaign songs, see Derek B. Scott, "The US Presidential Campaign Songster, 1840–1900," in *Cheap Print and Popular Song in the Nineteenth Century: A Cultural History of the Songster*, ed. Paul Watt, Derek B. Scott, and Patrick Spedding (Cambridge: Cambridge University Press, 2017), 73–90.

9. Benjamin S. Schoening and Eric T. Kasper's monograph offers the most comprehensive study on the history of campaign music, spanning from the eighteenth to twenty-first century. Focusing on the eighteenth and nineteenth centuries, Laura Lohman's meticulous study on songs published in broadsides, newspapers, and song collections addresses election-related music, as well as political music more broadly. Billy Coleman covers similar terrain in his 2020 monograph. Adopting a deeply interdisciplinary conceptual framework, Justin Patch's monograph addresses the role of sound and affect in twenty-first-century campaigns. See Benjamin S. Schoening and Eric T. Kasper, *Don't Stop Thinking about the Music: The Politics of Songs and Musicians in Presidential Campaigns* (Lanham, MD: Lexington Books, 2012); Laura Lohman, *Hail Columbia! American Music and Politics in the Early Nation* (New York: Oxford University Press, 2020); Billy Coleman, *Harnessing Harmony: Music, Power, and Politics in the United States, 1788–1865* (Chapel Hill: University of North Carolina Press, 2020); and Justin Patch, *Discordant Democracy: Noise, Affect, Populism, and the Presidential Campaign* (New York: Routledge, 2019).

10. For more on race as a social construct, see Michael Omi and Howard Winant, *Racial Formation in the United States*, 3rd ed. (New York: Routledge, 2015).

11. Jennifer Lynn Stoever, *The Sonic Color Line: Race and the Cultural Politics of Listening* (New York: New York University Press, 2016), 11.

12. Nina Sun Eidsheim, *The Race of Sound: Listening, Timbre, and Vocality in African American Music* (Durham: Duke University Press, 2019).

13. Karl Hagstrom Miller, *Segregating Sound: Inventing Folk and Pop Music in the Age of Jim Crow* (Durham: Duke University Press, 2010), 1–2.

14. David Brackett, *Categorizing Sound: Genre and Twentieth-Century Popular Music* (Oakland: University of California Press, 2016), 18–20.

15. Ronald Radano and Philip V. Bohlman, "Introduction: Music and Race, Their Past, Their Presence," in *Music and the Racial Imagination*, ed. Ronald Radano and Philip V. Bohlman (Chicago: University of Chicago Press, 2000), 8; Josh Kun, *Audiotopia: Music, Race, and America* (Berkeley: University of California Press, 2005), 19–20.

16. Some of this material on Bill Clinton was published in my 2013 dissertation. See Dana Gorzelany-Mostak, "Pre-existing Music in United States Presidential Campaigns, 1972–2012," PhD diss., McGill University, 2013.

17. Robert Costa, "Songs for Campaign Seasons Past and Present," *Wall Street Journal*, October 2, 2008, http://online.wsj.com/article/SB122290103509796055.html

18. In 2016, *Rolling Stone* falsely claimed that the Hillary Clinton campaign paid $90,000 to a consulting firm to compile her playlist. See David Browne, "Complete Guide to the 2016 Candidates' Favorite Music," *Rolling Stone*, February 1, 2016, https://www.rollingstone.com/music/music-news/complete-guide-to-the-2016-candidates-favorite-music-240830/

19. David Maraniss, "Tooting His Own Horn: Clinton's Team Sees 'Arsenio' Gig as Triumph," *Washington Post*, June 5, 1992, C1.

20. Maureen Dowd, "The 1992 Campaign: Democrats; After Ordeal, Is Clinton Tempered Now, or Burned?," *New York Times*, February 2, 1992, sec. 1, pt. 1, 24, col. 1. Dowd stated, "The candidate was not flustered. He offered his trademark 'Elvis' look, featured heavily in his commercials, of biting his lower lip and crinkling his eyes a bit, a look meant to convey an appealing combination of decency and deviltry."

21. Jarman-Ivens, "Don't Cry, Daddy," 161–80; YouTube, "Bill Clinton Playing Saxophone on *Arsenio Hall Show* (HD)."

22. Greil Marcus, "The Elvis Strategy," *New York Times*, October 27, 1992, http://www.nytimes.com/1992/10/27/opinion/the-elvis-strategy.html. Cited in Marcus, *Double Trouble*, 50.

23. George Bush, Remarks Accepting the Presidential Nomination at the Republican National Convention in Houston [August 20, 1992], online by Gerhard Peters and John T. Woolley, American Presidency Project, https://www.presidency.ucsb.edu/node/266944. See also Marcus, "Elvis Strategy."

24. *People*, "The King & I: Sure, Carville Got the Credit, but Clinton May Really Owe It All to Elvis," December 28, 1992–January 4, 1993, 114–15. Quoted in Chris Gray, "Elvis: 30 Famous Quotes about the King," *Houston Press*, January 4, 2011, https://www.houstonpress.com/music/elvis-30-famous-quotes-about-the-king-6772855

25. Maraniss, "Tooting His Own Horn." For Clinton's performance of "God Bless the Child" see YouTube, "Bill Clinton on Arsenio Hall (June 1992)," Video, 1:12:52, posted by Clinton Warriner, n.d., https://www.youtube.com/watch?v=kWbNK5JvTb8

26. Ron Givens, "Saxophonists Rate Bill Clinton's Musical Ability," *Entertainment Weekly*, June 19, 1992, https://ew.com/article/1992/06/19/saxophonists-rate-bill-clintons-musical-ability/

27. Givens, "Saxophonists."

28. Andrew Ross, *No Respect: Intellectuals and Popular Culture* (New York: Routledge, 1989), 81.

29. Ingrid Monson, "The Problem with White Hipness: Race, Gender, and Cultural Conceptions in Jazz Historical Discourse," *Journal of the American Musicological Society* 48, no. 3 (Autumn 1995): 399.

30. Some of the preexisting tunes used in campaigns between the mid-nineteenth and early twentieth centuries became popular through their performance in minstrel shows.

31. Eric Weisbard, "Proxy Music," *Village Voice*, October 24, 2000, https://www .villagevoice.com/2000/10/24/proxy-music. During the performance, Bush mock-strummed a guitar emblazoned with the words "The Prez." See Ben Sisario, "George Bush, Soul Man? Footage from an Inauguration Concert Is Restored," *New York Times*, December 5, 2018, https://www.nytimes.com/2018/12/05/arts/music/bush-atw ater-inauguration-concert.html

32. Susan Sontag, *Notes on "Camp"* (New York: Picador, 1964), 22.

33. Richard Goldstein, "Sweet William, Sex and Sensibility: The Clinton Touch," *Village Voice*, October 27, 1992, 29–33. Quoted in Marcus, *Double Trouble*, 46.

34. For more on Elvis impersonation, see Francesca Brittan, "Women Who 'Do Elvis': Authenticity, Masculinity, and Masquerade," *Journal of Popular Music Studies* 18, no. 2 (August 2006): 167–90, https://doi.org/10.1111/j.1533-1598.2006.00087.x; and Eric Lott, "All the King's Men: Elvis Impersonators and White Working-Class Masculinity," in *Race and the Subject of Masculinities*, ed. Harry Stecopoulos and Michael Uebel (Durham: Duke University Press, 1997), 192–230.

35. I assembled this playlist by looking at press coverage of Clinton's rallies. See, for example, Maureen Dowd, "The 1992 Campaign: Behind the Scenes; The Faces Behind the Face That Clinton's Smile Masks," *New York Times*, October 25, 1992, A1; Steven Stark, "The Campaigns and Pop Culture," *Evening Sun*, September 4, 1992, 19A; Martin Walker, "Music Carries the Message at the Democrats' Rallies-cum-Rock Concerts; Taking Care of Business—the Clinton Way," *Ottawa Citizen*, October 30, 1992, A6. For a more recent study on popular songs and campaigning, see Courtney Blankenship and Stan Renard, "Pop Songs on Political Platforms," *Journal of Popular Music Studies* 29, no. 3 (2017), https://doi.org/10.1111/jpms.12222. See also Bloomberg, "What the Voters are Streaming," *Bloomberg Politics*, February 19, 2016, https://www .bloomberg.com/politics/graphics/2016-voter-spotify-listens/

36. Nostalgia is broadly conceived as "a preference (general liking, positive atti-tude, or favorable affect) toward objects (people, places, or things) that were more common (popular, fashionable, or widely circulated) when one was younger (in early adulthood, in adolescence, in childhood, or even before birth)." Morris B. Holbrook and Robert M. Schindler, "Echoes of the Dear Departed Past: Some Work in Progress on Nostalgia," in *Advances in Consumer Research* 18, ed. Rebecca H. Holman and Michael R. Solomon (Provo, UT: Association for Consumer Research, 1991), 330–33, https://www.acrwebsite.org/volumes/7181

37. William J. Havlena and Susan L. Holak, "'The Good Old Days': Observations on Nostalgia and Its Role in Consumer Behavior," in *Advances in Consumer Research*

18, ed. Rebecca H. Holman and Michael R. Solomon (Provo, UT: Association for Consumer Research, 1991), 323–29, https://www.acrwebsite.org/volumes/7180

38. Morris B. Holbrook and Robert M. Schindler, "Some Exploratory Findings on the Development of Musical Tastes," *Journal of Consumer Research* 16, no. 1 (June 1989): 119–24.

39. Randall Rothenberg, "Advertising; the Past Is Now the Latest Craze," *New York Times*, November 29, 1989, http://www.nytimes.com/1989/11/29/business/the-media-business-advertising-the-past-is-now-the-latest-craze.html

40. Havlena and Holak, "Good Old Days," 323–29.

41. See Philip Abbott, "A 'Long and Winding Road': Bill Clinton and the 1960s," *Rhetoric & Public Affairs* 9, no. 1 (2006): 1–20.

42. Fred Davis, *Yearning for Yesterday: A Sociology of Nostalgia* (New York: Free Press, 1979), 101.

43. Chris Kaltenbach, "Clinton Proves Himself a Rock and Roll President," *Baltimore Sun*, June 3, 1997, https://www.baltimoresun.com/news/bs-xpm-1997-06-03-1997154115-story.html. In 1997, VH1 released a special titled *Bill Clinton: Rock & Roll President*, which features Clinton talking about his musical experiences during his formative years.

44. Michael P. Jeffries, "Is Obama Really the Hip-Hop President?," *The Atlantic*, January 26, 2011, https://www.theatlantic.com/entertainment/archive/2011/01/is-obama-really-the-hip-hop-president/70061/

45. Aleks Eror, "Sorry Obama but Donald Trump Is America's First Hip-Hop President," Highsnobiety, n.d., https://www.highsnobiety.com/p/donald-trump-hip-hop-president/

46. Chris R. Morgan, "Beto Wants to Be Our First Punk President," *American Conservative*, March 25, 2019, https://www.theamericanconservative.com/articles/beto-wants-to-be-our-first-punk-president-orourke/

47. Samuel L. Popkin, *The Reasoning Voter: Communication and Persuasion in Presidential Campaigns* (Chicago: University of Chicago Press, 1991), 7–21.

48. Lawrence Grossberg, *We Gotta Get Out of This Place: Popular Conservativism and Postmodern Culture* (New York: Routledge, 1992), 9; Bethany Klein, *As Heard on TV: Popular Music in Advertising* (Farnham, UK: Ashgate, 2009), 16.

49. Fabian Holt, *Genre in Popular Music* (Chicago: University of Chicago Press, 2007), 1. Ken McLeod notes how mainstream sports organizations use music to connect with an audience or to diversify their fan base (e.g., the NBA/hip-hop connection); *We Are the Champions: The Politics of Sports and Popular Music* (Farnham, UK: Ashgate, 2011). See also Don Cusic, "NASCAR and Country Music," *Studies in Popular Culture* 21, no. 1 (1998): 31–40.

50. Lawrence Grossberg, "Another Boring Day in Paradise: Rock and Roll and the Empowerment of Everyday Life," *Popular Music* 4 (January 1984): 252–56.

51. Keir Keightley, "Reconsidering Rock," in *The Cambridge Companion to Pop and Rock*, ed. Simon Frith, Will Straw, and John Street (Cambridge: Cambridge University Press, 2001), 109.

52. Abbott, "Long and Winding Road," 5–6.

53. YouTube, "Ted Cruz: 'My Music Tastes Changed on 9/11,'" Video, 1:24, posted by CBS This Morning, March 24, 2015, https://www.youtube.com/watch?v=nik-Ust mCjw

54. Brackett, *Categorizing Sound*, 20.

55. See Maiken Umbach and Matthew Humphrey, *Authenticity: The Cultural History of a Political Concept* (Cham: Palgrave Macmillan, 2018).

56. Theodor W. Adorno, "On Popular Music," in *Cultural Theory and Popular Culture: A Reader*, 2nd ed., ed. John Storey (Athens: University of Georgia Press, 1998), 200–201.

57. Simon Frith, "Music and Identity," in *Questions of Cultural Identity*, ed. Stuart Hall and Paul du Gay (London: Sage, 1996), 114.

58. Kun, *Audiotopia*, 17.

59. See Richard Middleton, "Introduction: Locating the Popular Music Text," in *Reading Pop: Approaches to Textual Analysis in Popular Music*, ed. Richard Middleton (Oxford: Oxford University Press, 2000), 13.

60. See Middleton, "Introduction," 13.

61. Simon Frith, *Music for Pleasure: Essays in the Sociology of Pop* (New York: Routledge, 1988), 123; Kun, *Audiotopia*, 17.

62. John M. Murphy, "Inventing Authority: Bill Clinton, Martin Luther King, Jr., and the Orchestration of Rhetorical Traditions," *Quarterly Journal of Speech* 83, no. 1 (1997): 71–89, https://doi.org/10.1080/00335639709384172

63. Barack Obama's engagement with music in 2008 and 2012 attracted the attention of many scholars. See Travis L. Gosa, "Not Another Remix: How Obama Became the First Hip-Hop President," *Journal of Popular Music Studies* 22, no. 4 (2010): 389–415, https://doi.org/10.1111/j.1533-1598.2010.01252.x; Travis L. Gosa, "'The Audacity of Dope': Rap Music, Race, and the Obama Presidency," in *The Iconic Obama, 2007–2009: Essays on Media Representations of the Candidate and New President*, ed. Nicholas A. Yanes and Derrais Carter (Jefferson, NC: McFarland, 2012), 85–96; Murray Forman, "Conscious Hip-Hop, Change, and the Obama Era," *American Studies Journal* 54 (2010), http://www.asjournal.org/54-2010/conscious-hip-hop/; Lester K. Spence, "Obama and the Future of Hip-Hop Politics," in *Stare in the Darkness: The Limits of Hip-Hop and Black Politics* (Minneapolis: University of Minnesota Press, 2011), 157–76; Michael P. Jeffries, "Obama as Hip-Hop Icon," in *Thug Life: Race, Gender, and the Meaning of Hip-Hop* (Chicago: University of Chicago Press, 2011), 199–206; Matthew F. Jordan, "Obama's iPod: Popular Music and the Perils of Postpolitical Populism," *Popular Communication* 11, no. 2 (2013): 99–115; Dana Gorzelany-Mostak, "Keepin' It Real (Respectable) in 2008: Barack Obama's Music Strategy and the Formation of Presidential Identity," *Journal of the Society for American Music* 10, no. 2 (May 2016): 113–48, https://doi.org/10.1017/S1752196316000043; Travis L. Gosa and Erik Nielson, eds., *The Hip Hop & Obama Reader* (New York: Oxford University Press, 2015); and Dana Gorzelany-Mostak and James Deaville, eds., special issue, *Music & Politics* 9, no. 2 (2015).

64. Eduardo Bonilla-Silva, *Racism without Racists: Color-Blind Racism and the*

Persistence of Racial Inequality in America, 6th ed. (Lanham: Rowman & Littlefield, 2021), 82.

65. Michael Tesler, *Post-Racial or Most-Racial?: Race and Politics in the Obama Era* (Chicago: University of Chicago Press, 2016).

66. Nell Irvin Painter, "What Whiteness Means in the Trump Era," *New York Times*, November 12, 2016, https://www.nytimes.com/2016/11/13/opinion/what-whiteness-means-in-the-trump-era.html

67. Ta-Nehisi Coates, "The First White President," *The Atlantic*, October 2017, https://www.theatlantic.com/magazine/archive/2017/10/the-first-white-president-ta-nehisi-coates/537909/

68. Critical race theory positions race as a socially constituted phenomenon that legitimizes structural inequalities, thereby reinforcing White supremacy and maintaining the subjugation of people of color.

69. Daniel Martinez HoSang and Joseph E. Lowndes, *Producers, Parasites, Patriots: Race and the New Right-Wing Politics of Precarity* (Minneapolis: University of Minnesota Press, 2019), 4, 6.

70. HoSang and Lowndes, *Producers, Parasites, Patriots*, 10–11.

71. HoSang and Lowndes, *Producers, Parasites, Patriots*, 4, 12, 53–54.

72. HoSang and Lowndes, *Producers, Parasites, Patriots*, 67–68.

73. Paul Elliott Johnson, "The Art of Masculine Victimhood: Donald Trump's Demagoguery," *Women's Studies in Communication* 40, no. 3 (2017): 230.

74. For more on user-generated videos and the 2008 campaign, see Carol Vernallis, "Audiovisual Change: Viral Web Media and the Obama Campaign," *Cinema Journal* 50, no. 4 (Summer 2011): 73–97; and Patch, *Discordant Democracy*.

75. Juan M. Floyd-Thomas and Anthony B. Pinn, eds., *Religion in the Age of Obama* (London: Bloomsbury, 2018); Gary Gerstle, "Civic Ideals, Race, and Nation in the Age of Obama," in *The Presidency of Barack Obama: A First Historical Assessment*, ed. Julian E. Zelizer (Princeton: Princeton University Press, 2018), 261–80; Anthony J. Lemelle Jr., *Black Masculinity and Sexual Politics* (New York: Routledge, 2010); Jerry Harris and Carl Davidson, "Obama: The New Contours of Power," *Race & Class* 50, no. 4 (2009): 1–19, https://doi.org/10.1177/0306396809102993; Vincent N. Pham, "Our Foreign President Barack Obama: The Racial Logics of Birther Discourses," *Journal of International and Intercultural Communication* 8, no. 2 (May 2015): 86–107, https://doi.org/10.1080/17513057.2015.1025327; Anthony Neal, *The Oral Presidency of Barack Obama* (Lanham, MD: Lexington Books, 2018); Tricia Rose, *The Hip Hop Wars: What We Talk about When We Talk about Hip Hop—and Why It Matters* (New York: BasicCivitas, 2008); H. Samy Alim and Geneva Smitherman, *Articulate While Black: Barack Obama, Language, and Race in the U.S.* (Oxford: Oxford University Press, 2012); Ron Walters, "Barack Obama and the Politics of Blackness," *Journal of Black Studies* 38, no. 1 (September 2007): 7–29; Gosa and Nielson, *Hip Hop & Obama*; Gosa, "Not Another Remix."

76. Dewey M. Clayton considers this strategy in the 2008 Obama campaign. See Dewey M. Clayton, *The Presidential Campaign of Barack Obama: A Critical Analysis of*

a *Racially Transcendent Strategy* (New York: Routledge, 2010). For a more comprehensive look at music in the 2016 campaign, see Sally Bick and Dana Gorzelany-Mostak, eds., "Music and the 2016 U.S. Presidential Campaign," special issue, *American Music* 35, no. 4 (Winter 2017); and Eric T. Kasper and Benjamin S. Schoening, eds., *You Shook Me All Campaign Long: Music in the 2016 Presidential Election and Beyond* (Denton: University of North Texas Press, 2018).

77. Negin Ghavami and Letitia Anne Peplau, "An Intersectional Analysis of Gender and Ethnic Stereotypes: Testing Three Hypotheses," *Psychology of Women Quarterly* 37, no. 1 (2013): 113–27, https://doi.org/10.1177/0361684312464203; Alice H. Eagly and Linda L. Carli, *Through the Labyrinth: The Truth about How Women Become Leaders* (Cambridge, MA: Harvard Business Press, 2007); Janis V. Sanchez-Hucles and Donald D. Davis, "Women and Women of Color in Leadership: Complexity, Identity, and Intersectionality," *American Psychologist* 65, no. 3 (2010): 171–81; Sarah Florini, "Tweets, Tweeps, and Signifyin': Communication and Cultural Performance on 'Black Twitter,'" *Television & New Media* 15, no. 3 (2014): 223–37, https://doi.org/10.1177/152 7476413480247; Gwendolyn D. Pough, *Check It While I Wreck It: Black Womanhood, Hip-Hop Culture, and the Public Sphere* (Boston: Northeastern University Press, 2004); Amanda R. Matos, "Alexandria Ocasio-Cortez and Cardi B Jump through Hoops: Disrupting Respectability Politics When You Are from the Bronx and Wear Hoops," *Harvard Journal of Hispanic Policy* 31 (January 2019): 89–93; Tasha S. Philpot and Hanes Walton Jr., "One of Our Own: Black Female Candidates and the Voters Who Support Them," *American Journal of Political Science* 51, no. 1 (January 2007): 49–62; Danielle Casarez Lemi and Nadia E. Brown, "The Political Implications of Colorism Are Gendered," *PS: Political Science & Politics* 53, no. 4 (October 2020): 669–73, https://doi.org/10.1017/S1049096520000761

78. Charles Tien, "The Racial Gap in Voting among Women: White Women, Racial Resentment, and Support for Trump," *New Political Science* 39, no. 4 (December 2017): 651–69, https://doi.org/10.1080/07393148.2017.1378296; Matthew C. MacWilliams, "Who Decides When the Party Doesn't? Authoritarian Voters and the Rise of Donald Trump," *PS: Political Science & Politics* 49, no. 4 (October 2016): 716–21; John Fea, *Believe Me: The Evangelical Road to Donald Trump* (Grand Rapids, MI: William B. Eerdmans, 2018); Peter Glick and Susan T. Fiske, "The Ambivalent Sexism Inventory: Differentiating Hostile and Benevolent Sexism," *Journal of Personality and Social Psychology* 70 (1996): 491–512, https://doi.org/10.1037/0022-3514.70.3.491; Robert P. Jones, *The End of White Christian America* (New York: Simon & Schuster, 2016); C. J. Pascoe, "Who Is a Real Man? The Gender of Trumpism," *Masculinities and Social Change* 6, no. 2 (2017): 119–41; C. J. Pascoe and Jocelyn Hollander, "Good Guys Don't Rape: Gender, Domination, and Mobilizing Rape," *Gender & Society* 30, no. 1 (2016): 67–79; Deborah Cameron, "Banter, Male Bonding, and the Language of Donald Trump," in *Language in the Trump Era: Scandals and Emergencies*, ed. Janet McIntosh and Norma Mendoza-Denton (Cambridge: Cambridge University Press, 2020), 158–67; Nicholas A. Valentino, Carly Wayne, and Marzia Oceno, "Mobilizing Sexism: The Interaction of Emotion and Gender Attitudes in the 2016 US Presidential Election," *Public Opinion Quarterly* 82, no. S1 (2018): 799–821; Ruth Frankenberg, "Local

Whitenesses, Localizing Whiteness," in *Displacing Whiteness: Essays in Social and Cultural Criticism*, ed. Ruth Frankenberg (Durham: Duke University Press, 1997), 1–34; Annelot Prins, "From Awkward Teen Girl to Aryan Goddess Meme: Taylor Swift and the Hijacking of Star Texts," *Celebrity Studies* 11, no. 1 (2020): 144–48, https://doi .org/10.1080/19392397.2020.1704431

79. Dan Scavino Jr., @DanScavino, Twitter post, September 6, 2020, 2:29 a.m., https://twitter.com/DanScavino/status/1302494021617680384

80. John Hartley, "Silly Citizenship," *Critical Discourse Studies* 7, no. 4 (2010): 233–48, https://doi.org/10.1080/17405904.2010.511826; John Hartley, *Digital Futures for Cultural and Media Studies* (Malden, MA: Wiley-Blackwell, 2012); Jenny L. Davis, Tony P. Love, and Gemma Killen, "Seriously Funny: The Political Work of Humor on Social Media," *New Media & Society* 20, no. 10 (2018): 3898–916, https://doi.org/10.1177 /1461444818762602; Whitney Phillips and Ryan M. Milner, *The Ambivalent Internet: Mischief, Oddity, and Antagonism Online* (Malden, MA: Polity, 2017); Whitney Phillips, *This Is Why We Can't Have Nice Things: Mapping the Relationship between Online Trolling and Mainstream Culture* (Cambridge, MA: MIT Press, 2016); Brian L. Ott and Greg Dickinson, *The Twitter Presidency: Donald J. Trump and the Politics of White Rage* (New York: Routledge, 2019); Raúl Pérez, "Racism without Hatred? Racist Humor and the Myth of 'Colorblindness,'" *Sociological Perspectives* 60, no. 5 (2017): 956–74.

81. HoSang and Lowndes, *Producers, Parasites, Patriots*; Magnus Hörnqvist, *The Pleasure of Punishment* (London: Routledge, 2021); Amy Louise Wood, *Lynching and Spectacle: Witnessing Racial Violence in America, 1890–1940* (Chapel Hill: University of North Carolina Press, 2009).

82. Vanessa Williamson and Isabella Gelfand, "Trump and Racism: What Do the Data Say?," Brookings, August 14, 2019; see also Griffin Sims Edwards and Stephen Rushin, "The Effect of President Trump's Election on Hate Crimes," January 14, 2018, available at SSRN, https://ssrn.com/abstract=3102652

83. HoSang and Lowndes, *Producers, Parasites, Patriots*, 3.

CHAPTER 1

Chapter 1 is based on the author's article, "Keepin' It Real (Respectable) in 2008: Barack Obama's Music Strategy and the Formation of Presidential Identity," *Journal of the Society for American Music* 10, no. 2 (May 2016): 113–48.

1. Alexander Mooney, "Obama Using 'White Guilt,' Nader Says," CNN, June 25, 2008, https://www.cnn.com/2008/POLITICS/06/25/nader.obama/index.html. See also Colorado Pols, "Nader Tells Rocky: Obama Trying to 'Talk White,'" June 25, 2008, https://www.coloradopols.com/diary/6516

2. BBC News, "Bush's iPod Reveals Music Tastes," April 13, 2005, http://news.bbc .co.uk/2/hi/4435639.stm

3. "Decision 2004/Bush vs. Kerry/Kerry Interview," Video, 9:00, Evening News [Tom Brokaw], NBC, October 28, 2004, Vanderbilt Television News Archive, http://tv news.vanderbilt.edu/program.pl?ID=769639 (accessed July 16, 2012).

4. Dana Gorzelany-Mostak, "'I've Got a Little List': Spotifying Mitt Romney and Barack Obama in the 2012 U.S. Presidential Election," *Music & Politics* 9, no. 2 (2015), http://dx.doi.org/10.3998/mp.9460447.0009.202

5. Naomi Klein, *No Logo*, 10th anniversary ed. (New York: Picador, 2009), xxiii.

6. According to Ancestry.com, Obama's White mother, Stanley Ann Dunham, was a descendant of John Punch, a Black man who came to the colonies as an indentured servant, but later became enslaved for life in 1640. See Amanda Holpuch, "Barack Obama May Be Descendant of First African Slave in Colonial America," *The Guardian*, July 30, 2012, https://www.theguardian.com/world/us-news-blog/2012/jul/30/barack-obama-descendant-first-african

7. Grant Rindner, "Who Were Barack Obama's Parents?," Oprah Daily, November 16, 2020, https://www.oprahdaily.com/life/a34670592/barack-obamas-parents/

8. Cathleen Falsani, "Transcript: Barack Obama and the God Factor Interview [March 27, 2004]," Sojourners, February 21, 2012, https://sojo.net/articles/transcript-barack-obama-and-god-factor-interview. See also Juan M. Floyd-Thomas and Anthony B. Pinn, "Introduction," in *Religion in the Age of Obama*, ed. Juan M. Floyd-Thomas and Anthony B. Pinn (London: Bloomsbury, 2018), 7.

9. Gary Gerstle, "Civic Ideals, Race, and Nation in the Age of Obama," in *The Presidency of Barack Obama: A First Historical Assessment*, ed. Julian E. Zelizer (Princeton: Princeton University Press, 2018), 262.

10. Barack Obama, *Dreams from My Father: A Story of Race and Inheritance* (New York: Times Books, 1995).

11. Jerry Harris and Carl Davidson, "Obama: The New Contours of Power," *Race & Class* 50, no. 4 (2009): 2.

12. Evelyn Brooks Higginbotham introduced the concept of "politics of respectability" in *Righteous Discontent: The Women's Movement in the Black Baptist Church, 1880–1920* (Cambridge, MA: Harvard University Press, 1994).

13. FiveThirtyEight, "Obama and the Rev. Wright Controversy: What Really Happened," n.d., https://fivethirtyeight.com/videos/obama-and-the-rev-wright-controversy-what-really-happened/ (accessed September 1, 2022).

14. Brian Ross and Rehab El-Buri, "Obama's Pastor: God Damn America, U.S. to Blame for 9/11," ABC News, March 13, 2008, https://abcnews.go.com/Blotter/story?id=4443788

15. Max Perry Mueller, "Religion (and Race) Problems on the Way to the White House: Mitt Romney and Barack Obama's 'Faith' Speeches," in *Religion in the Age of Obama*, ed. Juan M. Floyd-Thomas and Anthony B. Pinn (London: Bloomsbury, 2018), 29. See also Barack Obama, "Transcript: Barack Obama's Speech on Race," NPR, March 18, 2008, https://www.npr.org/templates/story/story.php?storyId=88478467

16. Gerstle, "Civic Ideals," 265; see also Mueller, "Religion (and Race) Problems," 30–31.

17. Anthony B. Pinn, "In the Wake of Obama's Hope: Thoughts on Black Lives Matter, Moralism, and Re-imaging Race Struggle," in *Religion in the Age of Obama*, ed. Juan M. Floyd-Thomas and Anthony B. Pinn (London: Bloomsbury, 2018), 144.

18. Floyd-Thomas and Pinn, "Introduction," 5.

19. Tom Jensen, "A Deeper Look at the Birthers," Public Policy Polling, August 19, 2009, http://publicpolicypolling.blogspot.com/2009/08/deeper-look-at-birthers.html; Pew Research Center, "Growing Number of Americans Say Obama Is a Muslim," August 18, 2010, https://www.pewforum.org/2010/08/18/growing-number-of-americ ans-say-obama-is-a-muslim/

20. Vincent N. Pham, "Our Foreign President Barack Obama: The Racial Logics of Birther Discourses," *Journal of International and Intercultural Communication* 8, no. 2 (2015): 102.

21. Anthony Neal, *The Oral Presidency of Barack Obama* (Lanham, MD: Lexington, 2018), 1.

22. Since 2008, the topic of music and Obama has become fertile ground for scholars in the areas of musicology, media studies, political science, sociology, and Africana studies. Travis L. Gosa investigates the political capital of digital mixtapes with Obama-themed hip-hop (called "Obama-Hop") and the campaign-related activities of youth both on and offline: "Not Another Remix: How Obama Became the First Hip-Hop President," *Journal of Popular Music Studies* 22, no. 4 (2010): 389–415, https://doi.org/10.1111/j.1533-1598.2010.01252.x. Covering terrain similar to Gosa's, Lester K. Spence examines artists' Obama-inspired tracks and hip-hop's potential to engage with Black politics in "Obama and the Future of Hip-Hop Politics," in *Stare in the Darkness: The Limits of Hip-Hop and Black Politics* (Minneapolis: University of Minnesota Press, 2011), 157–76; and Erik Nielson, primarily focusing on Young Jeezy's track "My President," investigates the interdependence of Obama and gangsta-type themes in Obama-Hop: "'My President Is Black, My Lambo's Blue': The Obamafication of Rap?," *Journal of Popular Music Studies* 21, no. 4 (December 2009): 344–63. Turning to YouTube, Carol Vernallis explores the intertextual and aesthetic dimensions of viral media that emerged during the 2008 campaign: "Audiovisual Change: Viral Web Media and the Obama Campaign," *Cinema Journal* 50, no. 4 (Summer 2011): 73–97. Gosa and Nielson's edited volume, *The Hip Hop & Obama Reader* (New York: Oxford University Press, 2015), offers interdisciplinary perspectives on hip-hop in the age of Obama, including an outstanding essay by Murray Forman ("Obama/Time: The President in the Hip Hop Nation," 155–75), who investigates how the assertion of musical tastes and age identity allowed the candidate to locate himself in relation to specific classes and constituencies. Richard Daniel Blim's dissertation addresses campaign advertising and the candidate's own iPod, as well as user-generated, Obama-themed mashups and hip-hop offerings: "The Electoral Collage: Mapping Barack Obama's Mediated Identities in the 2008 Election," in "Patchwork Nation: Collage, Music, and American Identity," PhD diss., University of Michigan–Ann Arbor, 2013, 364–450. My work departs from that of Gosa, Nielson, and Spence in that my primary focus lies with popular songs and their signifying potential, rather than with newly composed music and the cultural currency it brings to campaigns. Gosa and Spence focus on the hip-hop community's response to Obama's candidacy, whereas I, like H. Samy Alim and Geneva Smitherman, Michael P. Jeffries, and Forman, am interested in exploring how the candidate situated himself in relation to this community through the deployment of linguistic and cultural markers of blackness; see H. Samy Alim

and Geneva Smitherman, *Articulate While Black: Barack Obama, Language, and Race in the U.S.* (Oxford: Oxford University Press, 2012); Michael P. Jeffries, "The King's English: Obama, Jay Z, and the Science of Code Switching," in *The Hip Hop & Obama Reader*, 243–61; and "Obama as Hip-Hop Icon," in *Thug Life: Race, Gender, and the Meaning of Hip-Hop* (Chicago: University of Chicago Press, 2011), 117–50; and Forman, "Obama/Time." And rather than focusing on the populist appeal of the candidate's iPod, as thoughtfully explored by Blim and Matthew F. Jordan, I read the candidate's list of favorite songs and rally set lists through the construct of respectability and investigate the reception of his personal tastes and public playlist among specific blocs of voters; see Blim, "The Electoral Collage"; and Matthew F. Jordan, "Obama's iPod: Popular Music and the Perils of Postpolitical Populism," *Popular Communication* 11, no. 2 (2013): 99–115.

23. Murray Forman, "Conscious Hip-Hop, Change, and the Obama Era," *American Studies Journal* 54, no. 3 (2010), http://www.asjournal.org/54-2010/conscious-hip-hop/#

24. Shaun Ossei-Owusu, "Barack Obama's Anomalous Relationship with the Hip-Hop Community," in *The Obama Phenomenon: Toward a Multiracial Democracy*, ed. Charles P. Henry, Robert L. Allen, and Robert Chrisman (Urbana: University of Illinois Press, 2011), 224.

25. Quoted in David Mills, "Sister Souljah's Call to Arms: The Rapper Says the Riots Were Payback. Are You Paying Attention?," *Washington Post*, May 13, 1992, https://www.washingtonpost.com/wp-dyn/content/article/2010/03/31/AR2010033101709.html

26. Bill Clinton, "Remarks of Governor Bill Clinton," Rainbow Coalition National Convention, Washington, DC, June 13, 1992, http://www.ibiblio.org/pub/academic/political-science/speeches/clinton.dir/c23.txt

27. C-SPAN, "Rap Artist's Response to Clinton Remarks," Video, 20:24, June 16, 1992, https://www.c-span.org/video/?26613-1/rap-artists-response-clinton-remarks

28. Tricia Rose, *The Hip Hop Wars: What We Talk about When We Talk about Hip Hop—and Why It Matters* (New York: BasicCivitas, 2008), 7–14.

29. For more on twenty-first-century hip-hop's engagement with electoral politics, see S. Craig Watkins, *Hip Hop Matters: Politics, Pop Culture, and the Struggle for the Soul of a Movement* (Boston: Beacon, 2005), 154–56; and the following chapters in Gosa and Nielson, *The Hip Hop & Obama Reader*: Jeffrey O. G. Ogbar, "Message from the Grassroots: Hip Hop Activism, Millennials, and the Race for the White House" (31–53); Bakari Kitwana and Elizabeth Méndez Berry, "It's Bigger Than Barack: Hip Hop Political Organizing, 2004–2013" (54–69); and Travis L. Gosa and Erik Nielson, "'There Are No Saviors': An Interview with Kevin Powell" (70–87).

30. Quoted in Keli Goff, *Party Crashing: How the Hip-Hop Generation Declared Political Independence* (New York: BasicCivitas, 2008), 18–19.

31. Gosa, "Not Another Remix."

32. Citing historian and journalist James G. Spady's description of hip-hop as an "art form/forum," Alim and Smitherman show that the community did not blindly embrace the charismatic candidate simply because he was Black and spoke their

language, but rather welcomed his candidacy as an opportunity to initiate conversations regarding the broader political issues that impact Black communities; see "'My President's Black, My Lambo's Blue': Hip Hop, Race, and the Culture Wars," in *Articulate While Black*, 136–37. Nonetheless, Obama's candidacy was not universally embraced by the hip-hop community. Several artists voiced their critique in song; see Travis L. Gosa, "'The Audacity of Dope': Rap Music, Race, and the Obama Presidency," in *The Iconic Obama, 2007–2009: Essays on Media Representations of the Candidate and New President*, ed. Nicholas A. Yanes and Derrais Carter (Jefferson, NC: McFarland, 2012), 85–96. At the 2008 meeting of the National Hip-Hop Political Convention, an organization cofounded by journalist Rosa Clemente, former Black Panther turned activist Dhoruba Bin Wahad cautioned participants to be wary of Black politicians who may only reaffirm the corrupt system of government and institutional hierarchies that perpetuate White supremacy; see Ogbar, "Message from the Grassroots," 37–38.

33. Ryan Chiachiere, "Imus Called Women's Basketball Team 'Nappy-Headed Hos,'" *Media Matters*, April 4, 2007, https://www.mediamatters.org/msnbc/imus-called-womens-basketball-team-nappy-headed-hos

34. Jake Tapper and Jerry Tully, "Rap Mogul Takes on Obama," ABC News, April 16, 2007, http://abcnews.go.com/GMA/story?id=3045077

35. Deborah Solomon, "Hip-Hop Guru," *New York Times*, April 29, 2007, http://www.nytimes.com/2007/04/29/magazine/29wwlnQ4.t.html?pagewanted=print

36. YouTube, "USA President Barack Obama Opinion on Hip-Hop & Rap 2008" [Barack Obama, interview with Jeff Johnson on BET's political special "What's in It for Us?," aired January 8, 2008], Video, 3:49, posted by starrground, February 3, 2008, https://www.youtube.com/watch?v=pFSVG7jRp_g. Transcription by author. The MySpace page "Hip Hop for Obama," no longer available, contained quotations, video footage, and artists' statements: http://www.myspace.com/hiphopforobama

37. Travis L. Gosa and Erik Nielson, "The State of Hip Hop in the Age of Obama," in *The Hip Hop & Obama Reader*, 5; see also Nielson, "My President Is Black."

38. Jann S. Wenner, "A Conversation with Barack Obama," *Rolling Stone*, July 10–24, 2008, https://www.rollingstone.com/culture/culture-news/a-conversation-with-barack-obama-51394/

39. Gabe Meline, "Hip-Hop President: How Will Obama's Presidency Change the Face of Hip-Hop?," Bohemian.com, December 31, 2008, https://bohemian.com/hip-hop-president-1/

40. Sway Calloway, "Barack Obama Gives a Shout-Out to Hip-Hop," *MTV*, September 27, 2008, http://www.mtv.com/news/1595820/barack-obama-gives-a-shout-out-to-hip-hop/

41. Bakari Kitwana, *The Hip Hop Generation: Young Blacks and the Crisis in African American Culture* (New York: BasicCivitas, 2002), xiv.

42. Barack Obama, Interview with Angie Martinez, Hot 97, WQHT, June 27, 2007. This interview is cited in Peter Hamby, "Barack Obama Gets Name-Dropped in Hip-Hop," *CNN*, August 17, 2007, http://www.cnn.com/2007/POLITICS/08/17/obama.hip.hop/index.html

43. YouTube, "Barack Obama on Ellen," Video, 1:25, posted by BarackObamadotcom, October 30, 2007, https://www.youtube.com/watch?v=RsWpvkLCvu4&t=8s

44. "USA President Barack Obama Opinion on Hip-Hop & Rap 2008."

45. Wenner, "Conversation with Barack Obama."

46. For another reading on Obama's engagement with hip-hop artists, see Michael P. Jeffries, "'Where Ya At?' Hip-Hop's Political Locations in the Obama Era," in *The Cambridge Companion to Hip-Hop*, ed. Justin A. Williams (Cambridge: Cambridge University Press, 2015), 316–20.

47. See Ben Smith, "Obama Camp Condemns Song: Ludacris 'Should Be Ashamed,'" Ben Smith (blog), Politico, July 30, 2008, https://www.politico.com/blogs/ben-smith/2008/07/obama-camp-condemns-song-ludacris-should-be-ashamed-01 0659; and Julie Bosman, "The Inner Obama," The Caucus (blog), *New York Times*, June 24, 2008, https://thecaucus.blogs.nytimes.com/2008/06/24/the-inner-obama/

48. Rose, *Hip Hop Wars*, 129.

49. riley in nc, July 30, 2008, 2:13 p.m., comment on Smith, "Obama Camp Condemns Song."

50. For a report on the speech and the gesture, see Ari Melber, "Obama Meets Jay-Z in YouTube Mashup Slamming Clinton & Debate," *Huffington Post*, April 17, 2008, https://www.huffpost.com/entry/obama-meets-jay-z-in-yout_b_97342. For the speech, see YouTube, "Barack Obama in Raleigh, NC," Video, 4:10, posted by BarackObamadotcom, April 17, 2008, https://www.youtube.com/watch?v=FlR9DNf qGD4. For more on Obama's gesture and Jay-Z's song, see Spence, "Obama and the Future," 157–59.

51. For more on Obama's code-switching strategies, see Alim and Smitherman, "My President's Black"; and Jeffries, "The King's English," 243–61.

52. The lyrics in the chorus of Jay-Z's song are "You gotta get, that, dirt off your shoulder." Obama states, "You gotta" and then completes the phrase with the gesture. Jay-Z, The Black Album, Roc-A-Fella Records B0001528-02, 2003, CD.

53. Spence, "Obama and the Future," 159.

54. Melber, "Obama Meets Jay-Z."

55. YouTube, "Barack Gets That Dirt off His Shoulders," Video, 1:18, posted by Bill3948, April 17, 2008, https://www.youtube.com/watch?v=yel8IjOAdSc

56. YouTube, "Obama Dirt off Your Shoulder Remix," Video, 1:36, posted by jarts, April 18, 2008, https://www.youtube.com/watch?v=7j2g2axmnY8

57. For more on how hip-hop artists made Obama an "honorary member of the hip-hop community" and appropriated his image, see Gosa, "Not Another Remix," 398–403; and for more on "coolness" and Obama's postsoul identity, see Ossei-Owusu, "Barack Obama's Anomalous Relationship," 219–23.

58. Claire Cain Miller, "How Obama's Internet Campaign Changed Politics," Bits (blog), *New York Times*, November 7, 2008, https://bits.blogs.nytimes.com/2008/11/07/how-obamas-internet-campaign-changed-politics/

59. Caroline E. Dadas, "Inventing the Election: Civic Participation and Presidential Candidates' Websites," *Computers and Composition* 25, no. 4 (2008): 416–31.

60. Carol Vernallis, "Audiovisual Change."

61. Gregory Phillips, "The Campaign Song Comeback," From Fay to Z (blog), *Fayetteville Observer*, October 29, 2008, http://blogs.fayobserver.com/faytoz (no longer available).

62. Several right-leaning websites questioned the accuracy of the biographical sketch Obama provided in this speech and criticized his fanciful rewriting of history. The Obama campaign later admitted that the candidate wrongly credited the Kennedy family for his father's scholarship, and that when referring to Selma, Obama was actually referring to the civil rights movement in general as opposed to the Selma march.

63. Keith D. Miller, *Voice of Deliverance: The Language of Martin Luther King, Jr. and Its Sources* (New York: Free Press, 1992), 18–25.

64. Barack Obama, Selma Voting Rights March Commemoration Speech, March 4, 2007, American Rhetoric Online Speech Bank, https://www.americanrhetoric.com /speeches/barackobama/barackobamabrownchapel.htm

65. Ron Walters, "Barack Obama and the Politics of Blackness," *Journal of Black Studies* 38, no. 1 (September 2007): 7–29.

66. John M. Murphy examines how Bill Clinton similarly deployed this strategy; see "Inventing Authority: Bill Clinton, Martin Luther King, Jr., and the Orchestration of Rhetorical Traditions," *Quarterly Journal of Speech* 83, no. 1 (1997): 75. See also Mueller, "Religion (and Race) Problems," 23.

67. Wenner, "Conversation with Barack Obama"; "USA President Barack Obama Opinion on Hip-Hop & Rap 2008"; Calloway, "Barack Obama Gives a Shout-Out"; Barack Obama, Interview Hot 97; Jeff Chang, "Barack Obama: The Vibe Interview," *Vibe*, September 2007; Jon Coplon, "White House DJ Battle," *Blender*, July 30, 2008, https://web.archive.org/web/20080814151724/http://www.blender.com/WhiteHouse DJBattle/articles/39518.aspx. This *Blender* poll took place after Clinton conceded the Democratic nomination to Obama.

68. Blim, "The Electoral Collage," 404–8; see also Jordan, "Obama's iPod." Several magazines, news outlets, and blogs, including *Seventeen* and NPR, discussed the contents of the candidates' lists. For an article that dissects Obama's 2008 rally music and offers an expert's analysis, see Margaret Talev, "Soul of the Obama Campaign Is in the Soundtrack," McClatchy, October 31, 2008, https://www.mcclatchydc.com/news/polit ics-government/article24507895.html. The expert is Mark Anthony Neal, a professor of African and African American studies at Duke University.

69. Forman, "Obama/Time," 163.

70. There are likely other crossovers between Obama's list of favorites (as recounted in the interviews cited above) and his rally playlists, but I have only indicated here the artists whose music I am fairly certain he used at his official rallies. Obama may have also cited additional artists as favorites in his other interviews. The music of Wonder, Crow, and West was also featured on *Yes We Can: Voices of a Grassroots Movement*, a compilation CD released by the campaign in order to raise funds for the general election. See *Yes We Can: Voices of a Grassroots Movement*, Hidden Beach, B001IF269Y, 2008, CD.

71. Dave Beard, "'Celebration' and 'There's Hope' on Obama's Setlist," Boston.com, January 5, 2008, http://www.boston.com/news/politics/politicalintelligence/2008/01

/celebrationand.html (no longer available). Slate (and other websites) posted lists of the songs Obama used on the campaign trail. See Christopher Beam, "Barack Obama's iTunes Playlist," Trailhead (blog), Slate, January 26, 2008, https://slate.com/news-and -politics/2008/01/barack-obama-s-itunes-playlist.html

72. Dave Hoekstra, "The Soul of a President," *Chicago Sun-Times*, January 11, 2009.

73. Hoekstra, "Soul of a President."

74. For a more nuanced economic and cultural history, see Suzanne E. Smith, *Dancing in the Street: Motown and the Cultural Politics of Detroit* (Cambridge, MA: Harvard University Press, 1999), 138.

75. Stevie Wonder, *Signed, Sealed & Delivered*, Tamla, TS304, 1970, LP. "Signed, Sealed, Delivered I'm Yours," words and music by Stevie Wonder, Syreeta Wright, Lee Garrett, and Lula Mae Hardaway.

76. Jeff Zeleny, "Long by Obama's Side, an Adviser Fills a Role That Exceeds His Title," *New York Times*, October 26, 2008, https://www.nytimes.com/2008/10/27/us /politics/27axelrod.html?r=1

77. Wenner, "Conversation with Barack Obama." *Innervisions* (1973) predates *Fulfillingness' First Finale* (1974).

78. Carol Marin, "Thanks to Hillary for Being a Winner at Heart," *Chicago Sun-Times*, May 11, 2008.

79. Philippa Roberts and Jane Cunningham, "Feminisation of Brands," *Marketing*, September 2, 2008; see also Katherine Adam and Charles Derber, *The New Feminized Majority: How Democrats Can Change America with Women's Values* (Boulder, CO: Paradigm, 2008).

80. Paul Gipson, the president of a steelworkers' union, made the following remarks in a speech introducing Clinton: "I truly believe that that's going to take an individual that has testicular fortitude. . . . That's exactly right. That's what we gotta have." See Catherine Price, "Hillary's 'Testicular Fortitude,'" Salon, May 1, 2008, https://www.sa lon.com/2008/05/01/hillary_s_testicles/. Easley is quoted in Fernando Suarez, "N.C. Governor: Hillary Makes Rocky Look Like 'Pansy,'" CBS News, April 28, 2008, https:// www.cbsnews.com/news/nc-governor-hillary-makes-rocky-look-like-pansy/

81. Douglas Kellner, "Barack Obama and Celebrity Spectacle," *International Journal of Communication* 3 (2009): 715–41.

82. Maureen Dowd, "¿Quién Es Less Macho?," *New York Times*, February 24, 2008, https://www.nytimes.com/2008/02/24/opinion/24dowd.html; Marie Wilson, "Leading Like a Girl: For Men Only?," *Huffington Post*, April 15, 2008, https://www .huffpost.com/entry/leading-like-a-girl-for-m_b_96753; Michael Scherer, "Hillary Is from Mars, Obama Is from Venus," Salon, July 12, 2007, https://www.salon.com/2007 /07/12/obama_hillary/

83. For more on the concept of the mythic presidency, see Patricia S. Misciagno, "Rethinking the Mythic Presidency," *Political Communication* 13, no. 3 (1996): 329–44.

84. Bryan Garman, "Models of Charity and Spirit: Bruce Springsteen, 9/11, and the War on Terror," in *Music in the Post-9/11 World*, ed. Jonathan Ritter and J. Martin Daughtry (New York: Routledge, 2007), 71–89.

85. For more on sentimentality and Black music, see chapters 2 and 3 in Mitchell

Morris, *The Persistence of Sentiment: Display and Feeling in Popular Music of the 1970s* (Berkeley: University of California Press, 2013).

86. Mayfield's "Move on Up" does not deal with romantic attachment, but the opening invocation, "Hush now child and don't you cry," is reminiscent of a lullaby, a genre historically identified with the maternal feminine.

87. Scherer, "Hillary Is from Mars."

88. Jackson Katz, *Leading Men: Presidential Campaigns and the Politics of Manhood* (Northampton, MA: Interlink, 2013), 4.

89. Adam and Derber, *New Feminized Majority*, 139.

90. Frank Rudy Cooper, "Our First Unisex President?: Black Masculinity and Obama's Feminine Side," *Denver University Law Review* 86, no. 3 (2009): 633.

91. For more on Obama's appropriation of hip-hop culture in his speeches, see Alim and Smitherman, "My President's Black." See also Sanford K. Richmond, "Paint the White House Black!! A Critical Discourse Analysis Look at Hip Hop's Social, Cultural, and Political Influence on the Presidency of Barack Obama," *Western Journal of Black Studies* 37, no. 4 (Winter 2013): 249–57.

92. Emma Cannen, "Avant-Garde Militarism and a Post-Hip-Hop President," *International Feminist Journal of Politics* 16, no. 2 (2014): 268.

93. Barack Obama, "Text of Obama's Fatherhood Speech," Politico, June 15, 2008, http://www.politico.com/news/stories/0608/11094.html

94. Anthony J. Lemelle Jr., *Black Masculinity and Sexual Politics* (New York: Routledge, 2010), xiv.

95. YouTube, "Crush on Obama. (with LYRICS)," Video, 3:24, posted by The Key of Awesome, February 17, 2008, https://www.youtube.com/watch?v=dyjXt1zSXHU

96. Nedra Pickler, "Obama's Girls Aren't Fans of YouTube's Obama Girl," *The Sun*, August 22, 2007, https://www.sbsun.com/2007/08/22/obamas-girls-arent-fans-of-you tubes-obama-girl/

97. Michael Falcone, "Obama on 'Obama Girl,'" The Caucus (blog), *New York Times*, August 20, 2007, http://thecaucus.blogs.nytimes.com/2007/08/20/obama-on -obama-girl/

98. Kyle-Anne Shiver, "Women Voters and the Obama Crush," American Thinker, March 11, 2008, https://www.americanthinker.com/articles/2008/03/women_voters _and_the_obama_cru.html

99. Quoted in Nick Miller, "The Good Wife," *Sydney Morning Herald*, May 27, 2012, https://www.smh.com.au/world/the-good-wife-20120526-1zbs5.html

100. Michelle Cottle, "Wife Lessons: Why Michelle Obama Is No Hillary Clinton," *New Republic*, March 26, 2008, 23.

101. Simon Frith, *Sound Effects: Youth, Leisure, and the Politics of Rock 'n' Roll* (New York: Pantheon, 1981), 123.

102. This informant attended the Harrisonburg, Virginia, rally at James Madison University on October 28, 2008. All statements from interviews are copied verbatim without correcting spelling/grammar/punctuation.

103. Peter Wicke, *Rock Music: Culture, Aesthetics, and Sociology*, trans. Rachel Fogg (Cambridge: Cambridge University Press, 1990), ix.

104. Richard Middleton, "'From Me to You': Popular Music as Message," in *Studying Popular Music* (Milton Keynes: Open University Press, 1990), 232.

105. Question: "Because he used 'Signed, Sealed, Delivered I'm Yours' for his campaign, we now often associate this song with Barack Obama, but the song has been around a long time. What else does this song make you think about?" This informant attended the Harrisonburg, Virginia, rally at James Madison University on October 28, 2008.

106. Satinder P. Gill, "Entrainment and Musicality in the Human System Interface," *Artificial Intelligence and Society* 21, no. 4 (June 2007): 568.

107. Katz, *Leading Men*, 3.

108. The Center for Responsive Politics website tracks federal campaign contributions and lobbying activity. "Donor Demographics by Gender," July 13, 2009, https://www.opensecrets.org/pres08/donordemCID_compare.php%7B?%7Dcycle=2008 (no longer available).

109. Caroline A. Streeter, "Obama Jungle Fever: Interracial Desire on the Campaign Trail," in Yanes and Carter, *Iconic Obama*, 167–83, esp. 171–72.

110. YouTube, "Democratic Debate—Saturday Night Live" [Season 33, episode 5, February 23, 2008], Video, 9:24, posted by Saturday Night Live, October 3, 2013, https://www.youtube.com/watch?v=AdHc6aX2gEs. See also Bernard Goldberg, *A Slobbering Love Affair: The True (and Pathetic) Story of the Torrid Romance between Barack Obama and the Mainstream Media* (Washington, DC: Regnery, 2009).

111. Mark Leibovich, "The Other Man of the Hour," *Washington Post*, July 27, 2004, http://www.washingtonpost.com/wp-dyn/articles/A16606-2004Jul26.html

112. Goff, *Party Crashing*, 34.

113. Gosa, "Not Another Remix," 398.

114. For further discussion on how Obama constructed his American identity, see Etse Sikanku and Nicholas A. Yanes, "The Modern *E Pluribus Unum* Man: How Obama Constructed His American Identity from His Global Background," in Yanes and Carter, *Iconic Obama*, 16–27.

115. Talev, "Soul of the Obama Campaign."

116. Lemelle, *Black Masculinity*, 2.

117. For more on Obama in 2012, see Dana Gorzelany-Mostak and James Deaville, eds., special issue, *Music & Politics* 9, no. 2 (2015), https://quod.lib.umich.edu/m/mp/9460447.0009.2*?rgn=main;view=fulltext. Also see Jeffries, "Where Ya At?," 314–26; and Erik Nielson, "How Hip-Hop Fell Out of Love with Obama," *The Guardian*, August 23, 2012, http://www.theguardian.com/music/2012/aug/23/why-hip-hop-deserting-obama

CHAPTER 2

1. Rupert Murdoch, @rupertmurdoch, Twitter post, October 7, 2015, 8:59 p.m., https://twitter.com/rupertmurdoch/status/651924724960874497

2. Ben Carson radio ad, SoundCloud, November 5, 2015, https://soundcloud.com
/abcpolitics/ben-carson-radio-ad

3. Katherine Faulders, "Listen to Ben Carson's New Rap Ad Aimed at African-
American Voters," ABC News, November 5, 2015, https://abcnews.go.com/Politics/lis
ten-ben-carsons-rap-ad-aimed-african-american/story?id=34988082

4. Tessa Stuart, "Listen to Ben Carson's Rap Campaign Ad," *Rolling Stone*,
November 5, 2015, https://www.rollingstone.com/politics/politics-news/listen-to-ben
-carsons-rap-campaign-ad-40435/. See also All Things Considered, "Meet the Man
behind the Ben Carson Rap," NPR, November 7, 2015, https://www.npr.org/2015/11/07
/455150311/meet-the-man-behind-the-ben-carson-rap

5. Ben Carson radio ad.

6. "It feels like a McDonald's Commercial." Mark S. Luckie, @marksluckie,
Twitter post, November 5, 2015, 9:58 a.m., https://twitter.com/marksluckie/status/66
2282744345530373

7. "That Ben Carson radio spot is essentially a political payday loan ad." Jamil
Smith, @JamilSmith, Twitter post, November 5, 2015, 9:07 a.m., https://twitter.com/Ja
milSmith/status/662269986124222466

8. Issie Lapowsky, "Twitter Reacts to the Ben Carson Rap That Shouldn't Exist,"
Wired, November 5, 2015, https://www.wired.com/2015/11/twitter-reacts-to-the-ben
-carson-rap-that-shouldnt-exist/

9. See Joanna Love, "Political Pop and Commercials That Flopped: Early Lessons
from the 2016 Presidential Race," Trax on the Trail, January 14, 2016, https://www.tra
xonthetrail.com/2016/01/14/political-pop-and-commercials-that-flopped-early-lesso
ns-from-the-2016-presidential-race/

10. Philip Bump, "Talib Kweli Has Some Thoughts on Ben Carson's New 'Urban'
Ad: He Thinks Jeb Bush Might Have Done Better," *Washington Post*, November 5,
2015, https://www.washingtonpost.com/news/the-fix/wp/2015/11/05/talib-kweli-has
-some-thoughts-on-ben-carsons-new-urban-ad/

11. Loren Kajikawa, "'My Name Is': Signifying Whiteness, Rearticulating Race," in
Sounding Race in Rap Songs (Oakland: University of California Press, 2015), 127.

12. SoundCloud, "Panderdom—Ben Carson Rap Ad Spoof," posted by aaronnemo,
n.d., https://soundcloud.com/aaronnemo/ben-carson-rap-ad-spoof#t=0:00. See also
Aaron Nemo, "Listen to the Spoof of Ben Carson's Hip-Hop Radio Ad," HuffPost,
November 9, 2015, https://www.huffpost.com/entry/spoof-ben-carson-rap_n_563e8
d78e4b0307f2cadbdf5?ncid=tweetlnkushpmg00000067. Other remixes/parodies followed Carson's ad. See YouTube, "Ben Carson's Rap Ad, Fixed," Video, 1:15, posted by
Slate, June 18, 2018, https://www.youtube.com/watch?v=B_cSm87SJKE&t=32s

13. Nick Gass, "Ben Carson's 15 Most Controversial Quotes," Politico, October 9,
2015, https://www.politico.com/story/2015/10/ben-carson-controversial-quotes-21
4614

14. Carson later disavowed the ad during a January 2016 campaign stop in Creston,
Iowa. He stated, "I did not approve that, and when it came out, I said, why did you put
that out? What are you thinking? . . . I was horrified. It was done by people who have

no concept of the black community and what they were doing." See Sam Frizell, "Ben Carson 'Horrified' By His Own Campaign Ad," *Time*, January 22, 2016, https://time .com/4191428/ben-carson-rap-advertisement-radio/

15. "We need to reestablish faith in our communities and the values and principles that got us through slavery, that got us through Jim Crow, and segregation, and all kinds of horrible things that were heaped upon us. . . . Why were we able to get through those? Because of our faith, because of our family, because of our values, and as we allow the hip-hop community to destroy those things for us, and as we grasp onto what's politically correct and not what is correct, we continue to deteriorate." Interview on the R & B radio station WBLS, April 5, 2015, quoted in Leslie Larson, "Ben Carson Blasts Hip-Hop for Hurting African-American Communities," *Business Insider*, April 6, 2015, http://www.businessinsider.com/ben-carson-blasts-hip-hop-20 15-4

16. Drew Millard, "Ben Carson's Rap Radio Ad Is an Embarrassment for Everyone," Vice, November 5, 2015, https://www.vice.com/en/article/8gkkdg/ben-carsons-rap-ad -republicans-dont-understand-hip-hop-115

17. C-SPAN, "Carson Prayer Speech," Video, 26:51, February 7, 2013, https://www .c-span.org/video/?c4353213/user-clip-carson-prayer-speech

18. Robert Samuels, "Ben Carson: From Inspiring to Polarizing," *Washington Post*, January 2, 2016, https://www.washingtonpost.com/sf/national/2016/01/02/deciderscarson/

19. Wolf Blitzer, "Carson: There's a Reason Dictators 'Take the Guns First,'" CNN, October 8, 2015, https://www.cnn.com/videos/politics/2015/10/08/ben-carson-gun-co ntrol-nazi-germany-intvw-wolf.cnn; Ben Carson and Candy Carson, *A More Perfect Union: What We the People Can Do to Reclaim Our Constitutional Liberties* (New York: Sentinel, 2015); Gass, "Ben Carson's 15 Most Controversial Quotes."

20. Jesse J. Holland and Bill Barrow, "Ben Carson Stands by Statement That Egyptian Pyramids Built to Store Grain," PBS NewsHour, November 5, 2015, https:// www.pbs.org/newshour/politics/presidential-candidate-ben-carson-stands-belief-py ramids-built-store-grain

21. Lawrence M. Krauss, "Ben Carson's Scientific Ignorance," *New Yorker*, September 28, 2015, https://www.newyorker.com/news/news-desk/ben-carsons -scientific-ignorance; Emily Cadei, "The World Through Ben Carson's Surgical Magnifying Glass," *Newsweek Global*, November 3, 2015.

22. See, for example, Allan Smith, "The Day Ben Carson's Campaign Died," *Business Insider*, March 7, 2016, https://www.businessinsider.com/ben-carson-presid ent-campaign-why-2016-2

23. Michael Tesler, *Post-Racial or Most-Racial?: Race and Politics in the Obama Era* (Chicago: University of Chicago Press, 2016).

24. Maulana Karenga, "Jesse Jackson and the Presidential Campaign: The Invitation and Oppositions of History," *Black Scholar* 15, no. 5 (September–October 1984): 57–71.

25. Dewey M. Clayton, *The Presidential Campaign of Barack Obama: A Critical Analysis of a Racially Transcendent Strategy* (New York: Routledge, 2010), 42–44.

26. H. Samy Alim and Geneva Smitherman, *Articulate While Black: Barack Obama, Language, and Race in the U.S.* (Oxford: Oxford University Press, 2012); Murray

Forman, "Obama/Time: The President in the Hip Hop Nation," in *The Hip Hop & Obama Reader*, ed. Travis L. Gosa and Erik Nielson (New York: Oxford University Press, 2015), 155–75; Michael P. Jeffries, "'Where Ya At?' Hip-Hop's Political Locations in the Obama Era," in *The Cambridge Companion to Hip-Hop*, ed. Justin A. Williams (Cambridge: Cambridge University Press, 2015), 314–26. For more on Obama and hip-hop, see Gosa and Nielson, *The Hip Hop & Obama Reader*.

27. Ryan Teague Beckwith, "Ben Carson Launches 2016 Presidential Campaign," *Time*, May 4, 2015, http://time.com/3845489/ben-carson-campaign-launch

28. In some instances, prerecorded tracks accompany the live singers.

29. C-SPAN, "Ben Carson Presidential Campaign Announcement," Video, 1:08:10, C-SPAN, May 4, 2015, https://www.c-span.org/video/?325722-1/dr-ben-carson-presid ential-campaign-announcement

30. Selected of God website, https://www.selectedofgod.com (accessed May 20, 2021).

31. Veritas includes Jeff Anderson, tenor; James Berrian, baritone; Andrew Goodwin, tenor; Jordan Johnson, tenor; and Scott Lawrence, bass.

32. *8 Mile*, directed by Curtis Hanson (2002; Universal City, CA: Universal Pictures, 2003), DVD.

33. Hunter Schwarz, "The 9 Best Moments from Ben Carson's Bizarre and Glorious Campaign Launch/Concert," *Washington Post*, May 4, 2015, https://www.washington post.com/news/the-fix/wp/2015/05/04/the-9-best-moments-from-ben-carsons-bizar re-and-glorious-campaign-launch/?utm_term=.46dba35e26d2

34. As Mickey Hess has posited, Eminem inverts the narratives of Black rappers in order to frame his whiteness as a disadvantage in his quest to become a hip-hop artist. See Mickey Hess, "Hip-Hop Realness and the White Performer," *Critical Studies in Media Communication* 22, no. 5 (December 2005): 372. See also Kajikawa, "My Name Is," 118–42.

35. See "Neurosurgeon Demographics and Statistics in the US," Zippia, https:// www.zippia.com/neurosurgeon-jobs/demographics/ (accessed October 1, 2022).

36. See Ben Carson and Candy Carson, *America the Beautiful: Rediscovering What Made This Nation Great* (Grand Rapids, MI: Zondervan, 2013); and Carson and Carson, *A More Perfect Union*.

37. See James Hamblin, "Who Is Dr. Ben Carson? And Why Is He Sort of Running for President?," Politico, April 21, 2014, https://www.politico.com/magazine/story /2014/04/who-is-dr-ben-carson-105875/; Eminem, *Lose Yourself*, Shady/Interscope Records, 2002, CD.

38. I am grateful to my colleague Eric Smialek for drawing my attention to the significance of this omission.

39. Eminem, "Lose Yourself."

40. Jerma A. Jackson, *Singing in My Soul: Black Gospel Music in a Secular Age* (Chapel Hill: University of North Carolina Press, 2004), 2.

41. YouTube, "Mosh (Dirty Version) by Eminem | Eminem," Video, 5:18, posted by EminemMusic, n.d., https://www.youtube.com/watch?v=9wRLd5l7WYE

42. Diamond Alexis, "Eminem Scalped Donald Trump in His Hip Hop Awards Cypher and the Internet Is Floored," BET, October 10, 2017, https://www.bet.com/art

icle/q61ycv/eminem-scalped-donald-trump-in-his-hip-hop-awards-cypher. Eminem made the following remarks in the Billboard interview with Paul Rosenberg: "At the end of the day, if I did lose half my fan base, then so be it, because I feel like I stood up for what was right and I'm on the right side of this. I don't see how somebody could be middle class, busting their ass every single day, paycheck to paycheck, who thinks that that fucking billionaire is gonna help you." See Dan Rys, "Eminem and New Def Jam CEO Paul Rosenberg on Early 'Broke Days,' Courting Controversy and Hip-Hop's Future," Billboard, January 25, 2018, https://www.billboard.com/music/features/eminem-paul-rosenberg-interview-billboard-cover-story-2018-8095496/. In August 2018, Eminem addressed backlash over the performance in a track titled "The Ringer" on *Kamikaze (2018)*. See Jordan Darville, "Eminem Expresses Regret for Anti-Trump Freestyle, Claims He Was Questioned by Secret Service," Fader, August 31, 2018, https://www.thefader.com/2018/08/31/eminem-regret-anti-trump-freestyle-secret-service-interview

43. Quoted in Chris Norris, "Artist of the Year," *Spin*, January 2001, https://web.archive.org/web/20030608212512/http://www.spin.com/new/magazine/jan2001eminem2.html

44. Simon Stow, "On the Existential Politics of Hip-Hop (Or, the Concept of Irony with Continual Reference to Eminem)," *Brolly* 2, no. 2 (2019): 111, https://www.journals.lapub.co.uk/index.php/brolly/article/view/1197/1060

45. Marcia Alesan Dawkins, "Close to the Edge: The Representational Tactics of Eminem," *Journal of Popular Culture* 43, no. 3 (2010): 463–85.

46. Kajikawa, "My Name Is," 128.

47. See Olivia Nuzzi, "How Pepe the Frog Became a Nazi Trump Supporter and Alt-Right Symbol," Daily Beast, May 26, 2016, https://www.thedailybeast.com/how-pepe-the-frog-became-a-nazi-trump-supporter-and-alt-right-symbol

48. Kajikawa, "My Name Is," 134.

49. Stow, "On the Existential Politics of Hip-Hop," 118.

50. YouTube, "Chrysler 'Imported from Detroit' Campaign: Super Bowl Commercial with Eminem," Video, 2:18, posted by Cause Marketing, October 30, 2016, https://www.youtube.com/watch?v=mYsFUFgOEmM

51. For more on this ad, see David Kiley, "The Inside Story: Chrysler's Risky Eminem Super Bowl Commercial," Auto Blog, February 8, 2011, http://www.autoblog.com/2011/02/08/chrysler-eminem-super-bowl-ad

52. Michael Wayland, "Chrysler Gospel Remix of 'Lose Yourself' by Eminem Celebrates Detroit, Benefits Charities," MLive, August 2, 2011, https://www.mlive.com/news/detroit/2011/08/video_chrysler_releases_gospel.html

53. YouTube, "Selected of God Choir—Lose Yourself (Official Music Video)," Video, 4:07, posted by SoundofGospel, July 29, 2011, https://www.youtube.com/watch?v=sg4lSGGOfzE. The song was released on iTunes on August 2, 2011.

54. Veritas website, http://veritasfive.com/bio (accessed June 2, 2021).

55. John Stauffer and Benjamin Soskis, *The Battle Hymn of the Republic: A Biography of the Song That Marches On* (Oxford: Oxford University Press, 2013), 18.

56. "Ben Carson Presidential Campaign Announcement."

57. Ben Carson, "Announcement of Candidacy Music Hall Center for the Performing Arts," Detroit, MI, May 4, 2015, http://www.p2016.org/carson/carson0504 15spt.html

58. Carson, "Announcement of Candidacy."

59. Although the medley songs' blending of the sacred and civic may have appealed to Carson's team, the usage in a campaign context suggests they are unaware of the songs' complex histories, and how these histories might complicate a reading of the songs as espousing conservative Christian values. For example, "God Bless America," Sheryl Kaskowitz argues, represents the White mainstream, yet encompasses a rich and complex history—Kate Smith's Armistice Day broadcast, association with the civil rights and labor movements, appropriation by the Christians who fought against secularity during the 1960s, Congress's "spontaneous" performance at the Capitol Building on September 11, and post-9/11 ubiquity during baseball's seventh-inning stretch, just to name a few. See Sheryl Kaskowitz, *God Bless America: The Surprising History of an Iconic Song* (New York: Oxford University Press, 2013), 3–11.

60. See "John Brown's Body," [Broadside] *Songs Sung at the Reunion of the 23d Regiment, O. V. I., at Fremont, O., Sept. 14, 1877* (Journal Steam Print, 1877), Kenneth S. Goldstein American Song Broadsides, Middle Tennessee State University Digital Collections, https://digital.mtsu.edu/digital/collection/p15838coll19/id/3100

CHAPTER 3

1. Moded_Corroded, @Moded_Corroded, Twitter post, February 13, 2019, 11:21 a.m., https://twitter.com/Moded_Corroded/status/1095719579735605249

2. YouTube, "Petty," Video, 1:32, posted by SOLMEMES, May 30, 2018, https://www.youtube.com/watch?v=BIK10JFs4GA; for Cameron J's original video, see YouTube, "PETTY SONG—the Starrkeisha Cheer Squad!—@TheKingOfWeird," Video, 1:29, posted by Randome Guye, April 4, 2016, https://www.youtube.com/watch?v=xMU5C-fEXA8. The song includes several musical quotations, including "Work" by Rihanna and Drake, "Work from Home" by Fifth Harmony, "Formation" by Beyoncé, and "Hello" by Adele. I could not locate the origins of the video featuring female politicians, but the version cited here has a closing frame that names "Solent Greenis Productions." The 2019 Twitter post is no longer available.

3. Lauren Michele Jackson, "We Need to Talk about Digital Blackface in Reaction GIFs," *Teen Vogue*, August 2, 2017, https://www.teenvogue.com/story/digital-blackface-reaction-gifs

4. Negin Ghavami and Letitia Anne Peplau, "An Intersectional Analysis of Gender and Ethnic Stereotypes: Testing Three Hypotheses," *Psychology of Women Quarterly* 37, no. 1 (2013): 113.

5. According to the music critics who weighed in on this article, "Ms. Harris is far and away the most hip-hop-minded of all the candidates." See Astead Herndon, Jon Caramanica, and Jon Pareles, "What Do Rally Playlists Say About the Candidates?,"

New York Times, August 19, 2019, https://www.nytimes.com/interactive/2019/08/19/us/politics/presidential-campaign-songs-playlists.html

6. In 2019, Harris expressed regret over the "unintended consequences" of this policy. See Katie Galioto, "Kamala Harris Expresses 'Regret' over California Truancy Law," Politico, April 17, 2019, https://www.politico.com/story/2019/04/17/kamala-harris-regrets-truancy-law-1279788

7. Lara Bazelon, "Kamala Harris Was Not a 'Progressive Prosecutor,'" *New York Times*, January 17, 2019, https://www.nytimes.com/2019/01/17/opinion/kamala-harris-criminal-justice.html

8. Kamala Harris, *The Truths We Hold: An American Journey* (New York: Penguin, 2019), 49–50. See German Lopez, "Kamala Harris's Controversial Record on Criminal Justice, Explained," Vox, January 23, 2019, https://www.vox.com/future-perfect/2019/1/23/18184192/kamala-harris-president-campaign-criminal-justice-record; and Lee Fang, "In Her First Race, Kamala Harris Campaigned as Tough on Crime—and Unseated the Country's Most Progressive Prosecutor," *The Intercept*, February 7, 2019, https://theintercept.com/2019/02/07/kamala-harris-san-francisco-district-attorney-crime/

9. Emily Bazelon, "Kamala Harris, a 'Top Cop' in the Era of Black Lives Matter," *New York Times Magazine*, May 25, 2016, https://www.nytimes.com/2016/05/29/magazine/kamala-harris-a-top-cop-in-the-era-of-black-lives-matter.html

10. Niels Lesniewski, "The Legislative Record of Kamala Harris Shows a Loyal Democrat and Trump Counterpuncher," Roll Call, August 12, 2020, https://rollcall.com/2020/08/12/the-legislative-record-of-kamala-harris-shows-a-loyal-democrat-and-trump-counter-puncher/. The Development, Relief, and Education for Alien Minors (DREAM) Act was a bill intended to grant temporary conditional residency and a pathway to citizenship to undocumented immigrants who arrived in the United States when they were minors. The bill never passed, but the term "DREAMer" is sometimes used to refer to undocumented youth. The nonpartisan site GovTrack ranked Harris as the "most politically left compared to all senators" for the year 2019. See GovTrack.us, "Sen. Kamala Harris's 2019 Report," last updated January 18, 2020, https://www.govtrack.us/congress/members/kamala_harris/412678/report-card/2019 (accessed July 2, 2021).

11. Kelly Dittmar, "Black Women in American Politics, 2019," Center for American Women and Politics, https://cawp.rutgers.edu/sites/default/files/resources/black-women-politics-2019.pdf (accessed June 25, 2021).

12. Lisa Lerer and Jennifer Medina, "What Does This Country Demand of Black Women in Politics?," *New York Times*, December 8, 2019, https://www.nytimes.com/2019/12/08/us/politics/kamala-harris-black-women.html

13. See Alice H. Eagly and Linda L. Carli, *Through the Labyrinth: The Truth about How Women Become Leaders* (Cambridge, MA: Harvard Business Press, 2007); and Janis V. Sanchez-Hucles and Donald D. Davis, "Women and Women of Color in Leadership: Complexity, Identity, and Intersectionality," *American Psychologist* 65, no. 3 (2010): 171–81.

14. For more on Harris as reformer, see Lopez, "Kamala Harris's Controversial Record."

15. One appeal many might remember is the video where Harris joined prominent Indian producer/actor/writer Mindy Kaling to cook masala dosas on YouTube. In many respects, Harris sidelined this aspect of her identity during the primary campaign, possibly because of the controversy that surrounded Obama's citizenship in 2008 or out of a desire to downplay the "perpetual foreigner" stereotype. For more on Harris's multiracial identity and the 2020 campaign, see Nisha Chittal, "The Kamala Harris Identity Debate Shows How America Still Struggles to Talk about Multiracial People," Vox, August 14, 2020, https://www.vox.com/identities/2020/8/14/21366307/kamala-harris-black-south-asian-indian-identity

16. Media studies professor Meredith Clark refers to "Black Twitter" as "a network of culturally connected communicators using the platform to draw attention to issues of concern to black communities." See Whitelaw Reid, "Black Twitter 101: What Is It? Where Did It Originate? Where Is It Headed?," *UVA Today*, November 28, 2018, https://news.virginia.edu/content/black-twitter-101-what-it-where-did-it-originate-where-it-headed

17. Sarah Florini, "Tweets, Tweeps, and Signifyin': Communication and Cultural Performance on 'Black Twitter,'" *Television & New Media* 15, no. 3 (2014): 224, https://doi.org/10.1177/1527476413480247

18. Florini, "Tweets, Tweeps, and Signifyin,'" 224.

19. YouTube, "Mood Mix with Senator Kamala Harris," Video, 2:35, posted by The Late Show with Stephen Colbert, January 14, 2019, https://www.youtube.com/watch?v=Qo2482G1gog; Stephen Colbert, @StephenAtHome, Twitter post, January 14, 2019, 10:04 p.m., https://twitter.com/StephenAtHome/status/1085009849992335360. See also Harris's post: Kamala Harris, @KamalaHarris, Twitter post, January 14, 2019, 10:03 p.m., https://twitter.com/KamalaHarris/status/1085009675744145408: "One nation under a groove. Gettin' down just for the funk of it."

20. Dana Gorzelany-Mostak, "'I've Got a Little List': Spotifying Mitt Romney and Barack Obama in the 2012 U.S. Presidential Election," *Music & Politics* 9, no. 2 (2015), http://dx.doi.org/10.3998/mp.9460447.0009.202

21. "The Official Hillary 2016 Playlist," Spotify playlist, https://open.spotify.com/playlist/43JJ50RsHoyUXj8eI8FaPQ?si=51d02bb487eb4fc2

22. Harris also sings the Marley song.

23. Paul Messaris, *Visual "Literacy": Image, Mind, and Reality* (Boulder, CO: Westview, 1994), 32–33. Quoted in Shawn J. Parry-Giles, "Mediating Hillary Rodham Clinton: Television News Practices and Image-Making in the Postmodern Age," *Critical Studies in Media Communication* 17, no. 2 (2000): 216.

24. Shawn J. Parry-Giles and Trevor Parry-Giles, *Constructing Clinton: Hyperreality and Presidential Image-Making in Postmodern Politics* (New York: Peter Lang, 2002), 28.

25. Obama even made use of a distorted version of Romney's patriotic turn in one of his 2012 campaign ads. See YouTube, "Obama for America TV Ad: 'Firms,'" Video,

0:32, posted by BarackObamadotcom, July 14, 2012, https://www.youtube.com/watch?v=Ud3mMj0AZZk

26. Karlyn Kohrs Campbell, *Man Cannot Speak for Her*, vol. 1, *A Critical Study of Early Feminist Rhetoric* (New York: Greenwood, 1989), 13.

27. Campbell, *Man Cannot Speak*, 13–14.

28. Katherine Adam and Charles Derber, *The New Feminized Majority: How Democrats Can Change America with Women's Values* (Boulder, CO: Paradigm, 2008), 6–7, 62. Feminized values, Adam and Derber argue, "are universalistic and require attention to values linked to racial and class injustice" (90).

29. Susana Leyva, @SusanaLeyva, Twitter post, January 14, 2019, 10:47 p.m., https://twitter.com/SusanaLeyva/status/1085020718990049281

30. "You know Phife is dead, right?," #YHMP Des, @youheardmedawg, Twitter post, January 24, 2019, 7:42 a.m., https://twitter.com/youheardmedawg/status/1088416874612903940

31. See "With all due respect Senator Harris—Give it up. This is as phony as the 'hot-sauce in my purse' routine," Kitty Farmer #ForeverSanders, @4SacredHoop, Twitter post, January 15, 2019, 9:11 p.m., https://twitter.com/4SacredHoop/status/1085358790285975558; "Authenticity: FAIL," Black Bruce Wayne, @bushido49ers, Twitter post, January 15, 2019, 7:11 p.m., https://twitter.com/bushido49ers/status/1085328712147468289; and "I didn't think there could be a worse video of a Dem 2020 candidate than @SenWarren's 'I'm going to get me a beer' video. I was wrong," Cathy Buffaloe, @cathybuffaloe, Twitter post, January 15, 2019, 2:04 p.m., https://twitter.com/cathybuffaloe/status/1085251467869650946

32. Zach, @zcr86, Twitter post, January 14, 2019, 11:45 p.m., https://twitter.com/zcr86/status/1085035107340165120

33. "You are the Paul Ryan of 2019. Cops shouldn't try to relate to the public." Sans Culottes, @Cloutassent, Twitter post, January 15, 2019, https://twitter.com/Cloutassent/status/1085340526445056000. See Kevin Robillard, "Paul Ryan Pics Spark Dumbbell Debate," Politico, October 11, 2012, https://www.politico.com/story/2012/10/paul-ryan-pics-spark-dumbbell-debate-082296

34. Eternity Martis, "The Politics of Being Black and Loud," *Fader*, June 28, 2016, https://www.thefader.com/2016/06/28/the-politics-of-being-black-and-loud

35. For more on rap and the Michael Dunn trial, see William Cheng, "Black Noise, White Ears: Resilience, Rap, and the Killing of Jordan Davis," *Current Musicology*, no. 102 (2018): 115–89, https://doi.org/10.7916/cm.v0i102.5367

36. See, for example, Michael P. Jeffries, "Hip-Hop Authenticity in Black and White," in *Thug Life: Race, Gender, and the Meaning of Hip-Hop* (Chicago: University of Chicago Press, 2011), 117–50.

37. "Kamala does not do anything for black people. Actually voted for things that hurt the black community. And, while we are at it, she is NOT black." Plebeian Jane, @PlebeianJane, Twitter post, January 14, 2019, 10:40 p.m., https://twitter.com/PlebeianJane/status/1085018882631495680; "She graduated High School in Montreal. She's almost as Canadian as Senator Cruz." Grumpy In General, @GrumpyInGeneral, Twitter post, January 14, 2019, 10:08 p.m., https://twitter.com/GrumpyInGeneral/sta

tus/1085010845262905344. Ted Cruz was born in Calgary, Canada, where his mother and father worked in the oil industry. Cruz's father was born in Cuba and later became a US citizen. His mother was born in Delaware. Children born to US parents abroad are considered natural-born citizens. Donald Trump tried to make Cruz's citizenship status a sticking point in 2016, but according to legal experts, he was eligible. See David G. Savage, "Is Ted Cruz, Born in Canada, Eligible for the Presidency? Legal Experts Say Yes," *Los Angeles Times*, January 8, 2016, https://www.latimes.com/nation/la-na -natural-born-president-20160108-story.html; and Domenico Montanaro, "Is Ted Cruz Allowed to Run Since He Was Born In Canada?," NPR, March 23, 2015, https:// www.npr.org/sections/itsallpolitics/2015/03/23/394713013/is-ted-cruz-allowed-to -run-since-he-was-born-in-canada

38. "Hmm I was expecting something from . . . The Police." Mound—big structural bayleef, @PITmounD, Twitter post, January 15, 2019, 10:01 a.m., https://twitter.com/PI TmounD/status/1085190334097682434

39. BeatgrrrlRoseFlag of Palestinian Territories, @Beatgrrrl, Twitter post, January 15, 2019, 2:40 p.m., https://twitter.com/Beatgrrrl/status/1085260450239983616

40. "What was your favorite song/mix while you were servicing Willie Brown on your way to where you are now. Asking for a friend." Cynthia McGrath, @ CynthiaMcGrath6, Twitter post, January 16, 2019, 12:25 a.m., https://twitter.com/Cyn thiaMcGrath6/status/1085407584213979136

41. "You would have put Bob Marley & the Wailers in jail for smoking weed." Irate Plebeian, @postabsurdist, Twitter post, January 15, 2019, 10:44 p.m., https://twitter .com/postabsurdist/status/1085382343307743234

42. Norma Linda Livella, @NormaLivella, Twitter post, January 16, 2019, 10:58 p.m., https://twitter.com/NormaLivella/status/1085748103167102980

43. Lily Adams, @adamslily, Twitter post, January 22, 2019, 7:04 p.m., https://twitt er.com/adamslily/status/1087863537756717056

44. See YouTube, "Barack Obama on Ellen," Video, 1:25, posted by Barack Obamadotcom, October 30, 2007, https://www.youtube.com/watch?v=RsWpv kLCvu4&t=8s

45. AnonymousQ1776, Twitter post, January 2, 2019, https://twitter.com/Anon ymousQ17763/status/1081085429401690118. For the original video, see YouTube, "Phoenix—Lisztomania—Boston University Brat Pack Mashup," Video, 4:20, posted by Julian Jensen, October 1, 2010, https://www.youtube.com/watch?v=Qj2Xald7NYQ

46. Alexandria Ocasio-Cortez, @AOC, Twitter post, January 4, 2019, https://twitter .com/AOC/status/1081234130841600000

47. iamcardib, Instagram post, January 16, 2019, https://www.instagram.com/p/Bs tmkvDFGAm

48. Aris Folley, "Dem Senators Debate Whether to Retweet Cardi B Video Criticizing Trump over Shutdown," The Hill, January 17, 2019, https://thehill.com/blo gs/in-the-know/in-the-know/425904-dem-senators-publicly-debate-whether-to-retw eet-cardi-b-ripping

49. Harmeet Kaur, "Cardi B and Tomi Lahren Are Feuding over the Government Shutdown," CNN, January 21, 2019, https://www.cnn.com/2019/01/20/entertainme

nt/cardi-b-tomi-lahren-twitter-feud. See also Isabelia Herrera, "AOC Defends Cardi B against Critics: Don't Mess with Bronx Women or You'll Get Roasted," Remezcla, January 21, 2019, https://remezcla.com/music/cardi-b-alexandria-ocasio-cortez-gover nment-shutdown/

50. Gary Trust, "Cardi B 'Moves' to No. 1 on Billboard Hot 100 with 'Bodak Yellow,' Post Malone Debuts at No. 2 with 'Rockstar,'" *Billboard*, September 25, 2017, https:// www.billboard.com/articles/columns/chart-beat/7973958/cardi-b-no-1-hot-100-post -malone-portugal-the-man

51. Sherri Williams, "Cardi B: *Love & Hip Hop*'s Unlikely Feminist Hero," *Feminist Media Studies* 17, no. 6 (2017): 1114–17.

52. Williams, "Cardi B," 1116.

53. Williams, "Cardi B," 1115. See also Gwendolyn D. Pough, *Check It While I Wreck It: Black Womanhood, Hip-Hop Culture, and the Public Sphere* (Boston: Northeastern University Press, 2004), 76. Pough's work investigates the rhetorical practices of Black women who participate in hip-hop culture. To bring wreck is to "disrupt dominant masculine discourses, break into the public sphere, and in some way impact or influence the U.S. imaginary, even if that influence is fleeting" (12).

54. Charlotte Colombo, "Kamala Harris Isn't as Feminist as You Think," *Prospect*, January 29, 2021, https://www.prospectmagazine.co.uk/world/kamala-harris-isnt-as -feminist-as-you-think-united-states-vie-president

55. Sidney Madden, "The Business of Being Cardi B," NPR, April 5, 2018, https:// www.npr.org/sections/therecord/2018/04/05/599592959/the-business-of-being-cardi -b

56. Amanda R. Matos, "Alexandria Ocasio-Cortez and Cardi B Jump through Hoops: Disrupting Respectability Politics When You Are from the Bronx and Wear Hoops," *Harvard Journal of Hispanic Policy* 31 (January 2019): 89.

57. "Sorry, I think this is a publicity stunt to get the 'black' vote and celebrity endorsement." Fateemi, @FatimaKatumbusi, Twitter post, January 24, 2019, 6:29 a.m., https://twitter.com/FatimaKatumbusi/status/1088398354206273536

58. DNC, @theroguednc, Twitter post, January 23, 2019; reposted on The Hill, Facebook Page, January 23, 2019, https://www.facebook.com/kamalaisacop/photos/a. 2237469469799315/2238155336397395

59. Irving "Abolish ICE" Lang, @irvingjlang, Twitter post, January 23, 2019, 2:33 a.m., https://twitter.com/irvingjlang/status/1087976645007429633

60. Faith Karimi, "Alexandria Ocasio-Cortez Responds to Dance Video Critics with More Dancing," CNN, January 4, 2019, https://www.cnn.com/2019/01/04/polit ics/ocasio-cortez-dancing-video-trnd/index.html

61. RenéMiette, @MieteRene, Twitter post, January 22, 2019, 9:40 p.m., https://twit ter.com/MieteRene/status/1087902919557566471

62. Scott #BLM #ACAB #AbolishThePolice Menor, @smenor, Twitter post, January 23, 2019, 6:04 a.m., https://twitter.com/smenor/status/1088029610237816833

63. Amashinobi, @amashinobi, Twitter post, January 23, 2019, 6:12 a.m., https://tw itter.com/amashinobi/status/1088031595410481153

64. Regina G. Lawrence and Melody Rose, *Hillary Clinton's Race for the White*

House: Gender Politics and the Media on the Campaign Trail (Boulder, CO: Lynne Rienner, 2010), 8.

65. "This is the 'just chillin in Cedar Rapids' of 2019." Phil, @chillestphil, Twitter post, January 22, 2019, 10:41 p.m., https://twitter.com/chillestphil/status/108791811571 8086656; "Nice try. . . . not as cringe as 'pokemon go go go to the polls' but also not as cool as Bill Clinton playing sax on Arsenio." [Includes "How do you do, fellow kids?" meme.] Correcting the Record with Guillotines, @SetPixels, Twitter post, January 24, 2019, 7:21 p.m., https://twitter.com/SetPixels/status/1088592750390300674. These are all statements made by Hillary Clinton that were generally considered cringe-worthy, as they revealed her to be either out of touch or insincere in her attempts to connect with the average voter. These one-off remarks quickly circulated as memes. See Vann R. Newkirk II, "On Hillary Clinton's Pandering," *The Atlantic*, April 19, 2016, https://www.theatlantic.com/politics/archive/2016/04/hillary-clinton-pandering-ra dio/479004/; Kaleigh Rogers, "Hillary Clinton Accidentally Became a Vine Meme," Motherboard, August 14, 2015, https://www.vice.com/en/article/vvbwmj/hillary-cli nton-accidentally-became-a-vine-meme; and James Grebey, "Hillary Clinton Wants People to 'Pokemon-Go-to the Polls,'" Insider, July 14, 2016, https://www.insider.com /hillary-clinton-wants-people-to-pokemon-go-to-the-polls-2016-7

66. Ivory Lamont, @Squeeze1975, Twitter post, January 26, 2019, 11:02 p.m., https://twitter.com/Squeeze1975/status/1089372953106620417

67. YouTube, "Kamala Harris Talks 2020 Presidential Run, Legalizing Marijuana, Criminal Justice Reform + More," Video, 44:18, posted by Breakfast Club Power 105.1 FM, February 11, 2019, https://www.youtube.com/watch?v=Kh_wQUjeaTk&t=2326s

68. Victim of capitalism, @joshieecs, Twitter post, February 11, 2019, 5:01 p.m., https://twitter.com/joshieecs/status/1095080317768081413

69. black norma, @BLUafro, Twitter post, February 12, 2019, 6:44 p.m., https://twit ter.com/BLUafro/status/1095468642999914496

70. Realist, @knewvemb, Twitter post, February 13, 2019, 12:27 a.m., https://twitter .com/knewvemb/status/1095555126444609536

71. AntMoon325, @AntWadley325, Twitter post, February 13, 2019, 5:40 a.m., https://twitter.com/AntWadley325/status/1095633724765597697

72. Negro Mis-Education Camp Fugitive, @TheWokePost, Twitter post, February 12, 2019, 11:51 p.m., https://twitter.com/TheWokePost/status/1095545955145973762

73. EbonyEnchantress, @JanetSnackson, Twitter post, February 12, 2019, 6:16 p.m., https://twitter.com/JanetSnackson/status/1095461701091250176

74. Corey Cross, @cocropoker, Twitter post, February 13, 2019, 6:47 a.m., https://tw itter.com/cocropoker/status/1095650644269109248

75. Florini, "Tweets, Tweeps, and Signifyin,'" 224.

76. Alice Ashton Filmer, "Bilingual Belonging and the Whiteness of (Standard) English(es)," *Qualitative Inquiry* 13, no. 6 (2007): 761.

77. For more on the meanings attached to "good English" during the Trump era, see H. Samy Alim and Geneva Smitherman, "'Perfect English' and White Supremacy," in *Language in the Trump Era: Scandals and Emergencies*, ed. Janet McIntosh and Norma Mendoza-Denton (Cambridge: Cambridge University Press, 2020): 226–36.

78. Geneva Smitherman, *Talkin That Talk: Language, Culture, and Education in African America* (New York: Routledge, 2000), 26.

79. D Alex, @D_Alex_connect, Twitter post, February 13, 2019, 11:21 a.m., https://twitter.com/D_Alex_connect/status/1095719714540658690

80. Anuxperience, @Anuxperience1, Twitter post, February 12, 2019, 9:44 p.m., https://twitter.com/Anuxperience1/status/1095514053936586752

81. Quoted in John Wagner, "Kamala Harris's Jamaican Father Wasn't Amused by Her Joke about Marijuana Use," *Washington Post*, February 21, 2019, https://www.washingtonpost.com/politics/kamala-harriss-jamaican-father-wasnt-amused-by-her-joke-about-marijuana-use/2019/02/21/2d722658-35cb-11e9-af5b-b51b7ff322e9_story.html; see also David Martosko, "Her Grandparents 'Must Be Turning in Their Grave,'" *Daily Mail*, February 20, 2019, https://www.dailymail.co.uk/news/article-6725403/Kamala-Harris-Jamaican-father-slams-fraudulent-stereotype-linking-family-pot-smoking.html

82. Bastestain, @TommyIsBS, Twitter post, February 13, 2019, 4:11 a.m., https://twitter.com/TommyIsBS/status/1095611363693596672

83. Wade, @WadeFightClub7, Twitter post, February 12, 2019, 6:56 p.m., https://twitter.com/WadeFightClub7/status/1095471706163081216

84. Peter Beinart, "Progressives Have Short Memories," *The Atlantic*, December 4, 2019, https://www.theatlantic.com/ideas/archive/2019/12/kamala-harris-was-impossible-bind/602971/. See also these earlier critiques of Harris's record: Briahna Gray, "A Problem for Kamala Harris: Can a Prosecutor Become President in the Age of Black Lives Matter?," *The Intercept*, January 20, 2019, https://theintercept.com/2019/01/20/a-problem-for-kamala-harris-can-a-prosecutor-become-president-in-the-age-of-black-lives-matter/; and Conor Friedersdorf, "When Kamala Was a Top Cop," *The Atlantic*, August 25, 2019, https://www.theatlantic.com/ideas/archive/2019/08/kamala-cop-record/596758/

85. Amanda Marcotte, "Sympathy for the K-Hive: Kamala Harris Ran a Bad Campaign—and Faced Remarkable Online Spite," Salon, December 3, 2019, https://www.salon.com/2019/12/03/sympathy-for-the-k-hive-kamala-harris-ran-a-bad-campaign-and-faced-remarkable-online-spite/. See also Ashley Reese, "Did the 'Kamala Is a Cop' Meme Help Tank Harris's Campaign?," Jezebel, December 3, 2019, https://jezebel.com/did-the-kamala-is-a-cop-meme-help-tank-harriss-campaign-1840056843

86. Camille Squires, "Kamala Was a Cop. Black People Knew It First," Mother Jones, December 9, 2019, https://www.motherjones.com/politics/2019/12/kamala-was-a-cop-black-people-knew-it-first/

87. Jill Filipovic, "Kamala Harris' Candidacy Requires a Nuanced Debate about Her Record, Race and Gender. Is the Left Ready?," *Think*, January 22, 2019, https://www.nbcnews.com/think/opinion/kamala-harris-candidacy-requires-nuanced-debate-about-her-record-race-ncna961301

88. John B, comment on Astead W. Herndon, "Kamala Harris Is Accused of Lying about Listening to Tupac. Here's What Actually Happened," *New York Times*, February 13, 2019, https://nyti.ms/3ATNs4E#permid=30611602

89. Ian Sams retweeted the *Breakfast Club* clip with "The rightwing is so desperate

to attack @KamalaHarris they're trying to make Reefergate happen. @djenvy asked what she listened to. @cthagod made a pot joke. Then she answered @djenvy's question. This really isn't that complicated. Just watch." See Ian Sams, @IanSams, Twitter post, February 12, 2019, https://twitter.com/IanSams/status/1095366221032239109

90. Jackson Katz, *Leading Men: Presidential Campaigns and the Politics of Manhood* (Northampton, MA: Interlink, 2013), 3.

91. Quoted in Lerer and Medina, "What Does This Country Demand?"

92. Tasha S. Philpot and Hanes Walton Jr., "One of Our Own: Black Female Candidates and the Voters Who Support Them," *American Journal of Political Science* 51, no. 1 (January 2007): 49.

93. Maya King, "Why Black Voters Never Flocked to Kamala Harris," Politico, December 4, 2019, https://www.politico.com/news/2019/12/04/kamala-harris-black-voters-2020-075651

94. A Tribe Called ADOS, @TribecalledDOS, February 13, 2019, 11:43 a.m., https://twitter.com/TribecalledDOS/status/1095725105118957568

95. Michael P. Jeffries, "The King's English: Obama, Jay Z, and the Science of Code Switching," in *The Hip Hop & Obama Reader*, ed. Travis L. Gosa and Erik Nielson (New York: Oxford University Press, 2015), 244.

96. Tricia Rose, *The Hip Hop Wars: What We Talk about When We Talk about Hip Hop—and Why It Matters* (New York, BasicCivitas, 2008).

97. YouTube, "USA President Barack Obama Opinion on Hip-Hop & Rap 2008" [Barack Obama, interview with Jeff Johnson on BET's political special "What's in It for Us?," aired January 8, 2008], Video, 3:49, posted by starrground, February 3, 2008, https://www.youtube.com/watch?v=pFSVG7jRp_g

98. Jann S. Wenner, "A Conversation with Barack Obama," *Rolling Stone*, July 10–24, 2008, https://www.rollingstone.com/culture/culture-news/a-conversation-with-barack-obama-51394/

99. See also Sway Calloway, "Barack Obama Gives a Shout-Out to Hip-Hop," *MTV*, September 27, 2008, http://www.mtv.com/news/1595820/barack-obama-gives-a-shout-out-to-hip-hop/

100. Gabe Meline, "Hip-Hop President: How Will Obama's Presidency Change the Face of Hip-Hop?," Bohemian, December 31, 2008, https://bohemian.com/hip-hop-president-1/.

101. Michael Evans, Facebook post, https://www.facebook.com/kamalaisacop/

102. PMbeers, @PMbeers, Twitter post, February 13, 2019, 4:28 p.m., https://twitter.com/PMbeers/status/1095796997490040832

103. See Bill Hutchinson, "From 'BBQ Becky' to 'Golfcart Gail,' List of Unnecessary 911 Calls Made on Blacks Continues to Grow," ABC News, October 19, 2018, https://abcnews.go.com/US/bbq-becky-golfcart-gail-list-unnecessary-911-calls/story?id=58584961

104. Luther Campbell, "Kamala Harris Can't Count on the Black Vote in 2020," *Miami New Times*, February 5, 2019, https://www.miaminewtimes.com/news/kamala-harris-cant-count-on-the-black-vote-to-win-in-2020-11068985; see also Christopher Cadelago, "A Rap Legend Ripped Kamala's Marriage to a White Man. Then She Won

Him Over," *Politico*, September 3, 2019, https://www.politico.com/story/2019/09/03/kamala-harris-luther-campbell-2020-1479890

105. Danielle Casarez Lemi and Nadia E. Brown, "The Political Implications of Colorism Are Gendered," *PS: Political Science & Politics* 53, no. 4 (October 2020): 670.

106. Byron D'Andra Orey and Yu Zhang, "Melanated Millennials and the Politics of Black Hair," *Social Science Quarterly* 100, no. 6 (2019): 2458–76, https://doi.org/10.1111/ssqu.12694

107. "Kamala Harris Campaign Playlist," Spotify playlist, https://open.spotify.com/playlist/5uDxWcRvjzkUtjakgRUN3V

108. Morgan Gstalter, "Harris Dances with Drum Line, Leads Chant at SC Convention," The Hill, June 22, 2019, https://thehill.com/homenews/campaign/449842-harris-dances-with-drum-line-leads-chant-at-sc-convention/

109. Jon Dolan, "If Playlists Won Elections, Kamala Harris Would Be an Easy Frontrunner," *Rolling Stone*, June 25, 2019, https://www.rollingstone.com/politics/politics-news/kamala-harris-playlist-851861/. See "Kamala's Summer Playlist," Spotify playlist, https://open.spotify.com/playlist/5LBdQplc4UcClnFcIYxzCc?si=yLhWox4xQNiT-XZRlqxndw&nd=1. Not surprisingly, this list does include hip-hop.

110. Lily Adams, @adamslily, Twitter post, December 3, 2019, 8:36 p.m., https://twitter.com/adamslily/status/1202038829332516864

111. Jeneé Osterheldt, "Beyoncé's 'Homecoming' Netflix Documentary Is Black History," *Boston Globe*, April 17, 2019, https://www.bostonglobe.com/arts/music/2019/04/17/beyonce-homecoming-netflix-documentary-black-history/3c58KdpBpsn5BnLVJdb7rI/story.html

112. Erin E. Evans, "Beyoncé's 'Before I Let Go' Challenge Is Here—Now Get Your Steps in Order before the Summer," NBC News, April 23, 2019, https://www.nbcnews.com/news/nbcblk/beyonc-s-i-let-go-challenge-here-now-get-your-n997736

113. Osterheldt, "Beyoncé's 'Homecoming.'"

114. ANGELA RYE: Best rapper alive?

KAMALA HARRIS: Tupac.

RYE: He's not a . . . you say he lives on, he's not alive.

HARRIS: I know, I keep doing that.

RYE: You say . . . Listen, West Coast girls think Tupac lives on, I'm with you, I'm with you. So, Tupac, keep going.

HARRIS: I keep doing that. Um, who would I say? I mean, there's so many, I mean, you know, I . . . There are some that I . . . I would not mention right now because they should stay in their lane, but, um, others I <laughs> . . . .

See Aron A., "Kamala Harris Gets Flamed after Revealing Her Choice for 'Best Rapper Alive,'" HNHH, September 26, 2020, https://www.hotnewhiphop.com/kamala-harris-calls-tupac-the-best-rapper-alive-news.118534.html; and YouTube, "EXCLUSIVE: Kamala Harris Talks to Angela Rye about Breonna Taylor, RBG, and a Black Agenda," Video, 37:16, posted by Angela Rye, September 25, 2020, https://www.youtube.com/watch?v=snf_XcjVyWY

115. Judy Kurtz, "Trump Campaign Sets Aside Debate Ticket for Tupac after Harris

Calls Him Her Favorite Living Rapper," The Hill, October 7, 2020, https://thehill.com/blogs/in-the-know/in-the-know/520057-trump-campaign-sets-aside-debate-ticket-for-tupac-after-harris/

116. Lerer and Medina, "What Does This Country Demand?"

117. *The American Heritage Dictionary of the English Language*, 4th ed. (Boston: Houghton Mifflin, 2000). Cited in Catalyst, "The Double-Bind Dilemma for Women in Leadership: Damned If You Do, Doomed If You Don't" [2007 report], July 15, 2007, https://www.catalyst.org/research/the-double-bind-dilemma-for-women-in-leadership-damned-if-you-do-doomed-if-you-dont/

118. Rose and Lawrence discuss the impact such "contradictory demands" had on Hillary Clinton during her 2008 presidential bid. See *Hillary Clinton's Race*, 9.

119. Erin C. Cassese, "Intersectional Stereotyping in Political Decision Making," Oxford Research Encyclopedias, March 26, 2019, https://doi.org/10.1093/acrefore/9780190228637.013.773

CHAPTER 4

1. Matt Wilstein, "Trump Begs Suburban Women: 'Will You Please Like Me?,'" *Daily Beast*, October 13, 2020, https://www.thedailybeast.com/trump-begs-suburban-women-will-you-please-like-me

2. Facebook, "Fox News National Interview," Video, 10:54, posted by Camille & Haley, October 31, 2020, https://www.facebook.com/CamilleandHaley/videos/1077977639305618

3. USA Freedom Kids website, https://www.usafreedomkids.com (accessed July 5, 2021).

4. YouTube, "The Official Donald Trump Jam [Freedom's Call]," Video, 2:15, posted by Fox 10 Phoenix, January 13, 2016, https://www.youtube.com/watch?v=vPRfP_TEQ-g

5. For a thoughtful analysis of the USA Freedom Kids' Trump performance, see Quentin Vieregge, "Ameritude," in *You Shook Me All Campaign Long: Music in the 2016 Presidential Election and Beyond*, ed. Eric T. Kasper and Benjamin S. Schoening (Denton: University of North Texas Press, 2018), 185–214.

6. Time, "45 Americans Who Defined the Election," https://time.com/2016-election-americans/ (accessed September 1, 2022).

7. Jimmy Kimmel, @jimmykimmel, Twitter post, January 21, 2016, 11:26 a.m., https://twitter.com/jimmykimmel/status/690208834204229632?lang=en; YouTube, "Please Welcome: The USA Freedom Grown-Ups," Video, 3:30, posted by The Late Show with Stephen Colbert, August 5, 2016, https://www.youtube.com/watch?v=8UOKh00-GuY

8. Inae Oh, "Watch a Group of 'Freedom Kids' Perform a Horrifying Song at a Donald Trump Rally," *Mother Jones*, January 14, 2016, http://www.motherjones.com/politics/2016/01/freedom-girls-donald-trump-rally/; Jon Blistein, "Trump Campaign Enlists Children to Sweeten Jingoist, Racist Message," *Rolling Stone*, January 14, 2016,

https://www.rollingstone.com/politics/politics-news/trump-campaign-enlists-children-to-sweeten-jingoist-racist-message-2-223823/; Madeleine Davies, "The Dad/Manager behind Trump's Creepy Girl Group Just Really Loves Freedom," Jezebel, January 15, 2016, https://jezebel.com/the-dad-manager-behind-trumps-creepy-girl-group-just-re-1753265199

9. Peter Weber, "Stephen Colbert Showcases New Song to Mock Donald Trump for Stiffing Trio of Young Girls," The Week, August 5, 2016, https://theweek.com/speedreads/641149/stephen-colbert-showcases-new-song-mock-donald-trump-stiffing-trio-young-girls

10. Justin Moyer, "Trump-Loving USA Freedom Kid's Dad: 'To Me, Freedom Is Everything,'" Washington Post, January 15, 2016, https://www.washingtonpost.com/news/morning-mix/wp/2016/01/15/manager-of-trump-loving-usa-freedom-kids-to-me-freedom-is-everything/. See also Melissa Chan, "This Guy Wrote Donald Trump's 'USA Freedom Kids' Song," Time, January 14, 2016, http://time.com/4181383/donald-trump-usa-freedom-kids/

11. These three comments were posted in response to Breitbart TV, "Watch: Pro-Trump 'USA Freedom Kids'—'Enemies of Freedom Face the Music,'" Breitbart, January 14, 2016, http://www.breitbart.com/video/2016/01/14/watch-pro-trump-usa-freedom-kids-enemies-of-freedom-face-the-music/

12. Dana Gorzelany-Mostak, "Hearing Girls, Girls, Girls on the 2016 Campaign Trail," Journal of Popular Music Studies 29, no. 3 (2017): 4–6, https://doi.org/10.1111/jpms.12235

13. See, for example, this playlist of Trump's 2020 rally music compiled online: Apple Music, Trump Rally Playlist, posted by Steve Robinson, https://music.apple.com/us/playlist/trump-rally-playlist/pl.u-jV89b7DFqvgN6V (accessed September 1, 2022). There are forty-five songs on the list; only three are performed by female artists.

14. See Vieregge, "Ameritude," as well as two other chapters in Kasper and Schoening, You Shook Me All Campaign Long: Kate Zittlow Rogness, "This Is Our Fight Song," 215–38; and David Wilson, "'Pub Fight' Politics," 317–46.

15. Ruth Frankenberg, "Local Whitenesses, Localizing Whiteness," in Displacing Whiteness: Essays in Social and Cultural Criticism, ed. Ruth Frankenberg (Durham: Duke University Press, 1997), 6.

16. See Dana Gorzelany-Mostak, "Hearing Jackie Evancho in the Age of Donald Trump," in "Music and the 2016 U.S. Presidential Campaign," ed. Sally Bick and Dana Gorzelany-Mostak, special issue, American Music 35, no. 4 (Winter 2017): 467–77.

17. Charles Tien, "The Racial Gap in Voting among Women: White Women, Racial Resentment, and Support for Trump," New Political Science 39, no. 4 (2017): 656–57, https://doi.org/10.1080/07393148.2017.1378296. See also Michael Tesler, Post-Racial or Most-Racial?: Race and Politics in the Obama Era (Chicago: University of Chicago Press, 2016).

18. Matthew C. MacWilliams, "Who Decides When the Party Doesn't? Authoritarian Voters and the Rise of Donald Trump," PS: Political Science & Politics 49, no. 4 (October 2016): 716–21.

19. MacWilliams, "Who Decides."

20. John Fea, *Believe Me: The Evangelical Road to Donald Trump* (Grand Rapids, MI: William B. Eerdmans, 2018), 15.

21. Fea, *Believe Me*, 25.

22. Louis Nelson, "Trump: 'I Am the Law and Order Candidate,'" Politico, July 11, 2016, https://www.politico.com/story/2016/07/trump-law-order-candidate-225372

23. Justin Gest, Tyler Reny, and Jeremy Mayer, "Roots of the Radical Right: Nostalgic Deprivation in the United States and Britain," *Comparative Political Studies* 51, no. 13 (2018): 1695.

24. Donald Trump speech, Announcement of Candidacy, New York, NY, June 16, 2015, http://www.p2016.org/trump/trump061615sp.html

25. C. J. Pascoe, "Who Is a Real Man? The Gender of Trumpism," *Masculinities and Social Change* 6, no. 2 (2017): 131–32. See also C. J. Pascoe and Jocelyn A. Hollander, "Good Guys Don't Rape: Gender, Domination, and Mobilizing Rape," *Gender & Society* 30, no. 1 (2016): 67–79.

26. Wilstein, "Trump Begs Suburban Women."

27. Jennifer Brown, "They've Been Called Soccer Moms, Rage Moms and Zoom Moms. Why the Colorado Suburban-Women Vote Is So Important," *Colorado Sun*, October 21, 2020, https://coloradosun.com/2020/10/21/colorados-suburban-women -vote/. Political scientist Sara Chatfield is quoted in this article.

28. Reid Wilson, "On The Trail: Trump Presents Vision of the Suburbs Decades out of Date," The Hill, August 19, 2020, https://thehill.com/homenews/state-watch/512570 -on-the-trail-trump-presents-vision-of-the-suburbs-decades-out-of-date

29. David A. Fahrenthold, "Trump Recorded Having Extremely Lewd Conversation about Women in 2005," *Washington Post*, October 7, 2016, https://www.washingtonpo st.com/politics/trump-recorded-having-extremely-lewd-conversation-about-women -in-2005/2016/10/07/3b9ce776-8cb4-11e6-bf8a-3d26847eeed4_story.html

30. Patrick Healy and Maggie Haberman, "Donald Trump Opens New Line of Attack on Hillary Clinton: Her Marriage," *New York Times*, September 30, 2016, https://www.nytimes.com/2016/10/01/us/politics/donald-trump-interview-bill-hilla ry-clinton.html?_r=0

31. Deborah Cameron, "Banter, Male Bonding, and the Language of Donald Trump," in *Language in the Trump Era: Scandals and Emergencies*, ed. Janet McIntosh and Norma Mendoza-Denton (Cambridge: Cambridge University Press, 2020), 165.

32. Cameron, "Banter, Male Bonding," 165.

33. Nicholas A. Valentino, Carly Wayne, and Marzia Oceno, "Mobilizing Sexism: The Interaction of Emotion and Gender Attitudes in the 2016 US Presidential Election," *Public Opinion Quarterly* 82, no. S1 (2018): 801.

34. Peter Glick and Susan T. Fiske, "The Ambivalent Sexism Inventory: Differentiating Hostile and Benevolent Sexism," *Journal of Personality and Social Psychology* 70 (1996): 491.

35. Glick and Fiske, "Ambivalent Sexism Inventory," 492. For a discussion of this research in conjunction with Trump, see Emily Crockett, "Why Misogyny Won," Vox, November 15, 2016, http://www.vox.com/identities/2016/11/15/13571478/trump -president-sexual-assault-sexism-misogyny-won

36. In 2012, the sisters went under the name First Love Band. YouTube, "Game On—Original Song for Rick Santorum by Camille & Haley," Video, 2:25, posted by C&H Backstage, March 6, 2012, https://www.youtube.com/watch?v=U7pv7sO5Gng

37. Randy Krehbiel, "Tulsa Sisters' Santorum Song Big Hit on YouTube," *Tulsa World*, March 9, 2012, https://tulsaworld.com/news/local/govt-and-politics/tulsa-sist ers-santorum-song-big-hit-on-youtube/article_cadb73e9-84f6-5b89-b1d8-d04a2492 2866.html

38. Camille & Haley website, http://camilleandhaley.com/bio/ (accessed July 2, 2021). See also Facebook: https://www.facebook.com/CamilleandHaley/; Twitter: @ CamilleandHaley; Instagram: @camilleandhaley; and YouTube: @CamilleandHaley. For the sisters' solo ventures, see YouTube: @CamilleHarris; and 2 For Christ website, https://liftwithchrist.org

39. Camille & Haley website, http://camilleandhaley.com (accessed July 2, 2021).

40. Camille & Haley website, http://camilleandhaley.com (accessed July 2, 2021).

41. Barbara Welter, "The Cult of True Womanhood: 1820–1860," *American Quarterly* 18, no. 2, pt. 1 (Summer 1966): 152.

42. Laurie Stras, "She's So Fine, or Why Girl Singers (Still) Matter," in *She's So Fine: Reflections on Whiteness, Femininity, Adolescence and Class in 1960s Music*, ed. Laurie Stras (Farnham, UK: Ashgate, 2010), 3. For more on juvenation strategies, see Gaylyn Studlar, *Precocious Charms: Stars Performing Girlhood in Classical Hollywood Cinema* (Berkeley: University of California Press, 2012), 92.

43. Fea, *Believe Me*, 16.

44. Camille & Haley website, http://camilleandhaley.com/trump/ (accessed July 2, 2021).

45. Welter, "Cult of True Womanhood," 152.

46. In interviews, the girls stress the importance of showing respect for authority, including parents, God, police, and government. See Ford Fischer, @FordFischer, [News2Share], Twitter post, June 18, 2020, 10:13 p.m., https://twitter.com/FordFischer /status/1273801120431976453

47. YouTube, "Patriotic Concert 2018—Camille & Haley," Video, 1:02:30, posted by Camille & Haley, June 14, 2020, https://www.youtube.com/watch?v=RSJlWknyq-E&t =1235s

48. Samuel Francis Smith and Henry Carey (att.), "America (My Country, 'Tis of Thee)," in *A Second Book in Vocal Music* (New York, Boston, and Chicago: Silver, Burdett and Company, 1901), https://archive.org/details/america_my_country_tis_of _thee/mode/1up

49. John Philip Sousa, "Stars and Stripes Forever" (Cincinnati, New York, and Chicago: John Church Company, 1898), https://repository.duke.edu/dc/hasm/b0367

50. Dan Fogelberg, "Leader of the Band" (New York: Hickory Grove Music, 1981).

51. Cal Perry, @CalNBC, Twitter post, June 17, 2020, 8:45 p.m., https://twitter.com /CalNBC/status/1273416410283290625. YouTube, "KEEP AMERICA GREAT (Official Music Video)—Trump 2020 Song by Camille & Haley," Video, 1:59, posted by Camille & Haley, June 20, 2020, https://www.youtube.com/watch?v=FAvFFYu1RGM

52. Laura Mulvey, "Visual Pleasure and Narrative Cinema," *Screen* 16, no. 3 (1975): 6–18.

53. See National Women's Prayer and Voting Army website, https://www.national womenspva.com (accessed July 2, 2021).

54. YouTube, "Pro-Trump Girl Band Performs 'Keep America Great' Ahead of Tulsa Rally," Video, 0:47, posted by Breitbart News, June 18, 2020, https://www.youtu be.com/watch?v=cYyNMSrWqmM

55. Richard Dyer, "White," *Screen* 29, no. 4 (Autumn 1988): 44.

56. Laurie Stras, "Voice of the Beehive: Vocal Technique at the Turn of the 1960s," in *She's So Fine: Reflections on Whiteness, Femininity, Adolescence and Class in 1960s Music*, ed. Laurie Stras (Farnham, UK: Ashgate, 2010), 35–38.

57. A. T, @YouMatter2082, Twitter post, July 22, 2020, 2:02 a.m., https://twitter .com/YouMatter2082/status/1285817488073265162

58. Joel Heyman, @JoelHeyman, Twitter post, June 18, 2020, 12:55 p.m., https://twi tter.com/JoelHeyman/status/1273660593291968514

59. "Wow what a lovely bully you are! So proud aren't you? Grow up!" A. T, @ YouMatter2082, Twitter post, July 22, 2020, 2:00 a.m., https://twitter.com/YouMatter 2082/status/1285817086573449216

60. Stras, "She's So Fine," 5.

61. Svetlana Boym, *The Future of Nostalgia* (New York: Basic Books, 2001), xiii.

62. Robert P. Jones, *The End of White Christian America* (New York: Simon & Schuster, 2016), 47.

63. Annelot Prins, "From Awkward Teen Girl to Aryan Goddess Meme: Taylor Swift and the Hijacking of Star Texts," *Celebrity Studies* 11, no. 1 (2020): 144–48, https:// doi.org/10.1080/19392397.2020.1704431

64. dan shapiro, @dannyshap, Twitter post, June 18, 2020, 2:37 p.m., https://twitter .com/dannyshap/status/1273686289401823233

65. rodney pryor, @canisdeum, Twitter post, June 20, 2020, 11:12 p.m., https://twitt er.com/canisdeum/status/1274540625803612160

66. Nestor "the boss" Gomez, @soloyochapin, Twitter post, June 17, 2020, 9:56 p.m., https://twitter.com/soloyochapin/status/1273434504795951104

67. jcarrington, @jcarrington, Twitter post, June 17, 2020, 8:59 p.m., https://twit ter.com/jcarrington/status/1273419947180347392; "German Youth Display (1940)," Video, 1:36, posted by British Pathé, n.d., https://www.youtube.com/watch?v=g7u5Kn j5Uj4&t=12s (accessed July 30, 2021).

68. Jack Hutton, @jackhutton, Twitter post, June 17, 2020, 9:06 p.m., https://twitter .com/jackhutton/status/1273421832440254464

69. GM, @WasOnceLou, Twitter post, June 17, 2020, 9:20 p.m., https://twitter.com /WasOnceLou/status/1273425298231607296

70. Robert Eimstad, @beimstad, Twitter post, June 20, 2020, 12:27 p.m., https://twi tter.com/beimstad/status/1274378318796787712.

71. jcarrington Twitter post.

72. Mash PRESIDENT BIDEN, @ThisWasMash, Twitter post, June 17, 2020, 10:07 p.m., https://twitter.com/ThisWasMash/status/1273437076873150465

73. YouTube, "KEEP AMERICA GREAT (2020 Police Brutality Edition)—Trump Song by Camille & Haley," Video, 2:15, posted by Marc Webb, June 29, 2020, https://www.yo utube.com/watch?v=BLITHkac96M

74. Russell Drew, @RussOnPolitics, Twitter post, June 17, 2020, 10:37 p.m., https:// twitter.com/RussOnPolitics/status/1273444728760123396

75. Tara O'Donnell, @deathadderdiva, Twitter post, June 17, 2020, 8:48 p.m., https://twitter.com/deathadderdiva/status/1273417338679955456

76. MURRAY, @murray_nyc, Twitter post, June 18, 2020, 12:10 a.m., https://twitter .com/murray_nyc/status/1273468111535079433

77. The phrase "drinking the Kool-Aid" is often used in common parlance to refer to someone who acts on blind faith.

78. Russell Drew Twitter post.

79. Marie Conner, @thistallawkgirl, Twitter post, June 17, 2020, 10:31 p.m., https:// twitter.com/thistallawkgirl/status/1273443180432719872

80. Natalie Gontcharova, "The Story behind the Viral Photo of a Kent State Graduate Bringing a Gun on Campus," Refinery 29, May 15, 2018, https://www.refiner y29.com/en-us/2018/05/199241/kent-state-girl-with-gun-viral-photo

81. Gina Ciliberto and Stephanie Russell-Kraft, "They Invaded the Capitol Saying 'Jesus Is My Savior. Trump Is My President,'" Sojourners, January 7, 2021, https://sojo .net/articles/they-invaded-capitol-saying-jesus-my-savior-trump-my-president

82. Ciliberto and Russell-Kraft, "They Invaded the Capitol."

83. Mary R. Jackman, The Velvet Glove: Paternalism and Conflict in Gender, Class, and Race Relations (Berkeley: University of California Press, 1994), 9.

84. Haley Harris married Nick Gaglione in February 2022.

85. Joan Rivière, "Womanliness as Masquerade," in Feminist Theory: A Reader, 3rd ed., ed. Wendy K. Kolmar and Frances Bartowski (Boston: McGraw-Hill, 2010), 132.

86. Facebook, "Fox News National Interview."

CHAPTER 5

1. Elena Schneider and Brent D. Griffiths, "At Pennsylvania Rally, Trump Endorses Himself," Politico, March 10, 2018, https://www.politico.com/story/2018/03 /10/trump-pennsylvania-rally-rick-saccone-keep-america-great-454169

2. Friedrich Nietzsche, The Genealogy of Morals, vol. 13 of The Complete Works of Friedrich Nietzsche, ed. Oscar Levy, trans. Horace B. Samuel and J. M. Kennedy (Edinburgh: Foulis, 1913), 79.

3. John Cassidy, "Hillary Clinton's 'Basket of Deplorables' Gaffe," New Yorker, September 11, 2016, https://www.newyorker.com/news/john-cassidy/hillary-clintons -basket-of-deplorables-gaffe

4. For more on remix culture and political campaigns, see Ragnhild Brøvig-Hanssen and Aram Sinnreich, "Do You Wanna Build a Wall? Remix Tactics in the Age of Trump," Popular Music and Society 43, no. 5 (2020): 535–49, https://doi.org/10.1080

/03007766.2019.1650990; and Virginia Kuhn, "Remix in the Age of Trump," *Journal of Contemporary Rhetoric* 7, nos. 2–3 (2017): 87–93.

5. YouTube, "Awesome Trump Entrance—Miami FL Rally—Les Deplorables 9/16/2016," Video, 2:14, posted by R Powerhouse, September 17, 2016, https://www.yout ube.com/watch?v=UjZy2_wSuZg

6. For more on the "Les Deplorables" meme and Trump's use of musical theater, see Naomi Graber, "Do You Hear the People Sing? Theater and Theatricality in the Trump Campaign," in "Music and the 2016 U.S. Presidential Campaign," ed. Sally Bick and Dana Gorzelany-Mostak, special issue, *American Music* 35, no. 4 (Winter 2017): 435–45. See also Marva Barnett, "'Deplorables' Meme Gets It Wrong (from the HuffPost)," Marva Barnett (blog), https://www.marvabarnett.com/news-event/deplor ables-meme-gets-it-wrong-from-the-huffpost/ (accessed September 6, 2021).

7. John Hartley, "Silly Citizenship," *Critical Discourse Studies* 7, no. 4 (2010): 241, https://doi.org/10.1080/17405904.2010.511826

8. Jenny L. Davis, Tony P. Love, and Gemma Killen, "Seriously Funny: The Political Work of Humor on Social Media," *New Media & Society* 20, no. 10 (2018): 3899, https://doi.org/10.1177/1461444818762602

9. Hartley, "Silly Citizenship," 244. See also Davis, Love, and Killen, "Seriously Funny," 3899–900.

10. Giovanni Luca Ciampaglia, Azadeh Nematzadeh, Filippo Menczer, and Alessandro Flammini, "How Algorithmic Popularity Bias Hinders or Promotes Quality," *Scientific Reports* 8 (2018), 1; Kazutoshi Sasahara, Wen Chen, Hao Peng, Giovanni Luca Ciampaglia, Alessandro Flammini, and Filippo Menczer, "Social Influence and Unfollowing Accelerate the Emergence of Echo Chambers," *Journal of Computational Social Science* 4 (2021): 381–402, https://doi.org/10.1007/s42001-020 -00084-7

11. John Hartley refers to these acts of cocreating content as "DIY Citizenship." See *Uses of Television* (London: Routledge, 1999), 179.

12. Whitney Phillips and Ryan M. Milner, *The Ambivalent Internet: Mischief, Oddity, and Antagonism Online* (Malden, MA: Polity, 2017), 10–12.

13. Justin Patch, "This Is What Democracy Sounds Like," in *You Shook Me All Campaign Long: Music in the 2016 Presidential Election and Beyond*, ed. Eric T. Kasper and Benjamin S. Schoening (Denton: University of North Texas Press, 2018), 21.

14. Footloose (Original Motion Picture Soundtrack), Columbia CK 65781, 1999 [reissue], CD. For another reading of this incident and its aftermath, see Justin Patch, "Footloose: Political Transformations of a Song and Its Meaning," Trax on the Trail, October 25, 2020, https://www.traxonthetrail.com/2020/10/25/footloose-political-tra nsformations-of-a-song-and-its-meaning/

15. Alexis Benveniste, "The Meaning and History of Memes," *New York Times*, January 26, 2022, https://www.nytimes.com/2022/01/26/crosswords/what-is-a-meme.html

16. Braxton D. Shelley, "Music, Memes, and Digital Antiphony," paper presented at the Radcliffe Institute for Advanced Study, March 23, 2020, YouTube video, 57:46, posted by Harvard Radcliffe Institute, https://www.youtube.com/watch?v=PYXXwPd OpYA

17. At some protests across the country, protesters tore down statues of Confederate generals and enslavers, and in response, President Trump signed an executive order to quell such acts. See "Protecting American Monuments, Memorials, and Statues and Combating Recent Criminal Violence," Executive Order 13933, Federal Register (National Archives), June 26, 2020, https://www.federalregister.gov/documents/2020/07/02/2020-14509/protecting-american-monuments-memorials-and-statues-and-combating-recent-criminal-violence

18. Juliana Menasce Horowitz, Kim Parker, Anna Brown, and Kiana Cox, "Amid National Reckoning, Americans Divided on Whether Increased Focus on Race Will Lead to Major Policy Change," Pew Research Center, October 6, 2020, https://www.pewresearch.org/social-trends/2020/10/06/amid-national-reckoning-americans-divided-on-whether-increased-focus-on-race-will-lead-to-major-policy-change/

19. Lessie B. Branch, *Optimism at All Costs: Black Attitudes, Activism, and Advancement in Obama's America* (Amherst: University of Massachusetts Press, 2018), 1–4.

20. Jonathan Levinson, Conrad Wilson, and Ryan Haas, "50 Days of Protest in Portland," *OPB*, July 19, 2020, https://www.opb.org/news/article/police-violence-portland-protest-federal-officers/

21. Levinson, Wilson, and Haas, "50 Days of Protest."

22. Roudabeh Kishi and Sam Jones, "Demonstrations and Political Violence in America: New Data for Summer 2020," Armed Conflict Location & Event Data Project, September 3, 2020, https://acleddata.com/2020/09/03/demonstrations-political-violence-in-america-new-data-for-summer-2020/

23. Hannah Ray Lambert, "Portland Protests: What Happened in 2020, What's Next in 2021," KOIN, December 31, 2020, https://www.koin.com/news/protests/portland-protests-what-happened-in-2020-whats-next-in-2021/

24. Shortly before the man's feet caught on fire, several incendiary devices were lofted by protesters, and police blocked hundreds of protesters who were marching to a southeast Portland police precinct. See Samantha Swindler, "Tensions at Portland Protest Flare Saturday after Molotov Cocktails Tossed Near Police Blocking March Route," Oregon Live, September 5, 2020, https://www.oregonlive.com/news/2020/09/portland-protest-declared-riot-soon-after-it-begins-in-se-portland-live-updates.html

25. Tayler Hansen, @TaylerUSA, Twitter post, September 6, 2020, 12:20 a.m., https://twitter.com/TaylerUSA/status/1302461688910770176. There is some conjecture over who recorded the footage.

26. Just a Humanist, @ClaudeL1979, Twitter post, September 6, 2020, 12:52 a.m., https://twitter.com/ClaudeL1979/status/1302469804683649024

27. Dan Scavino Jr., @DanScavino, Twitter post, September 6, 2020, 2:29 a.m., https://twitter.com/DanScavino/status/1302494021617680384. The Announcer video is credited to Steve Inman. See Steve Inman, @SteveInmanUIC, Twitter post, September 6, 2020, 1:59 a.m., https://twitter.com/SteveInmanUIC/status/1302486468414156800. Inman frequently posts videos that feature violent confrontations with his own commentary.

28. Donald J. Trump, @realDonaldTrump, Twitter post, September 6, 2020, 2:32 p.m., https://twitter.com/realDonaldTrump/status/1302675943241199618

29. As of January 2021.

30. Michael Scherer, "Trump Employs Images of Violence as Political Fuel for Reelection Fight," *Washington Post*, September 8, 2020, https://www.washingtonpost.com/politics/trump-violence-election/2020/09/08/0a7fa096-edf6-11ea-99a1-71343d03bc29_story.html

31. See, for example, David Caron, "Trump Shares 'Footloose' Dubbed Video of Portland Antifa Member Caught on Fire by Molotov Cocktail," Media Right, September 6, 2020, https://mediarightnews.com/trump-shares-footloose-dubbed-video-of-portland-antifa-member-caught-on-fire-by-molotov-cocktail/

32. Scavino retweeted the Announcer video twice. For the first retweet, see Dan Scavino Jr., @DanScavino, Twitter post, September 6, 2020, 2:20 a.m., https://twitter.com/DanScavino/status/1302491940177444865

33. Whitney Phillips, *This Is Why We Can't Have Nice Things: Mapping the Relationship between Online Trolling and Mainstream Culture* (Cambridge, MA: MIT Press, 2016), 27–28. See also Phillips and Milner, *Ambivalent Internet*, 42.

34. Steven Williams, "What Even Is Yacht Rock Anyway?," *Discogs* (blog), September 11, 2018, https://web.archive.org/web/20220504235315/https://blog.discogs.com/en/what-even-is-yacht-rock-anyway/

35. Jack Seale, "I Can Go for That: The Smooth World of Yacht Rock Review—Lushly Comforting," *The Guardian*, June 14, 2019, https://www.theguardian.com/tv-and-radio/2019/jun/14/i-can-go-for-that-the-smooth-world-of-yacht-rock-review-katie-puckrik-bbc-four

36. Brian L. Ott and Greg Dickinson, *The Twitter Presidency: Donald J. Trump and the Politics of White Rage* (New York: Routledge, 2019), 61.

37. Ott and Dickinson, *Twitter Presidency*, 64.

38. Bill Hickerson, @WDHickerson, Twitter post, September 6, 2020, 4:12 p.m., https://twitter.com/WDHickerson/status/1302701297389330432

39. Luvmyk9kids2, @luvmyk9kids2, Twitter post, September 6, 2020, 3:14 p.m., https://twitter.com/luvmyk9kids2/status/1302686744869875712

40. AH at the Beach, @beach_ah, Twitter post, September 6, 2020, 5:41 p.m., https://twitter.com/beach_ah/status/1302723723011616768

41. John Pahl, @nasdrovhyeh, Twitter post, September 8, 2020, 9:40 a.m., https://twitter.com/nasdrovhyeh/status/1303327292614213633

42. Leandro MV, @Leandromv1999, Twitter post, September 6, 2020, 2:30 a.m., https://twitter.com/Leandromv1999/status/1302494365735149573

43. Jaylon Crawford, @JaylonCrawford3, Twitter post, September 6, 2020, 9:20 p.m., https://twitter.com/JaylonCrawford3/status/1302778629693341698

44. Stephanie Amore, @Steffaneze, Twitter post, September 6, 2020, 6:13 p.m., https://twitter.com/Steffaneze/status/1302731552405753861

45. Eric Patterson, @Ericpatsof1, Twitter post, September 7, 2020, 10:01 a.m., https://twitter.com/Ericpatsof1/status/1302970132478787585

46. Gypsy Traveler Nana, @mlynwalker, Twitter post, September 6, 2020, 2:32 a.m., https://twitter.com/mlynwalker/status/1302494902203416576

47. Conservative Solutions, @Knight_90s, Twitter post, September 6, 2020, 4:18 p.m., https://twitter.com/Knight_90s/status/1302702621640347648

48. We are watching you, @flyingpeapod, Twitter post, September 6, 2020, 5:07 a.m., https://twitter.com/flyingpeapod/status/1302533938443956224

49. CFO, @GrandpaTMoney, Twitter post, September 6, 2020, 2:36 a.m., https://twitter.com/GrandpaTMoney/status/1302495821900906497

50. 911Dispatcher45, @911Dispatcher45, Twitter post, September 6, 2020, 2:32 a.m., https://twitter.com/911Dispatcher45/status/1302494893743448066

51. Daniel Martinez HoSang and Joseph E. Lowndes, *Producers, Parasites, Patriots: Race and the New Right-Wing Politics of Precarity* (Minneapolis: University of Minnesota Press, 2019), 12.

52. HoSang and Lowndes, *Producers, Parasites, Patriots*, 17.

53. HoSang and Lowndes, *Producers, Parasites, Patriots*, 10.

54. "Intellectual disability" is now the preferred term for what psychiatric and medical professionals previously called "mental retardation." The word "retard," slang for mental retardation, is now considered offensive and derogatory. I also want to note that pro-eugenics rhetoric is in no way exclusive to the Right. At the start of the twentieth century, political progressives advocated for eugenics as a science-backed solution for addressing societal issues. In recent years, politicians on both sides of the aisle have defaulted to ableist remarks in the characterization of their opponents. I am grateful to Meghan Schrader for giving some context for this rhetoric.

55. Richard Thompson Ford, "Sagging and Subordination," in *Dress Codes: How the Laws of Fashion Made History* (New York: Simon & Schuster, 2021), 196–220. See also Priya Elan, "Nine Years after Trayvon Martin's Killing, Hoodies Still Spark Debate," *The Guardian*, February 27, 2021, https://www.theguardian.com/fashion/2021/feb/27/trayvon-martin-hoodies-black-young-people

56. YouTube, "Trump: Oregon Leaders Must Clean Out 'Beehive of Terrorists,' Threatens to Send in National Guard," 2:35, Video, posted by The Oregonian, July 30, 2020, https://www.youtube.com/watch?v=rWZDLnPmeOU

57. Most of the pop songs listed in Table 6 are paired with either Hansen's or Inman's footage. In some instances, the posters subject the footage to various modifications. The music has been removed from some videos due to copyright infringement, and several videos are no longer available because the users' accounts have been suspended. See Ducky, @thatjerkme, Twitter post, September 6, 2020, 1:37 a.m., https://twitter.com/thatjerkme/status/1302481066968653824; Caleb Hull, @CalebJHull, Twitter post, September 6, 2020, 1:44 a.m., https://twitter.com/CalebJHull/status/1302482835564122112; Ducky, @thatjerkme, Twitter post, September 6, 2020, 2:01 a.m., https://twitter.com/thatjerkme/status/1302487043449249794; Drew Hernandez, @DrewHLive, Twitter post, September 6, 2020, 2:09 a.m., https://twitter.com/PainefulMemes/status/1302489089061654528; Thatoneguy_55, @Thatoneguy_55, Twitter post, September 6, 2020, 2:27 a.m., https://twitter.com/Thatoneguy_55/status/1302493578871013376;

Dan Scavino Jr., @DanScavino, Twitter post, September 6, 2020, 2:29 a.m., https://twi
tter.com/DanScavino/status/1302494021617680384; Drew Hernandez, @DrewHLive,
September 6, 2020, 2:30 a.m., https://twitter.com/PainefulMemes/status/13024943997
38322944; Caleb Hull, @CalebJHull, Twitter post, September 6, 2020, 2:37 a.m., https://
twitter.com/PainefulMemes/status/1302496148075294722; Erin, @ERINJEAN84,
Twitter post, September 6, 2020, 2:43 a.m., https://twitter.com/ERINJEAN84/status
/1302497642577047552; Down the Middle, @Americanlll, Twitter post, September 6,
2020, 2:49 a.m., https://twitter.com/Americanlll/status/1302499068694863873; Male
Loquitur: Chris James, @BluesClown, September 6, 2020, Twitter post, 3:38 a.m.,
https://twitter.com/BluesClown/status/1302511553460068352; SirWilliamScot5, @
SirWilliamScot5, Twitter post, September 6, 2020, 4:47 a.m., https://twitter.com/Sir
WilliamScot5/status/1302528856184758272; Dre Ina.m., @inam_dre, Twitter post,
September 6, 2020, 6:04 a.m., https://twitter.com/inam_dre/status/130254827644
5577216; Ron Duncan, @RonDuncan7, Twitter post, September 6, 2020, 9:25 a.m.,
https://twitter.com/RonDuncan7/status/1302598802897907712; robert foggiato, @
TheFoggiato, Twitter post, September 6, 2020, 2:10 p.m., https://twitter.com/thefoggia
to/status/1302670547944308736; Donald J. Trump, @realDonaldTrump, Twitter post,
September 6, 2020, 2:32 p.m., https://twitter.com/realDonaldTrump/status/13026759
43241199618; Christie, @brooklyns_us, Twitter post, September 6, 2020, 3:40 p.m.,
https://twitter.com/brooklyns_us/status/1302693178877849605; MarsTheDoomer,
@DoomerMars, Twitter post, September 6, 2020, 3:51 p.m., https://twitter.com/Doo
merMars/status/1302695861793689600; The Homestead Padre, @padrehomestead,
Twitter post, September 6, 2020, 8:05 p.m., https://twitter.com/JDManly18/status/1302
759764405952512; Rodrigo, @rodrigoloope, Twitter post, September 6, 2020, 9:36 p.m.,
https://twitter.com/rodrigoloope/status/1302782786076643329; Joshua Swanson, @
JoshuaSwanson16, Twitter post, September 6, 2020, 10:02 p.m., https://twitter.com/Jo
shuaSwanson15/status/1302789400464629760; Thomas Kellogg, @oldnickels, Twitter
post, September 7, 2020, 12:40 p.m., https://twitter.com/oldnickels/status/1302829095
001104391; Jeremy Lucius, @JeremyLucius, Twitter post, September 7, 2020, 7:13 p.m.,
https://twitter.com/JeremyLucius/status/1303109094606352390

58. Phillips, *This Is Why*, 30–31.

59. Karin M. Fierke, *Political Self-Sacrifice: Agency, Body and Emotion in
International Relations* (Cambridge: Cambridge University Press, 2012), 92–93.

60. Emma Hutchison, *Affective Communities in World Politics: Collective Emotions
after Trauma* (Cambridge: Cambridge University Press, 2016), xi.

61. Stan Link analyzes how sound-image misalignment works as a distancing strategy in horror films. See "Sympathy with the Devil? Music of the Psycho Post-*Psycho*,"
Screen 45, no. 1 (Spring 2004): 1–20. For more on how the relationship between spectator and film operates in the horror genre, see Joe Tompkins, "Pop Goes the Horror
Score: Left Alone in *The Last House on the Left*," in *Music in the Horror Film: Listening
to Fear*, ed. Neil Lerner (New York: Routledge, 2010), 98–113.

62. Phillips, *This Is Why*, 29–30.

63. Some women do weigh in on the videos, but the profile images and handles

suggest that the majority of the posters engaging in the conversation identify as male. For more on White rage, see Carol Anderson, *White Rage: The Unspoken Truth of Our Racial Divide* (New York: Bloomsbury, 2016).

64. YouTube, "Donald Trump, Knock the Hell out of Anyone Throwing a Tomato, Cedar Rapids, Iowa, 2/1/16," 0:15, Video, posted by Jerry Pace, February 1, 2016, https://www.youtube.com/watch?v=p5s9kpPZBbg&t=8s

65. Quoted in Ali Vitali, "Donald Trump on Nevada Protester: 'I'd Like to Punch Him,'" NBC News, February 23, 2016, https://www.nbcnews.com/politics/2016-election/donald-trump-nevada-protester-i-d-punch-him-n524011

66. Quoted in Morgan Gstalter, "Trump Jokes after Rallygoer Suggests Migrants Be Shot," The Hill, May 9, 2019, https://thehill.com/homenews/administration/442860-trump-jokes-after-rally-goer-suggests-migrants-be-shot

67. Raúl Pérez, "Racism without Hatred? Racist Humor and the Myth of 'Colorblindness,'" *Sociological Perspectives* 60, no. 5 (2017): 958.

68. John Hartley, *Digital Futures for Cultural and Media Studies* (Malden, MA: Wiley-Blackwell, 2012), 152–54.

69. Magnus Hörnqvist, *The Pleasure of Punishment* (London: Routledge, 2021), 4–5.

70. Hörnqvist, *Pleasure of Punishment*, 128, 133.

71. Hörnqvist, *Pleasure of Punishment*, 127–28; see Nietzsche, *Genealogy of Morals*, 73.

72. Friedrich Nietzsche, *Thus Spoke Zarathustra: A Book for All and None*, ed. Adrian Del Caro and Robert B. Pippin, trans. Adrian Del Caro (Cambridge: Cambridge University Press, 2006), 111.

73. Hörnqvist, *Pleasure of Punishment*, 132.

74. Hörnqvist, *Pleasure of Punishment*, 127–28; see Nietzsche, *Genealogy of Morals*, 73.

75. Hörnqvist, *Pleasure of Punishment*, 133.

76. HoSang and Lowndes, *Producers, Parasites, Patriots*, 17.

77. Elisabeth R. Anker, *Orgies of Feeling: Melodrama and the Politics of Freedom* (Durham: Duke University Press, 2014), 254, 152. Cited in Paul Elliott Johnson, "The Art of Masculine Victimhood: Donald Trump's Demagoguery," *Women's Studies in Communication* 40, no. 3 (2017): 239.

78. Johnson, "Art of Masculine Victimhood," 239.

79. Alicia Scott, "Rise of the Digital Lynch Mob: Black Anger, White Hostility, Public Shaming, Blame [Social] Media!," Medium, March 19, 2017, https://medium.com/the-2x-ceo/rise-of-the-digital-lynch-mob-6c308bf02dbd. Scott defines the phenomenon as follows: "The *Digital Lynch Mob* is essentially the onslaught of off-color commentary and nasty social trolling on a social media platform about a recent news headline. It's those posts, tweets, and videos that spark the hate-filled barrage of comments directed at one person or group of people, around a specific point."

80. Todd A. Heywood, "'It Was a Digital Lynching': Rep. Johnson Discusses Video and Punishment," Michigan Advance, December 10, 2020, https://michiganadvance

.com/2020/12/10/it-was-a-digital-lynching-rep-johnson-discusses-video-and-punish
ment/

81. Scott, "Rise of the Digital Lynch Mob."

82. HoSang and Lowndes, *Producers, Parasites, Patriots*, 17.

83. Amy Louise Wood, *Lynching and Spectacle: Witnessing Racial Violence in America, 1890–1940* (Chapel Hill: University of North Carolina Press, 2009), 7–8, 49.

84. Wood, *Lynching and Spectacle*, 49.

85. Domenico Montanaro, "How the 'Replacement' Theory Went Mainstream on the Political Right," NPR, May 17, 2022, https://www.npr.org/2022/05/17/1099223012/how-the-replacement-theory-went-mainstream-on-the-political-right. According to the US Census Bureau, non-Hispanic White residents made up less than half (49.9%) of the nation's under-age-fifteen population for the first time in 2018. See William H. Frey, "Less Than Half of US Children Under 15 Are White, Census Shows," Brookings, June 24, 2019, https://www.brookings.edu/research/less-than-half-of-us-children-under-15-are-white-census-shows/. See also "The 'Great Replacement' Theory, Explained," National Immigration Forum, December 2021, https://immigrationforum.org/wp-content/uploads/2021/12/Replacement-Theory-Explainer-1122.pdf

86. Janet McIntosh, "Language and Trump's White Nationalist Strongman Politics," in *Language in the Trump Era: Scandals and Emergencies*, ed. Janet McIntosh and Norma Mendoza-Denton (Cambridge: Cambridge University Press, 2020), 217–25.

87. Brandon Tensley, "The Dark Subtext of Trump's 'Good Genes' Compliment," CNN, September 22, 2020, https://www.cnn.com/2020/09/22/politics/donald-trump-genes-historical-context-eugenics/index.html

88. Tensley, "Dark Subtext."

89. Jennifer Brown, "They've Been Called Soccer Moms, Rage Moms and Zoom Moms. Why the Colorado Suburban-Women Vote Is So Important," *Colorado Sun*, October 21, 2020, https://coloradosun.com/2020/10/21/colorados-suburban-women-vote/

90. YouTube, "Trump: Oregon Leaders Must Clean Out 'Beehive of Terrorists'"; Ben Zimmer, "Where Does Trump's 'Invasion' Rhetoric Come From?," *The Atlantic*, August 6, 2019, https://www.theatlantic.com/entertainment/archive/2019/08/trump-immigrant-invasion-language-origins/595579

91. Wood, *Lynching and Spectacle*, 49.

92. Wood, *Lynching and Spectacle*, 9.

93. Kira Hall, Donna M. Goldstein, and Matthew Bruce Ingram, "The Hands of Donald Trump: Entertainment, Gesture, Spectacle," *Hau: Journal of Ethnographic Theory* 6, no. 2 (2016): 82; see also Ott and Dickinson, *Twitter Presidency*, 44.

94. Hall, Goldstein, and Ingram, "Hands of Donald Trump," 82.

95. Wood, *Lynching and Spectacle*, 11.

96. Wood, *Lynching and Spectacle*, 44.

97. Wood, *Lynching and Spectacle*, 8–9.

98. Wood, *Lynching and Spectacle*, 10–11.

99. Wood, *Lynching and Spectacle*, 40.

100. Pérez, "Racism without Hatred?," 958.

101. Wood, *Lynching and Spectacle*, 3, 9.

102. Ciampaglia et al., "How Algorithmic Popularity Bias Hinders or Promotes Quality," 5. See also Filippo Menczer, "Here's Exactly How Social Media Algorithms Can Manipulate You," Big Think, October 7, 2021, https://bigthink.com/the-present/social-media-algorithms-manipulate-you/

103. Karen Hao, "Troll Farms Reached 140 Million Americans a Month on Facebook before 2020 Election, Internal Report Shows," MIT Technology Review, September 16, 2021, https://www.technologyreview.com/2021/09/16/1035851/facebook-troll-farms-report-us-2020-election/

104. Hao, "Troll Farms."

105. Sasahara et al., "Social Influence and Unfollowing," 383.

106. Pérez, "Racism without Hatred?," 956–57. See also Ian Haney López, *Dog Whistle Politics: How Coded Racial Appeals Have Reinvented Racism and Wrecked the Middle Class* (New York: Oxford University Press, 2013).

107. McIntosh, "Language," 222.

BIBLIOGRAPHY

MEDIA

Apple Music. "Trump Rally Playlist [2020]." Posted by Steve Robinson. https://music
.apple.com/us/playlist/trump-rally-playlist/pl.u-jV89b7DFqvgN6V

C-SPAN. "Ben Carson Presidential Campaign Announcement." 1:08:10. May 4, 2015.
https://www.c-span.org/video/?325722-1/dr-ben-carson-presidential-campaign
-announcement

C-SPAN. "Carson Prayer Speech." 26:51. February 7, 2013. https://www.c-span.org/vid
eo/?c4353213/user-clip-carson-prayer-speech

C-SPAN. "Rap Artist's Response to Clinton Remarks." 20:24. June 16, 1992. https://
www.c-span.org/video/?26613-1/rap-artists-response-clinton-remarks

Eminem. Lose Yourself. Shady/Interscope Records, 2002, CD.

Facebook. "Fox News National Interview." 10:54. Posted by Camille & Haley, October
31, 2020. https://www.facebook.com/CamilleandHaley/videos/1077977639305618

Footloose (Original Motion Picture Soundtrack). Columbia CK 65781,1999 [Reissue],
CD.

Hanson, Curtis, dir. 8 Mile. 2002; Universal City, CA: Universal Pictures, 2003, DVD.

Jay-Z. The Black Album. Roc-A-Fella Records, B0001528-02, 2003, CD.

NBC. "Decision 2004/Bush vs. Kerry/Kerry Interview." 9:00. Evening News [Tom
Brokaw], NBC, October 28, 2004. Vanderbilt Television News Archive. http://tvne
ws.vandcrbilt.cdu/program.pl?ID=769639

Obama, Barack. Interview with Angie Martinez. WQHT, June 27, 2007.

SoundCloud. Ben Carson Radio Ad. Posted by ABC Politics, November 5, 2015. https://
soundcloud.com/abcpolitics/ben-carson-radio-ad

SoundCloud. "Panderdom—Ben Carson Rap Ad Spoof." Posted by aaronnemo, n.d.
https://soundcloud.com/aaronnemo/ben-carson-rap-ad-spoof#t=0:00

Spotify. "Kamala Harris Campaign Playlist." Spotify playlist. Posted by kamalaharris.
https://open.spotify.com/playlist/5uDxWcRvjzkUtjakgRUN3V

Spotify. "Kamala's Summer Playlist." Spotify playlist. Posted by kamalaharris. https://
open.spotify.com/playlist/5LBdQplc4UcClnFcIYxzCc?si=yLhWox4xQNiT-XZRlq
xndw&nd=1

Spotify. "The Official Hillary 2016 Playlist." Spotify playlist. Posted by Hillary Clinton.

https://open.spotify.com/playlist/43JJ50RsHoyUXj8eI8FaPQ?si=51d02bb487eb
4fc2

Wonder, Stevie. *Signed, Sealed & Delivered*. Tamla, TS304, 1970, LP.

Yes We Can: Voices of a Grassroots Movement. Hidden Beach, B001IF269Y, 2008, CD.

YouTube. "American President—Clinton Part 1 in the Arsenio Hall—1992." 7:16. Posted by Brian Lee, July 9, 2009. http://www.youtube.com/watch?v=itKPWt2RkII

YouTube. "Awesome Trump Entrance-Miami FL Rally- Les Deplorables 9/16/2016." 2:14. Posted by R Powerhouse, September 17, 2016. https://www.youtube.com/wat ch?v=UjZy2_wSuZg

YouTube. "Barack Gets That Dirt off His Shoulders." 1:18. Posted by Bill3948, April 17, 2008. https://www.youtube.com/watch?v=yel8IjOAdSc

YouTube. "Barack Obama in Raleigh, NC." 4:10. Posted by BarackObamadotcom, April 17, 2008. https://www.youtube.com/watch?v=FlR9DNfqGD4

YouTube. "Barack Obama on Ellen." 1:25. Posted by BarackObamadotcom, October 30, 2007. https://www.youtube.com/watch?v=RsWpvkLCvu4&t=8s

YouTube. "Ben Carson's Rap Ad, Fixed." 1:15. Posted by Slate, June 18, 2018. https://www.youtube.com/watch?v=B_cSm87SJKE&t=32s

YouTube. "Bill Clinton: Rock & Roll President." 41:44. Posted by John Cook, October 19, 2020. https://www.youtube.com/watch?v=cyS8aSoZLwM

YouTube. "Bill Clinton on Arsenio Hall (June 1992)." 1:12:52. Posted by Clinton Warriner, September 15, 2016. https://www.youtube.com/watch?v=kWbNK5JvTb8

YouTube. "Bill Clinton Playing Saxophone on Arsenio Hall Show (HD)." 1:42. Posted by JR85, April 23, 2016. https://www.youtube.com/watch?v=a_WuGDYawFQ

YouTube. "Chrysler 'Imported from Detroit' Campaign: Super Bowl Commercial with Eminem." 2:18. Posted by Cause Marketing, October 30, 2016. https://www.youtube .com/watch?v=mYsFUFgOEmM

YouTube. "Crush on Obama. (with LYRICS)." 3:24. Posted by The Key of Awesome, February 17, 2008. https://www.youtube.com/watch?v=dyjXt1zSXHU

YouTube. "Democratic Debate—Saturday Night Live." [Season 33, episode 5, February 23, 2008]. 9:24. Posted by Saturday Night Live, October 3, 2013. https://www.youtu be.com/watch?v=AdHc6aX2gEs

YouTube. "Donald Trump, Knock the Hell out of Anyone Throwing a Tomato, Cedar Rapids, Iowa, 2/1/16." 0:15. Posted by Jerry Pace, February 1, 2016. https://www.you tube.com/watch?v=p5s9kpPZBbg&t=8s

YouTube. "EXCLUSIVE: Kamala Harris Talks to Angela Rye about Breonna Taylor, RBG, and a Black Agenda." 37:16. Posted by Angela Rye, September 25, 2020. https://www .youtube.com/watch?v=snf_XcjVyWY

YouTube. "Game On—Original Song for Rick Santorum by Camille & Haley." 2:25. Posted by C&H Backstage, March 6, 2012. https://www.youtube.com/watch?v=U 7pv7sO5Gng

YouTube. "German Youth Display (1940)." 1:36. Posted by British Pathé, April 13, 2014. https://www.youtube.com/watch?v=g7u5Knj5Uj4&t=12s

YouTube. "Kamala Harris Talks 2020 Presidential Run, Legalizing Marijuana,

Criminal Justice Reform + More." 44:18. Posted by Breakfast Club Power 105.1 FM, February 11, 2019. https://www.youtube.com/watch?v=Kh_wQUjeaTk&t=2326s

YouTube. "KEEP AMERICA GREAT (2020 Police Brutality Edition)—Trump Song by Camille & Haley." 2:15. Posted by Marc Webb, June 29, 2020. https://www.youtube.com/watch?v=BLITHkac96M

YouTube. "KEEP AMERICA GREAT (Official Music Video)—Trump 2020 Song by Camille & Haley." 1:59. Posted by Camille & Haley, June 20, 2020. https://www.youtube.com/watch?v=FAvFFYu1RGM

YouTube. "Mood Mix with Senator Kamala Harris." 2:35. Posted by The Late Show with Stephen Colbert, January 14, 2019. https://www.youtube.com/watch?v=Qo2482G1gog

YouTube. "Mosh (Dirty Version) by Eminem | Eminem." 5:18. Posted by EminemMusic, September 10, 2009. https://www.youtube.com/watch?v=9wRLd5l7WYE

YouTube. "Obama Dirt off Your Shoulder Remix." 1:36. Posted by jarts, April 18, 2008. https://www.youtube.com/watch?v=7j2g2axmnY8

YouTube. "Obama for America TV Ad: 'Firms.'" 0:32. Posted by BarackObamadotcom, July 14, 2012. https://www.youtube.com/watch?v=Ud3mMj0AZZk

YouTube. "The Official Donald Trump Jam [Freedom's Call]." 2:15. Posted by Fox 10 Phoenix, January 13, 2016. https://www.youtube.com/watch?v=vPRfP_TEQ-g

YouTube. "Patriotic Concert 2018—Camille & Haley." 1:02:30. Posted by Camille & Haley, June 14, 2020. https://www.youtube.com/watch?v=RSJlWknyq-E&t=1235s

YouTube. "Petty." 1:32. Posted by SOLMEMES, May 30, 2018. https://www.youtube.com/watch?v=BIK10JFs4GA

YouTube. "PETTY SONG—the Starrkeisha Cheer Squad!—@TheKingOfWeird." 1:29. Posted by Randome Guye, April 4, 2016. https://www.youtube.com/watch?v=xMU5C-fEXA8

YouTube. "Phoenix—Lisztomania—Boston University Brat Pack Mashup." 4:20. Posted by Julian Jensen, October 1, 2010. https://www.youtube.com/watch?v=Qj2Xald7NYQ

YouTube. "Please Welcome: The USA Freedom Grown-Ups." 3:30. Posted by The Late Show with Stephen Colbert, August 5, 2016. https://www.youtube.com/watch?v=8UOKh00-GuY

YouTube. "Pro-Trump Girl Band Performs 'Keep America Great' Ahead of Tulsa Rally." 0:47. Posted by Breitbart News, June 18, 2020. https://www.youtube.com/watch?v=cYyNMSrWqmM

YouTube. "Selected of God Choir—Lose Yourself (Official Music Video)." 4:07. Posted by SoundofGospel, July 29, 2011. https://www.youtube.com/watch?v=sg4lSGGOfzE

YouTube. "Ted Cruz: My Music Tastes Changed on 9/11.'" 1:24. Posted by CBS This Morning, March 24, 2015. https://www.youtube.com/watch?v=nik-UstmCjw

YouTube. "Trump: Oregon Leaders Must Clean Out 'Beehive of Terrorists,' Threatens to Send in National Guard." 2:35. Posted by The Oregonian, July 30, 2020. https://www.youtube.com/watch?v=rWZDLnPmeOU

YouTube. "USA President Barack Obama Opinion on Hip-Hop & Rap 2008" [Barack Obama, interview with Jeff Johnson on BET's political special "What's in It for Us?" aired January 8, 2008]. 3:49. Posted by starrground, February 3, 2008. https://www.youtube.com/watch?v=pFSVG7jRp_g

PRINTED MUSIC

Fogelberg, Dan. "Leader of the Band." New York: Hickory Grove Music, 1981.
"John Brown's Body." [Broadside] *Songs Sung at the Reunion of the 23d Regiment, O. V. I., at Fremont, O., Sept. 14, 1877.* Journal Steam Print, 1877. Kenneth S. Goldstein American Song Broadsides. Middle Tennessee State University Digital Collections. https://digital.mtsu.edu/digital/collection/p15838coll19/id/3100
Smith, Samuel Francis, and Henry Carey (att.). "America (My Country, 'Tis of Thee)." In *A Second Book in Vocal Music.* New York, Boston, and Chicago: Silver, Burdett and Company, 1901. https://archive.org/details/america_my_country_tis_of_thee /mode/1up
Sousa, John Philip. "Stars and Stripes Forever." Cincinnati, New York, and Chicago: John Church Company, 1898. https://repository.duke.edu/dc/hasm/b0367

SPEECHES

Bush, George. Remarks Accepting the Presidential Nomination at the Republican National Convention in Houston [August 20, 1992]. Online by Gerhard Peters and John T. Woolley. The American Presidency Project. https://www.presidency.ucsb .edu/node/266944
Carson, Ben. Announcement of Candidacy, Music Hall Center for the Performing Arts, Detroit, MI, May 4, 2015. http://www.p2016.org/carson/carson050415spt .html
Clinton, Bill. "Remarks of Governor Bill Clinton." Rainbow Coalition National Convention, Washington, DC, June 13, 1992. http://www.ibiblio.org/pub/academic /political-science/speeches/clinton.dir/c23.txt
Obama, Barack. Selma Voting Rights March Commemoration Speech, March 4, 2007. American Rhetoric Online Speech Bank. https://www.americanrhetoric.com/spee ches/barackobama/barackobamabrownchapel.htm
Obama, Barack. "Text of Obama's Fatherhood Speech." Politico, June 15, 2008. http:// www.politico.com/news/stories/0608/11094.html
Obama, Barack. "Transcript: Barack Obama's Speech on Race." NPR, March 18, 2008. https://www.npr.org/templates/story/story.php?storyId=88478467
Trump, Donald. Announcement of Candidacy, New York, June 16, 2015. http://www .p2016.org/trump/trump061615sp.html

A., Aron. "Kamala Harris Gets Flamed after Revealing Her Choice for 'Best Rapper Alive.'" HNHH, September 26, 2020. https://www.hotnewhiphop.com/kamala-har ris-calls-tupac-the-best-rapper-alive-news.118534.html

Alexis, Diamond. "Eminem Scalped Donald Trump in His Hip Hop Awards Cypher and the Internet Is Floored." BET, October 10, 2017. https://www.bet.com/article/q6 1ycv/eminem-scalped-donald-trump-in-his-hip-hop-awards-cypher

All Things Considered. "Meet the Man behind the Ben Carson Rap." NPR, November 7, 2015. https://www.npr.org/2015/11/07/455150311/meet-the-man-behind-the-ben -carson-rap

Barnett, Marva. "'Deplorables' Meme Gets It Wrong (from the HuffPost)." Marva Barnett (blog), n.d. https://www.marvabarnett.com/news-event/deplorables-me me-gets-it-wrong-from-the-huffpost/. Accessed September 6, 2021.

Bazelon, Emily. "Kamala Harris, a 'Top Cop' in the Era of Black Lives Matter." *New York Times Magazine*, May 25, 2016. https://www.nytimes.com/2016/05/29/magazi ne/kamala-harris-a-top-cop-in-the-era-of-black-lives-matter.html

Bazelon, Lara. "Kamala Harris Was Not a 'Progressive Prosecutor.'" *New York Times*, January 17, 2019. https://www.nytimes.com/2019/01/17/opinion/kamala-harris-cri minal-justice.html

BBC News. "Bush's iPod Reveals Music Tastes." April 13, 2005. http://news.bbc.co.uk /2/hi/4435639.stm

Beam, Christopher. "Barack Obama's iTunes Playlist." Trailhead (blog), Slate, January 26, 2008. https://slate.com/news-and-politics/2008/01/barack-obama-s-itunes-pla ylist.html

Beard, Dave. "'Celebration' and 'There's Hope' on Obama's Setlist." Boston.com, January 5, 2008. http://www.boston.com/news/politics/politicalintelligence/2008 /01/celebrationand.html

Beckwith, Ryan Teague. "Ben Carson Launches 2016 Presidential Campaign." *Time*, May 4, 2015. http://time.com/3845489/ben-carson-campaign-launch

Beinart, Peter. "Progressives Have Short Memories." *The Atlantic*, December 4, 2019. https://www.theatlantic.com/ideas/archive/2019/12/kamala-harris-was-impossib le-bind/602971/

Benveniste, Alexis. "The Meaning and History of Memes." *New York Times*, January 26, 2022. https://www.nytimes.com/2022/01/26/crosswords/what-is-a-meme.html

Blistein, Jon. "Trump Campaign Enlists Children to Sweeten Jingoist, Racist Message." *Rolling Stone*, January 14, 2016. https://www.rollingstone.com/politics/politics-ne ws/trump-campaign-enlists-children-to-sweeten-jingoist-racist-message-2-223 823/

Blitzer, Wolf. "Carson: There's a Reason Dictators 'Take the Guns First.'" CNN, October 8, 2015. https://www.cnn.com/videos/politics/2015/10/08/ben-carson -gun-control-nazi-germany-intvw-wolf.cnn

Bloomberg. "What the Voters Are Streaming." *Bloomberg Politics*, May 27, 2016. https://www.bloomberg.com/politics/graphics/2016-voter-spotify-listens/

Bosman, Julie. "The Inner Obama." The Caucus (blog), *New York Times*, June 24, 2008. https://thecaucus.blogs.nytimes.com/2008/06/24/the-inner-obama/

Breitbart TV. "Watch: Pro-Trump 'USA Freedom Kids'—'Enemies of Freedom Face the Music.'" *Breitbart*, January 14, 2016. http://www.breitbart.com/video/2016/01/14/watch-pro-trump-usa-freedom-kids-enemies-of-freedom-face-the-music/

Brown, Jennifer. "They've Been Called Soccer Moms, Rage Moms and Zoom Moms. Why the Colorado Suburban-Women Vote Is So Important." *Colorado Sun*, October 21, 2020. https://coloradosun.com/2020/10/21/colorados-suburban-women-vote/

Browne, David. "Complete Guide to the 2016 Candidates' Favorite Music." *Rolling Stone*, February 1, 2016. https://www.rollingstone.com/music/music-news/complete-guide-to-the-2016-candidates-favorite-music-240830/

Bump, Philip. "Talib Kweli Has Some Thoughts on Ben Carson's New 'Urban' Ad: He Thinks Jeb Bush Might Have Done Better." *Washington Post*, November 5, 2015. https://www.washingtonpost.com/news/the-fix/wp/2015/11/05/talib-kweli-has-some-thoughts-on-ben-carsons-new-urban-ad/

Cadei, Emily. "The World Through Ben Carson's Surgical Magnifying Glass." *Newsweek Global*, November 3, 2015.

Cadelago, Christopher. "A Rap Legend Ripped Kamala's Marriage to a White Man. Then She Won Him Over." Politico, September 3, 2019. https://www.politico.com/story/2019/09/03/kamala-harris-luther-campbell-2020-1479890

Calloway, Sway. "Barack Obama Gives a Shout-Out to Hip-Hop." MTV, September 27, 2008. http://www.mtv.com/news/1595820/barack-obama-gives-a-shout-out-to-hip-hop/

Camille & Haley website. http://camilleandhaley.com

Campbell, Luther. "Kamala Harris Can't Count on the Black Vote in 2020." Miami New Times, February 5, 2019. https://www.miaminewtimes.com/news/kamala-harris-cant-count-on-the-black-vote-to-win-in-2020-11068985

Caron, David. "Trump Shares 'Footloose' Dubbed Video of Portland Antifa Member Caught on Fire by Molotov Cocktail." Media Right, September 6, 2020. https://mediarightnews.com/trump-shares-footloose-dubbed-video-of-portland-antifa-member-caught-on-fire-by-molotov-cocktail/

Cassidy, John. "Hillary Clinton's 'Basket of Deplorables' Gaffe." *New Yorker*, September 11, 2016. https://www.newyorker.com/news/john-cassidy/hillary-clintons-basket-of-deplorables-gaffe

Chan, Melissa. "This Guy Wrote Donald Trump's 'USA Freedom Kids' Song." *Time*, January 14, 2016. http://time.com/4181383/donald-trump-usa-freedom-kids/

Chang, Jeff. "Barack Obama: The Vibe Interview." *Vibe*, September 2007.

Chiachiere, Ryan. "Imus Called Women's Basketball Team 'Nappy-Headed Hos.'" Media Matters, April 4, 2007. https://www.mediamatters.org/msnbc/imus-called-womens-basketball-team-nappy-headed-hos

Chittal, Nisha. "The Kamala Harris Identity Debate Shows How America Still

Struggles to Talk about Multiracial People." Vox, August 14, 2020. https://www.vox
.com/identities/2020/8/14/21366307/kamala-harris-black-south-asian-indian-ide
ntity

Ciliberto, Gina, and Stephanie Russell-Kraft. "They Invaded the Capitol Saying 'Jesus
Is My Savior. Trump Is My President.'" *Sojourners*, January 7, 2021. https://sojo.net
/articles/they-invaded-capitol-saying-jesus-my-savior-trump-my-president

Coates, Ta-Nehisi. "The First White President." *The Atlantic*, October 2017. https://
www.theatlantic.com/magazine/archive/2017/10/the-first-white-president-ta-nehi
si-coates/537909/

Colombo, Charlotte. "Kamala Harris Isn't as Feminist as You Think." *Prospect*,
January 29, 2021. https://www.prospectmagazine.co.uk/world/kamala-harris-isnt
-as-feminist-as-you-think-united-states-vie-president

Colorado Pols. "Nader Tells Rocky: Obama Trying to 'Talk White.'" June 25, 2008.
https://www.coloradopols.com/diary/6516

Coplon, Jon. "White House DJ Battle." *Blender*, July 30, 2008. https://web.archive.org
/web/20080814151724/http://www.blender.com/WhiteHouseDJBattle/articles/395
18.aspx

Costa, Robert. "Songs for Campaign Seasons Past and Present." *Wall Street Journal*,
October 2, 2008. http://online.wsj.com/article/SB122290103509796055.html

Cottle, Michelle. "Wife Lessons." *New Republic*, March 26, 2008.

Crockett, Emily. "Why Misogyny Won." Vox, November 15, 2016. https://www.vox
.com/identities/2016/11/15/13571478/trump-president-sexual-assault-sexism-mis
ogyny-won

Darville, Jordan. "Eminem Expresses Regret for Anti-Trump Freestyle, Claims He
Was Questioned by Secret Service." Fader, August 31, 2018. https://www.thefader
.com/2018/08/31/eminem-regret-anti-trump-freestyle-secret-service-interview

Davies, Madeleine. "The Dad/Manager behind Trump's Creepy Girl Group Just Really
Loves Freedom." Jezebel, January 15, 2016. https://jezebel.com/the-dad-manager
-behind-trumps-creepy-girl-group-just-re-1753265199

Demby, Gene. "Let's Talk about Kamala Harris." NPR, October 14, 2020. https://www
.npr.org/2020/10/13/923369723/lets-talk-about-kamala-harris

Dolan, Jon. "If Playlists Won Elections, Kamala Harris Would Be an Easy Frontrunner."
Rolling Stone, June 25, 2019. https://www.rollingstone.com/politics/politics-news
/kamala-harris-playlist-851861/

Dowd, Maureen. "The Faces Behind the Face That Clinton's Smile Masks." *New York
Times*, October 25, 1992.

Dowd, Maureen. "The 1992 Campaign: Democrats; After Ordeal, Is Clinton Tempered
Now, or Burned?" *New York Times*, February 2, 1992.

Dowd, Maureen. "¿Quién Es Less Macho?" *New York Times*, February 24, 2008. https://
www.nytimes.com/2008/02/24/opinion/24dowd.html

Elan, Priya. "Nine Years after Trayvon Martin's Killing, Hoodies Still Spark Debate."
The Guardian, February 27, 2021. https://www.theguardian.com/fashion/2021/feb
/27/trayvon-martin-hoodies-black-young-people

Eror, Aleks. "Sorry Obama but Donald Trump Is America's First Hip-Hop President."

Highsnobiety, n.d. https://www.highsnobiety.com/p/donald-trump-hip-hop-presi
dent/

Evans, Erin E. "Beyoncé's 'Before I Let Go' Challenge Is Here—Now Get Your Steps in
Order before the Summer." NBC News, April 23, 2019. https://www.nbcnews.com
/news/nbcblk/beyonc-s-i-let-go-challenge-here-now-get-your-n997736

Fahrenthold, David A. "Trump Recorded Having Extremely Lewd Conversation
about Women in 2005." Washington Post, October 7, 2016. https://www.washingt
onpost.com/politics/trump-recorded-having-extremely-lewd-conversation-about
-women-in-2005/2016/10/07/3b9ce776-8cb4-11e6-bf8a-3d26847eeed4_story.html

Falcone, Michael. "Obama on 'Obama Girl.'" The Caucus (blog), New York Times,
August 20, 2007. http://thecaucus.blogs.nytimes.com/2007/08/20/obama-on-oba
ma-girl/

Falsani, Cathleen. "Transcript: Barack Obama and the God Factor Interview [March
27, 2004]." Sojourners, February 21, 2012. https://sojo.net/articles/transcript-barack
-obama-and-god-factor-interview

Fang, Lee. "In Her First Race, Kamala Harris Campaigned as Tough on Crime—and
Unseated the Country's Most Progressive Prosecutor." The Intercept, February 7,
2019. https://theintercept.com/2019/02/07/kamala-harris-san-francisco-district-at
torney-crime/

Faulders, Katherine. "Listen to Ben Carson's New Rap Ad Aimed at African-American
Voters." ABC News, November 5, 2015. https://abcnews.go.com/Politics/listen-ben
-carsons-rap-ad-aimed-african-american/story?id=34988082

Filipovic, Jill. "Kamala Harris' Candidacy Requires a Nuanced Debate about Her
Record, Race and Gender. Is the Left Ready?" Think, January 22, 2019. https://www
.nbcnews.com/think/opinion/kamala-harris-candidacy-requires-nuanced-debate
-about-her-record-race-ncna961301

Folley, Aris. "Dem Senators Debate Whether to Retweet Cardi B Video Criticizing
Trump over Shutdown." The Hill, January 17, 2019. https://thehill.com/blogs/in-the
-know/in-the-know/425904-dem-senators-publicly-debate-whether-to-retweet-ca
rdi-b-ripping

Freedland, Jonathan. "Hum Along with Bush; Country Music Sweeps the Campaign."
Washington Post, August 21, 1992.

Frey, William H. "Less Than Half of US Children Under 15 Are White, Census Shows."
Brookings, June 24, 2019. https://www.brookings.edu/research/less-than-half-of
-us-children-under-15-are-white-census-shows/

Friedersdorf, Conor. "When Kamala Was a Top Cop." The Atlantic, August 25, 2019.
https://www.theatlantic.com/ideas/archive/2019/08/kamala-cop-record/596758/

Frizell, Sam. "Ben Carson 'Horrified' by His Own Campaign Ad." Time, January 22,
2016. https://time.com/4191428/ben-carson-rap-advertisement-radio/

Galioto, Katie. "Kamala Harris Expresses 'Regret' over California Truancy Law."
Politico, April 17, 2019. https://www.politico.com/story/2019/04/17/kamala-harris
-regrets-truancy-law-1279788

Gass, Nick. "Ben Carson's 15 Most Controversial Quotes." Politico, October 9, 2015.
https://www.politico.com/story/2015/10/ben-carson-controversial-quotes-214614

Givens, Ron. "Saxophonists Rate Bill Clinton's Musical Ability." *Entertainment Weekly*, June 19, 1992. https://ew.com/article/1992/06/19/saxophonists-rate-bill-cl intons-musical-ability/

Goldstein, Richard. "Sweet William, Sex and Sensibility: The Clinton Touch." *Village Voice*, October 27, 1992.

Gontcharova, Natalie. "The Story behind the Viral Photo of a Kent State Graduate Bringing a Gun on Campus." Refinery 29, May 15, 2018. https://www.refinery29 .com/en-us/2018/05/199241/kent-state-girl-with-gun-viral-photo

Gray, Briahna. "A Problem for Kamala Harris: Can a Prosecutor Become President in the Age of Black Lives Matter?" *The Intercept*, January 20, 2019. https://theintercept .com/2019/01/20/a-problem-for-kamala-harris-can-a-prosecutor-become-preside nt-in-the-age-of-black-lives-matter/

Gray, Chris. "Elvis: 30 Famous Quotes about the King." *Houston Press*, January 4, 2011. https://www.houstonpress.com/music/elvis-30-famous-quotes-about-the-ki ng-6772855

Grebey, James. "Hillary Clinton Wants People to 'Pokemon-Go-to the Polls.'" Insider, July 14, 2016. https://www.insider.com/hillary-clinton-wants-people-to-pokemon -go-to-the-polls-2016-7

Gstalter, Morgan. "Harris Dances with Drum Line, Leads Chant at SC Convention." The Hill, June 22, 2019. https://thehill.com/homenews/campaign/449842-harris -dances-with-drum-line-leads-chant-at-sc-convention/

Gstalter, Morgan. "Trump Jokes after Rallygoer Suggests Migrants Be Shot." The Hill, May 9, 2019. https://thehill.com/homenews/administration/442860-trump-jokes -after-rally-goer-suggests-migrants-be-shot

Hamblin, James. "Who Is Dr. Ben Carson? And Why Is He Sort of Running for President?" Politico, April 21, 2014. https://www.politico.com/magazine/story/2014 /04/who-is-dr-ben-carson-105875/

Hamby, Peter. "Barack Obama Gets Name-Dropped in Hip-Hop." CNN, August 17, 2007. http://www.cnn.com/2007/POLITICS/08/17/obama.hip.hop/index.html

Hao, Karen. "Troll Farms Reached 140 Million Americans a Month on Facebook before 2020 Election, Internal Report Shows." MIT Technology Review, September 16, 2021. https://www.technologyreview.com/2021/09/16/1035851/facebook-troll -farms-report-us-2020-election/

Healy, Patrick, and Maggie Haberman. "Donald Trump Opens New Line of Attack on Hillary Clinton: Her Marriage." *New York Times*, September 30, 2016. https:// www.nytimes.com/2016/10/01/us/politics/donald-trump-interview-bill-hillary-cl inton.html?_r=0

Herndon, Astead W. "Kamala Harris Is Accused of Lying about Listening to Tupac. Here's What Actually Happened." *New York Times*, February 13, 2019. https://www .nytimes.com/2019/02/13/us/politics/kamala-harris-snoop-tupac.html#comment sContainer

Herndon, Astead, Jon Caramanica, and Jon Pareles. "What Do Rally Playlists Say about the Candidates?" *New York Times*, August 19, 2019. https://www.nytimes

.com/interactive/2019/08/19/us/politics/presidential-campaign-songs-playlists
.html

Herrera, Isabelia. "AOC Defends Cardi B against Critics: Don't Mess with Bronx Women or You'll Get Roasted." Remezcla, January 21, 2019. https://remezcla.com /music/cardi-b-alexandria-ocasio-cortez-government-shutdown/

Heywood, Todd A. "'It Was a Digital Lynching': Rep. Johnson Discusses Video and Punishment." Michigan Advance, December 10, 2020. https://michiganadvance .com/2020/12/10/it-was-a-digital-lynching-rep-johnson-discusses-video-and-pun ishment/

Hip Hop for Obama. MySpace. http://www.myspace.com/hiphopforobama. Accessed October 1, 2010.

Hoekstra, Dave. "The Soul of a President." *Chicago Sun-Times*, January 11, 2009.

Holland, Jesse J., and Bill Barrow. "Ben Carson Stands by Statement That Egyptian Pyramids Built to Store Grain." PBS NewsHour, November 5, 2015. https://www .pbs.org/newshour/politics/presidential-candidate-ben-carson-stands-belief-pyra mids-built-store-grain

Holpuch, Amanda. "Barack Obama May Be Descendant of First African Slave in Colonial America." *The Guardian*, July 30, 2012. https://www.theguardian.com/wo rld/us-news-blog/2012/jul/30/barack-obama-descendant-first-african

Hutchinson, Bill. "From 'BBQ Becky' to 'Golfcart Gail,' List of Unnecessary 911 Calls Made on Blacks Continues to Grow." ABC News, October 19, 2018. https://abcne ws.go.com/US/bbq-becky-golfcart-gail-list-unnecessary-911-calls/story?id=5858 4961

Jackson, Lauren Michele. "We Need to Talk about Digital Blackface in Reaction GIFs." *Teen Vogue*, August 2, 2017. https://www.teenvogue.com/story/digital-blackface-re action-gifs

Jeffries, Michael P. "Is Obama Really the Hip-Hop President?" *The Atlantic*, January 26, 2011. https://www.theatlantic.com/entertainment/archive/2011/01/is-obama-re ally-the-hip-hop-president/70061/

Kaltenbach, Chris. "Clinton Proves Himself a Rock and Roll President." *Baltimore Sun*, June 3, 1997. https://www.baltimoresun.com/news/bs-xpm-1997-06-03-1997 154115-story.html

Karimi, Faith. "Alexandria Ocasio-Cortez Responds to Dance Video Critics with More Dancing." CNN, January 4, 2019. https://www.cnn.com/2019/01/04/politics /ocasio-cortez-dancing-video-trnd/index.html

Kaur, Harmeet. "Cardi B and Tomi Lahren Are Feuding over the Government Shutdown." CNN, January 21, 2019. https://www.cnn.com/2019/01/20/entertainme nt/cardi-b-tomi-lahren-twitter-feud/

Kiley, David. "The Inside Story: Chrysler's Risky Eminem Super Bowl Commercial." Auto Blog, February 8, 2011. http://www.autoblog.com/2011/02/08/chrysler-emin em-super-bowl-ad

King, Maya. "Why Black Voters Never Flocked to Kamala Harris." Politico, December 4, 2019. https://www.politico.com/news/2019/12/04/kamala-harris-black-voters-20 20-075651

Kolbert, Elizabeth. "The 1992 Campaign: Media; Whistle-Stops a la 1992: Arsenio, Larry and Phil." *New York Times*, June 5, 1992. http://www.nytimes.com/1992/06/05/us/the-1992-campaign-media-whistle-stops-a-la-1992-arsenio-larry-and-phil.html

Krauss, Lawrence M. "Ben Carson's Scientific Ignorance." *New Yorker*, September 28, 2015. https://www.newyorker.com/news/news-desk/ben-carsons-scientific-ignorance

Krehbiel, Randy. "Tulsa Sisters' Santorum Song Big Hit on YouTube." *Tulsa World*, March 9, 2012. https://tulsaworld.com/news/local/govt-and-politics/tulsa-sisters-santorum-song-big-hit-on-youtube/article_cadb73e9-84f6-5b89-b1d8-d04a24922866.html

Kurtz, Judy. "Trump Campaign Sets Aside Debate Ticket for Tupac after Harris Calls Him Her Favorite Living Rapper." The Hill, October 7, 2020. https://thehill.com/blogs/in-the-know/in-the-know/520057-trump-campaign-sets-aside-debate-ticket-for-tupac-after-harris/

Lambert, Hannah Ray. "Portland Protests: What Happened in 2020, What's Next in 2021." KOIN, December 31, 2020. https://www.koin.com/news/protests/portland-protests-what-happened-in-2020-whats-next-in-2021/

Lapowsky, Issie. "Twitter Reacts to the Ben Carson Rap That Shouldn't Exist." Wired, November 5, 2015. https://www.wired.com/2015/11/twitter-reacts-to-the-ben-carson-rap-that-shouldnt-exist/

Larson, Leslie. "Ben Carson Blasts Hip-Hop for Hurting African-American Communities." *Business Insider*, April 6, 2015. http://www.businessinsider.com/ben-carson-blasts-hip-hop-2015-4

Leibovich, Mark. "The Other Man of the Hour." *Washington Post*, July 27, 2004. http://www.washingtonpost.com/wp-dyn/articles/A16606-2004Jul26.html

Lerer, Lisa, and Jennifer Medina. "What Does This Country Demand of Black Women in Politics?" *New York Times*, December 8, 2019. https://www.nytimes.com/2019/12/08/us/politics/kamala-harris-black-women.html

Lesniewski, Niels. "The Legislative Record of Kamala Harris Shows a Loyal Democrat and Trump Counterpuncher." Roll Call, August 12, 2020. https://rollcall.com/2020/08/12/the-legislative-record-of-kamala-harris-shows-a-loyal-democrat-and-trump-counter-puncher/

Levinson, Jonathan, Conrad Wilson, and Ryan Haas. "50 Days of Protest in Portland." *OPB*, July 19, 2020. https://www.opb.org/news/article/police-violence-portland-protest-federal-officers/

Lopez, German. "Kamala Harris's Controversial Record on Criminal Justice, Explained." Vox, January 23, 2019. https://www.vox.com/future-perfect/2019/1/23/18184192/kamala-harris-president-campaign-criminal-justice-record

Love, Joanna. "Political Pop and Commercials That Flopped: Early Lessons from the 2016 Presidential Race." Trax on the Trail, January 14, 2016. https://www.traxonthetrail.com/2016/01/14/political-pop-and-commercials-that-flopped-early-lessons-from-the-2016-presidential-race/

Madden, Sidney. "The Business of Being Cardi B." NPR, April 5, 2018. https://www
.npr.org/sections/therecord/2018/04/05/599592959/the-business-of-being-cardi-b

Maraniss, David. "Tooting His Own Horn: Clinton's Team Sees 'Arsenio' Gig as
Triumph." *Washington Post*, June 5, 1992.

Marcotte, Amanda. "Sympathy for the K-Hive: Kamala Harris Ran a Bad Campaign—
and Faced Remarkable Online Spite." Salon, December 3, 2019. https://www.salon
.com/2019/12/03/sympathy-for-the-k-hive-kamala-harris-ran-a-bad-campaign
-and-faced-remarkable-online-spite/

Marcus, Greil. "The Elvis Strategy." *New York Times*, October 27, 1992. http://www.ny
times.com/1992/10/27/opinion/the-elvis-strategy.html

Marin, Carol. "Thanks to Hillary for Being a Winner at Heart." *Chicago Sun-Times*,
May 11, 2008.

Martis, Eternity. "The Politics of Being Black and Loud." *Fader*, June 28, 2016. https://
www.thefader.com/2016/06/28/the-politics-of-being-black-and-loud

Martosko, David. "Her Grandparents 'Must Be Turning in Their Grave.'" *Daily Mail*,
February 20, 2019. https://www.dailymail.co.uk/news/article-6725403/Kamala-Ha
rris-Jamaican-father-slams-fraudulent-stereotype-linking-family-pot-smoking
.html

Melber, Ari. "Obama Meets Jay-Z in YouTube Mashup Slamming Clinton & Debate."
Huffington Post, April 17, 2008. https://www.huffpost.com/entry/obama-meets-jay
-z-in-yout_b_97342

Meline, Gabe. "Hip-Hop President: How Will Obama's Presidency Change the Face
of Hip-Hop?" Bohemian, December 31, 2008. https://bohemian.com/hip-hop-pre
sident-1/

Menczer, Filippo. "Here's Exactly How Social Media Algorithms Can Manipulate
You." Big Think, October 7, 2021. https://bigthink.com/the-present/social-media
-algorithms-manipulate-you/

Merica, Dan, Kyung Lah, Abby Phillip, and Jasmine Wright. "Kamala Harris Plots
Iowa Blitz as Campaign Stalls." CNN, September 19, 2019. https://www.cnn.com/20
19/09/19/politics/kamala-harris-iowa-strategy-2020-campaign/index.html

Millard, Drew. "Ben Carson's Rap Radio Ad Is an Embarrassment for Everyone." Vice,
November 5, 2015. https://www.vice.com/en/article/8gkkdg/ben-carsons-rap-ad
-republicans-dont-understand-hip-hop-115

Miller, Claire Cain. "How Obama's Internet Campaign Changed Politics." Bits (blog),
New York Times, November 7, 2008. https://bits.blogs.nytimes.com/2008/11/07
/how-obamas-internet-campaign-changed-politics/

Miller, Nick. "The Good Wife." *Sydney Morning Herald*, May 27, 2012. https://www
.smh.com.au/world/the-good-wife-20120526-1zbs5.html

Mills, David. "Sister Souljah's Call to Arms: The Rapper Says the Riots Were Payback.
Are You Paying Attention?" *Washington Post*, May 13, 1992. https://www.washingt
onpost.com/wp-dyn/content/article/2010/03/31/AR2010033101709.html

Montanaro, Domenico. "How the 'Replacement' Theory Went Mainstream on the
Political Right." NPR, May 17, 2022. https://www.npr.org/2022/05/17/1099223012
/how-the-replacement-theory-went-mainstream-on-the-political-right

Montanaro, Domenico. "Is Ted Cruz Allowed to Run Since He Was Born in Canada?" NPR, March 23, 2015. https://www.npr.org/sections/itsallpolitics/2015/03/23/3947 13013/is-ted-cruz-allowed-to-run-since-he-was-born-in-canada

Mooney, Alexander. "Obama Using 'White Guilt,' Nader Says." CNN, June 25, 2008. https://www.cnn.com/2008/POLITICS/06/25/nader.obama/index.html

Morgan, Chris R. "Beto Wants to Be Our First Punk President." *American Conservative*, March 25, 2019. https://www.theamericanconservative.com/articles/beto-wants-to -be-our-first-punk-president-orourke/

Morrison, Toni. "Comment." *New Yorker*, September 27, 1998. https://www.newyorker .com/magazine/1998/10/05/comment-6543

Moyer, Justin. "Trump-Loving USA Freedom Kid's Dad: 'To Me, Freedom Is Everything.'" *Washington Post*, January 15, 2016. https://www.washingtonpost.com /news/morning-mix/wp/2016/01/15/manager-of-trump-loving-usa-freedom-kids -to-me-freedom-is-everything/

National Immigration Forum. "The 'Great Replacement' Theory, Explained." December 2021. https://immigrationforum.org/wp-content/uploads/2021/12/Rep lacement-Theory-Explainer-1122.pdf

National Women's Prayer and Voting Army website. https://www.nationalwomenspva .com. Accessed July 2, 2021.

Nelson, Louis. "Trump: 'I Am the Law and Order Candidate.'" Politico, July 11, 2016. https://www.politico.com/story/2016/07/trump-law-order-candidate-225372

Nemo, Aaron. "Listen to the Spoof of Ben Carson's Hip-Hop Radio Ad." HuffPost, November 9, 2015. https://www.huffpost.com/entry/spoof-ben-carson-rap_n_563 e8d78e4b0307f2cadbdf5?ncid=tweetlnkushpmg00000067

Newkirk, Vann R., II. "On Hillary Clinton's Pandering." *The Atlantic*, April 19, 2016. https://www.theatlantic.com/politics/archive/2016/04/hillary-clinton-pandering -radio/479004/

Nielson, Erik. "How Hip-Hop Fell Out of Love with Obama." *The Guardian*, August 23, 2012. http://www.theguardian.com/music/2012/aug/23/why-hip-hop-deserti ng-obama

Norris, Chris. "Artist of the Year." *Spin*, January 2001. https://web.archive.org/web/20 030608212512/http://www.spin.com/new/magazine/jan2001eminem2.html

Nuzzi, Olivia. "How Pepe the Frog Became a Nazi Trump Supporter and Alt-Right Symbol." Daily Beast, May 26, 2016. https://www.thedailybeast.com/how-pepe-the -frog-became-a-nazi-trump-supporter-and-alt-right-symbol

Oh, Inae. "Watch a Group of 'Freedom Kids' Perform a Horrifying Song at a Donald Trump Rally." *Mother Jones*, January 14, 2016. http://www.motherjones.com/politi cs/2016/01/freedom-girls-donald-trump-rally/

Osterheldt, Jeneé. "Beyoncé's 'Homecoming' Netflix Documentary Is Black History." *Boston Globe*, April 17, 2019. https://www.bostonglobe.com/arts/music/2019/04/17 /beyonce-homecoming-netflix-documentary-black-history/3c58KdpBpsn5BnLVJ db7rI/story.html

Painter, Nell Irvin. "What Whiteness Means in the Trump Era." *New York Times*, November 13, 2016. https://www.nytimes.com/2016/11/13/opinion/what-whiteness -means-in-the-trump-era.html

Patch, Justin. "Footloose: Political Transformations of a Song and Its Meaning." Trax on the Trail, October 25, 2020. https://www.traxonthetrail.com/2020/10/25/footlo ose-political-transformations-of-a-song-and-its-meaning/

People. "The King & I: Sure, Carville Got the Credit, but Clinton May Really Owe It All to Elvis." December 28, 1992–January 4, 1993.

Phillips, Gregory. "The Campaign Song Comeback." From Fay To Z (blog), *Fayetteville Observer*, October 29, 2008. http://blogs.fayobserver.com/faytoz

Pickler, Nedra. "Obama's Girls Aren't Fans of YouTube's Obama Girl." *The Sun*, August 22, 2007. https://www.sbsun.com/2007/08/22/obamas-girls-arent-fans-of -youtubes-obama-girl/

Price, Catherine. "Hillary's 'Testicular Fortitude.'" Salon, May 1, 2008. https://www.sa lon.com/2008/05/01/hillary_s_testicles/

Reese, Ashley. "Did the 'Kamala Is a Cop' Meme Help Tank Harris's Campaign?" Jezebel, December 3, 2019. https://jezebel.com/did-the-kamala-is-a-cop-meme-he lp-tank-harriss-campaign-1840056843

Reid, Whitelaw. "Black Twitter 101: What Is It? Where Did It Originate? Where Is It Headed?" *UVA Today*, November 28, 2018. https://news.virginia.edu/content/black -twitter-101-what-it-where-did-it-originate-where-it-headed

Rindner, Grant. "Who Were Barack Obama's Parents?" Oprah Daily, November 16, 2020. https://www.oprahdaily.com/life/a34670592/barack-obamas-parents/

Robillard, Kevin. "Paul Ryan Pics Spark Dumbbell Debate." Politico, October 11, 2012. https://www.politico.com/story/2012/10/paul-ryan-pics-spark-dumbbell-debate -082296

Rogers, Kaleigh. "Hillary Clinton Accidentally Became a Vine Meme." Motherboard, August 14, 2015. https://www.vice.com/en/article/vvbwmj/hillary-clinton-acciden tally-became-a-vine-meme

Ross, Brian, and Rehab El-Buri. "Obama's Pastor: God Damn America, U.S. to Blame for 9/11." ABC News, March 13, 2008. https://abcnews.go.com/Blotter/story?id=44 43788

Rothenberg, Randall. "The Past Is Now the Latest Craze." *New York Times*, November 29, 1989. http://www.nytimes.com/1989/11/29/business/the-media-business-adver tising-the-past-is-now-the-latest-craze.html

Rys, Dan. "Eminem and New Def Jam CEO Paul Rosenberg on Early 'Broke Days,' Courting Controversy and Hip-Hop's Future." Billboard, January 25, 2018. https:// www.billboard.com/music/features/eminem-paul-rosenberg-interview-billboard -cover-story-2018-8095496/

Samuels, Robert. "Ben Carson: From Inspiring to Polarizing." *Washington Post*, January 2, 2016. https:// www.washingtonpost.com/sf/national/2016/01/02/decide rscarson/

Savage, David G. "Is Ted Cruz, Born in Canada, Eligible for the Presidency? Legal Experts Say Yes." *Los Angeles Times*, January 8, 2016. https://www.latimes.com/nat ion/la-na-natural-born-president-20160108-story.html

Scherer, Michael. "Hillary Is from Mars, Obama Is from Venus." Salon, July 12, 2007. https://www.salon.com/2007/07/12/obama_hillary/

Scherer, Michael. "Trump Employs Images of Violence as Political Fuel for Reelection Fight." *Washington Post*, September 8, 2020. https://www.washingtonpost.com/politics/trump-violence-election/2020/09/08/0a7fa096-edf6-11ea-99a1-71343d03bc29_story.html

Schneider, Elena, and Brent D. Griffiths. "At Pennsylvania Rally, Trump Endorses Himself." Politico, March 10, 2018. https://www.politico.com/story/2018/03/10/trump-pennsylvania-rally-rick-saccone-keep-america-great-454169

Schwarz, Hunter. "The 9 Best Moments from Ben Carson's Bizarre and Glorious Campaign Launch/Concert." *Washington Post*, May 4, 2015. https://www.washingtonpost.com/news/the-fix/wp/2015/05/04/the-9-best-moments-from-ben-carsons-bizarre-and-glorious-campaign-launch/?utm_term=.46dba35e26d2

Scott, Alicia. "Rise of the Digital Lynch Mob: Black Anger, White Hostility, Public Shaming, Blame [Social] Media!" Medium, March 19, 2017. https://medium.com/the-2x-ceo/rise-of-the-digital-lynch-mob-6c308bf02dbd

Seale, Jack. "I Can Go for That: The Smooth World of Yacht Rock Review—Lushly Comforting." *The Guardian*, June 14, 2019. https://www.theguardian.com/tv-and-radio/2019/jun/14/i-can-go-for-that-the-smooth-world-of-yacht-rock-review-katie-puckrik-bbc-four

Selected of God website. https://www.selectedofgod.com. Accessed May 20, 2021.

Shiver, Kyle-Anne. "Women Voters and the Obama Crush." American Thinker, March 11, 2008. https://www.americanthinker.com/articles/2008/03/women_voters_and_the_obama_cru.html

Sisario, Ben. "George Bush, Soul Man? Footage From an Inauguration Concert Is Restored." *New York Times*, December 5, 2018. https://www.nytimes.com/2018/12/05/arts/music/bush-atwater-inauguration-concert.html

Smith, Allan. "The Day Ben Carson's Campaign Died." *Business Insider*, March 7, 2016. https://www.businessinsider.com/ben-carson-president-campaign-why-2016-2

Smith, Ben. "Obama Camp Condemns Song: Ludacris 'Should Be Ashamed.'" Ben Smith (blog), Politico, July 30, 2008. https://www.politico.com/blogs/ben-smith/2008/07/obama-camp-condemns-song-ludacris-should-be-ashamed-010659

Solomon, Deborah. "Hip-Hop Guru." *New York Times Magazine*, April 29, 2007. http://www.nytimes.com/2007/04/29/magazine/29wwlnQ4.t.html?pagewanted=print

Stark, Steven. "The Campaigns and Pop Culture." *Evening Sun*, September 4, 1992.

Squires, Camille. "Kamala Was a Cop. Black People Knew It First." Mother Jones, December 9, 2019. https://www.motherjones.com/politics/2019/12/kamala-was-a-cop-black-people-knew-it-first/

Stuart, Tessa. "Listen to Ben Carson's Rap Campaign Ad." *Rolling Stone*, November 5, 2015. https://www.rollingstone.com/politics/politics-news/listen-to-ben-carsons-rap-campaign-ad-40435/

Suarez, Fernando. "N.C. Governor: Hillary Makes Rocky Look Like 'Pansy.'" CBS News, April 28, 2008. https://www.cbsnews.com/news/nc-governor-hillary-makes-rocky-look-like-pansy/

Swindler, Samantha. "Tensions at Portland Protest Flare Saturday after Molotov

Cocktails Tossed Near Police Blocking March Route." Oregon Live, September 5, 2020. https://www.oregonlive.com/news/2020/09/portland-protest-declared-riot -soon-after-it-begins-in-se-portland-live-updates.html

Talev, Margaret. "Soul of the Obama Campaign Is in the Soundtrack." McClatchy, October 31, 2008. https://www.mcclatchydc.com/news/politics-government/articl e24507895.html

Tapper, Jake, and Jerry Tully. "Rap Mogul Takes on Obama." ABC News, April 16, 2007. http://abcnews.go.com/GMA/story?id=3045077

Tensley, Brandon. "The Dark Subtext of Trump's 'Good Genes' Compliment." CNN, September 22, 2020. https://www.cnn.com/2020/09/22/politics/donald-trump-gen es-historical-context-eugenics/index.html

Time. "45 Americans Who Defined the Election." https://time.com/2016-election-am ericans/. Accessed September 1, 2022.

Trust, Gary. "Cardi B 'Moves' to No. 1 on Billboard Hot 100 with 'Bodak Yellow,' Post Malone Debuts at No. 2 with 'Rockstar.'" Billboard, September 25, 2017. https:// www.billboard.com/articles/columns/chart-beat/7973958/cardi-b-no-1-hot-100 -post-malone-portugal-the-man

USA Freedom Kids website. https://www.usafreedomkids.com. Accessed May 5, 2021.

Veritas website. http://veritasfive.com. Accessed June 2, 2021.

Vitali, Ali. "Donald Trump on Nevada Protester: 'I'd Like to Punch Him.'" NBC News, February 23, 2016. https://www.nbcnews.com/politics/2016-election/donald-tru mp-nevada-protester-i-d-punch-him-n524011

Wagner, John. "Kamala Harris's Jamaican Father Wasn't Amused by Her Joke about Marijuana Use." Washington Post, February 21, 2019. https://www.washingtonpo st.com/politics/kamala-harriss-jamaican-father-wasnt-amused-by-her-joke-abo ut-marijuana-use/2019/02/21/2d722658-35cb-11e9-af5b-b51b7ff322e9_story.html

Walker, Martin. "Music Carries the Message at the Democrats' Rallies-cum-Rock Concerts; Taking Care of Business—the Clinton Way." Ottawa Citizen, October 30, 1992.

Wayland, Michael. "Chrysler Gospel Remix of 'Lose Yourself' by Eminem Celebrates Detroit, Benefits Charities." MLive, August 2, 2011. https://www.mlive.com/news /detroit/2011/08/video_chrysler_releases_gospel.html

Weber, Peter. "Stephen Colbert Showcases New Song to Mock Donald Trump for Stiffing Trio of Young Girls." The Week, August 5, 2016. https://theweek.com/sp eedreads/641149/stephen-colbert-showcases-new-song-mock-donald-trump-stiffi ng-trio-young-girls

Weisbard, Eric. "Proxy Music." Village Voice, October 24, 2000. https://www.villagevo ice.com/2000/10/24/proxy-music

Wenner, Jann S. "A Conversation with Barack Obama." Rolling Stone, July 10–24, 2008. https://www.rollingstone.com/culture/culture-news/a-conversation-with-barack -obama-51394/

Williams, Steven. "What Even Is Yacht Rock Anyway?" Discogs (blog), September 11, 2018. https://web.archive.org/web/20220504235315/https://blog.discogs.com/en /what-even-is-yacht-rock-anyway/

Wilson, Marie. "Leading Like a Girl: For Men Only?" *Huffington Post*, April 15, 2008. https://www.huffpost.com/entry/leading-like-a-girl-for-m_b_96753

Wilson, Reid. "On the Trail: Trump Presents Vision of the Suburbs Decades out of Date." *The Hill*, August 19, 2020. https://thehill.com/homenews/state-watch/5125 70-on-the-trail-trump-presents-vision-of-the-suburbs-decades-out-of-date

Wilstein, Matt. "Trump Begs Suburban Women: 'Will You Please Like Me?'" *Daily Beast*, October 13, 2020. https://www.thedailybeast.com/trump-begs-suburban-wo men-will-you-please-like-me

Zeleny, Jeff. "Long by Obama's Side, an Adviser Fills a Role That Exceeds His Title." *New York Times*, October 26, 2008. https://www.nytimes.com/2008/10/27/us/polit ics/27axelrod.html?r=1

Zimmer, Ben. "Where Does Trump's 'Invasion' Rhetoric Come From?" *The Atlantic*, August 6, 2019. https://www.theatlantic.com/entertainment/archive/2019/08/tru mp-immigrant-invasion-language-origins/595579

BOOKS, DISSERTATIONS, AND ARTICLES

Abbott, Philip. "A 'Long and Winding Road': Bill Clinton and the 1960s." *Rhetoric & Public Affairs* 9, no. 1 (2006): 1–20.

Adam, Katherine, and Charles Derber. *The New Feminized Majority: How Democrats Can Change America with Women's Values.* Boulder, CO: Paradigm, 2008.

Adorno, Theodor W. "On Popular Music." In *Cultural Theory and Popular Culture: A Reader*, 2nd ed., edited by John Storey, 197–209. Athens: University of Georgia Press, 1998.

Alim, H. Samy, and Geneva Smitherman. *Articulate While Black: Barack Obama, Language, and Race in the U.S.* Oxford: Oxford University Press, 2012.

Alim, H. Samy, and Geneva Smitherman. "'My President's Black, My Lambo's Blue': Hip Hop, Race, and the Culture Wars." In *Articulate While Black: Barack Obama, Language, and Race in the U.S.*, 130–66. Oxford: Oxford University Press, 2012.

Alim, H. Samy, and Geneva Smitherman. "'Perfect English' and White Supremacy." In *Language in the Trump Era: Scandals and Emergencies*, edited by Janet McIntosh and Norma Mendoza-Denton, 226–36. Cambridge: Cambridge University Press, 2020.

Anderson, Carol. *White Rage: The Unspoken Truth of Our Racial Divide.* New York: Bloomsbury, 2016.

Anker, Elisabeth R. *Orgies of Feeling: Melodrama and the Politics of Freedom.* Durham: Duke University Press, 2014.

Blankenship, Courtney, and Stan Renard. "Pop Songs on Political Platforms." *Journal of Popular Music Studies* 29, no. 3 (2017). https://doi.org/10.1111/jpms.12222

Blim, Richard Daniel. "The Electoral Collage: Mapping Barack Obama's Mediated Identities in the 2008 Election." In "Patchwork Nation: Collage, Music, and American Identity," 364–450. PhD diss., University of Michigan–Ann Arbor, 2013.

Bonilla-Silva, Eduardo. *Racism without Racists: Color-Blind Racism and the Persistence of Racial Inequality in America*. 6th ed. Lanham: Rowman & Littlefield, 2021.

Boym, Svetlana. *The Future of Nostalgia*. New York: Basic Books, 2001.

Brackett, David. *Categorizing Sound: Genre and Twentieth-Century Popular Music*. Oakland: University of California Press, 2016.

Branch, Lessie B. *Optimism at All Costs: Black Attitudes, Activism, and Advancement in Obama's America*. Amherst: University of Massachusetts Press, 2018.

Brittan, Francesca. "Women Who 'Do Elvis': Authenticity, Masculinity, and Masquerade." *Journal of Popular Music Studies* 18, no. 2 (August 2006): 167–90. https://doi.org/10.1111/j.1533-1598.2006.00087.x

Brøvig-Hanssen, Ragnhild, and Aram Sinnreich. "Do You Wanna Build a Wall? Remix Tactics in the Age of Trump." *Popular Music and Society* 43, no. 5 (2020): 535–49. https://doi.org/10.1080/03007766.2019.1650990

Cameron, Deborah. "Banter, Male Bonding, and the Language of Donald Trump." In *Language in the Trump Era: Scandals and Emergencies*, edited by Janet McIntosh and Norma Mendoza-Denton, 158–67. Cambridge: Cambridge University Press, 2020.

Campbell, Karlyn Kohrs. *Man Cannot Speak for Her*. Vol. 1. *A Critical Study of Early Feminist Rhetoric*. New York: Greenwood, 1989.

Cannen, Emma. "Avant-Garde Militarism and a Post-Hip-Hop President." *International Feminist Journal of Politics* 16, no. 2 (2014): 255–77. https://doi.org/10.1080/14616742.2013.780375

Carson, Ben, and Candy Carson. *America the Beautiful: Rediscovering What Made This Nation Great*. Grand Rapids, MI: Zondervan, 2013.

Carson, Ben, and Candy Carson. *A More Perfect Union: What We the People Can Do to Reclaim Our Constitutional Liberties*. New York: Sentinel, 2015.

Cassese, Erin C. "Intersectional Stereotyping in Political Decision Making." Oxford Research Encyclopedias, March 26, 2019. https://doi.org/10.1093/acrefore/9780190228637.013.773

Cheng, William. "Black Noise, White Ears: Resilience, Rap, and the Killing of Jordan Davis." *Current Musicology*, no. 102 (April 2018): 115–89. https://doi.org/10.7916/cm.v0i102.5367

Ciampaglia, Giovanni Luca, Azadeh Nematzadeh, Filippo Menczer, and Alessandro Flammini. "How Algorithmic Popularity Bias Hinders or Promotes Quality." *Scientific Reports* 8 (2018): 1–7.

Clayton, Dewey M. *The Presidential Campaign of Barack Obama: A Critical Analysis of a Racially Transcendent Strategy*. New York: Routledge, 2010.

Coleman, Billy. *Harnessing Harmony: Music, Power, and Politics in the United States, 1788–1865*. Chapel Hill: University of North Carolina Press, 2020.

Cooper, Frank Rudy. "Our First Unisex President?: Black Masculinity and Obama's Feminine Side." *Denver University Law Review* 86 (2009): 633–61.

Crew, Danny O. *American Political Music: A State-by-State Catalog of Printed and Recorded Music Related to Local, State and National Politics, 1756–2004*. 2 vols. Jefferson, NC: McFarland, 2006.

Crew, Danny O. *Presidential Sheet Music: An Illustrated Catalogue of Published Music Associated with the American Presidency and Those Who Sought the Office.* Jefferson, NC: McFarland, 2001.

Cusic, Don. "NASCAR and Country Music." *Studies in Popular Culture* 21, no. 1 (1998): 31–40.

Dadas, Caroline E. "Inventing the Election: Civic Participation and Presidential Candidates' Websites." *Computers and Composition* 25, no. 4 (2008): 416–31.

Davis, Fred. *Yearning for Yesterday: A Sociology of Nostalgia.* New York: Free Press, 1979.

Davis, Jenny L., Tony P. Love, and Gemma Killen. "Seriously Funny: The Political Work of Humor on Social Media." *New Media & Society* 20, no. 10 (2018): 3898–916. https://doi.org/10.1177/1461444818762602

Dawkins, Marcia Alesan. "Close to the Edge: The Representational Tactics of Eminem." *Journal of Popular Culture* 43, no. 3 (2010): 463–85.

Durham, Aisha, Brittney C. Cooper, and Susana M. Morris. "The Stage Hip-Hop Feminism Built: A New Directions Essay." *Signs* 38, no. 3 (Spring 2013): 721–37.

Dyer, Richard. "White." *Screen* 29, no. 4 (1988): 44–65.

Eagly, Alice H., and Linda L. Carli. *Through the Labyrinth: The Truth about How Women Become Leaders.* Boston, MA: Harvard Business School Press, 2007.

Edwards, Griffin Sims, and Stephen Rushin. "The Effect of President Trump's Election on Hate Crimes." SSRN, January 14, 2018. https://ssrn.com/abstract=3102652

Eidsheim, Nina Sun. *The Race of Sound: Listening, Timbre, and Vocality in African American Music.* Durham: Duke University Press, 2019.

Fea, John. *Believe Me: The Evangelical Road to Donald Trump.* Grand Rapids, MI: William B. Eerdmans, 2018.

Fierke, Karin M. *Political Self-Sacrifice: Agency, Body and Emotion in International Relations.* Cambridge: Cambridge University Press, 2012.

Filmer, Alice Ashton. "Bilingual Belonging and the Whiteness of (Standard) English(es)." *Qualitative Inquiry* 13, no. 6 (2007): 747–65.

Florini, Sarah. "Tweets, Tweeps, and Signifyin': Communication and Cultural Performance on 'Black Twitter.'" *Television & New Media* 15, no. 3 (2014): 223–37. https://doi.org/10.1177/1527476413480247

Floyd-Thomas, Juan M., and Anthony B. Pinn. "Introduction." In *Religion in the Age of Obama,* edited by Juan M. Floyd-Thomas and Anthony B. Pinn, 1–18. London: Bloomsbury, 2018.

Floyd-Thomas, Juan M., and Anthony B. Pinn, eds. *Religion in the Age of Obama.* London: Bloomsbury, 2018.

Ford, Richard Thompson. "Sagging and Subordination." In *Dress Codes: How the Laws of Fashion Made History,* 196–220. New York: Simon & Schuster, 2021.

Forman, Murray. "Conscious Hip-Hop, Change, and the Obama Era." *American Studies Journal* 54, no. 3 (2010). http://www.asjournal.org/54-2010/conscious-hip-hop/#

Forman, Murray. "Obama/Time: The President in the Hip Hop Nation." In *The Hip Hop & Obama Reader,* edited by Travis L. Gosa and Erik Nielson, 155–75. New York: Oxford University Press, 2015.

Frankenberg, Ruth. "Local Whitenesses, Localizing Whiteness." In *Displacing Whiteness: Essays in Social and Cultural Criticism*, edited by Ruth Frankenberg, 1–34. Durham: Duke University Press, 1997.

Frith, Simon. "Music and Identity." In *Questions of Cultural Identity*, edited by Stuart Hall and Paul du Gay, 108–27. London: Sage, 1996.

Frith, Simon. *Music for Pleasure: Essays in the Sociology of Pop*. New York: Routledge, 1988.

Frith, Simon. *Sound Effects: Youth, Leisure, and the Politics of Rock 'n' Roll*. New York: Pantheon, 1981.

Garman, Bryan. "Models of Charity and Spirit: Bruce Springsteen, 9/11, and the War on Terror." In *Music in the Post-9/11 World*, edited by Jonathan Ritter and J. Martin Daughtry, 71–89. New York: Routledge, 2007.

Gerstle, Gary. "Civic Ideals, Race, and Nation in the Age of Obama." In *The Presidency of Barack Obama: A First Historical Assessment*, edited by Julian E. Zelizer, 261–80. Princeton: Princeton University Press, 2018.

Gest, Justin, Tyler Reny, and Jeremy Mayer. "Roots of the Radical Right: Nostalgic Deprivation in the United States and Britain." *Comparative Political Studies* 51, no. 13 (2018): 1694–719.

Ghavami, Negin, and Letitia Anne Peplau. "An Intersectional Analysis of Gender and Ethnic Stereotypes: Testing Three Hypotheses." *Psychology of Women Quarterly* 37, no. 1 (2013): 113–27. https://doi.org/10.1177/0361684312464203

Gill, Satinder P. "Entrainment and Musicality in the Human System Interface." *Artificial Intelligence and Society* 21, no. 4 (June 2007): 567–605.

Glick, Peter, and Susan T. Fiske. "The Ambivalent Sexism Inventory: Differentiating Hostile and Benevolent Sexism." *Journal of Personality and Social Psychology* 70, no. 3 (1996): 491–512. https://doi.org/10.1037/0022-3514.70.3.491

Goff, Keli. *Party Crashing: How the Hip-Hop Generation Declared Political Independence*. New York: BasicCivitas, 2008.

Goldberg, Bernard. *A Slobbering Love Affair: The True (and Pathetic) Story of the Torrid Romance between Barack Obama and the Mainstream Media*. Washington, DC: Regnery, 2009.

Gorzelany-Mostak, Dana. "Hearing Girls, Girls, Girls on the 2016 Campaign Trail." *Journal of Popular Music Studies* 29, no. 3 (2017). https://doi.org/10.1111/jpms.12235

Gorzelany-Mostak, Dana. "Hearing Jackie Evancho in the Age of Donald Trump." In "Music and the 2016 U.S. Presidential Campaign," edited by Sally Bick and Dana Gorzelany-Mostak. Special issue, *American Music* 35, no. 4 (Winter 2017): 467–77.

Gorzelany-Mostak, Dana. "'I've Got a Little List': Spotifying Mitt Romney and Barack Obama in the 2012 U.S. Presidential Election." *Music & Politics* 9, no. 2 (Summer 2015). https://doi.org/10.3998/mp.9460447.0009.202

Gorzelany-Mostak, Dana. "Keepin' It Real (Respectable) in 2008: Barack Obama's Music Strategy and the Formation of Presidential Identity." *Journal of the Society for American Music* 10, no. 2 (2016): 113–48. https://doi.org/10.1017/S1752196316000043

Gorzelany-Mostak, Dana. "Pre-existing Music in United States Presidential Campaigns, 1972–2012." PhD diss., McGill University, 2013.

Gorzelany-Mostak, Dana, and Sally Bick, eds. "Music and the 2016 U.S. Presidential Campaign." Special issue, *American Music* 35, no. 4 (Winter 2017).

Gorzelany-Mostak, Dana, and James Deaville, eds. Special issue, *Music & Politics* 9, no. 2 (Summer 2015). https://quod.lib.umich.edu/m/mp/9460447.0009.2*?rgn=main;view=fulltext

Gosa, Travis L. "'The Audacity of Dope': Rap Music, Race, and the Obama Presidency." In *The Iconic Obama, 2007–2009: Essays on Media Representations of the Candidate and New President*, edited by Nicholas A. Yanes and Derrais Carter, 85–96. Jefferson, NC: McFarland, 2012.

Gosa, Travis L. "Not Another Remix: How Obama Became the First Hip-Hop President." *Journal of Popular Music Studies* 22, no. 4 (2010): 389–415. https://doi.org/10.1111/j.1533-1598.2010.01252.x

Gosa, Travis L., and Erik Nielson, eds. *The Hip Hop & Obama Reader*. New York: Oxford University Press, 2015.

Gosa, Travis L., and Erik Nielson. "The State of Hip Hop in the Age of Obama." In *The Hip Hop & Obama Reader*, edited by Travis L. Gosa and Erik Nielson, 1–28. New York: Oxford University Press, 2015.

Gosa, Travis L., and Erik Nielson. "'There Are No Saviors': An Interview with Kevin Powell." In *The Hip Hop & Obama Reader*, edited by Travis L. Gosa and Erik Nielson, 70–87. New York: Oxford University Press, 2015.

Graber, Naomi. "Do You Hear the People Sing? Theater and Theatricality in the Trump Campaign." In "Music and the 2016 U.S. Presidential Campaign," edited by Sally Bick and Dana Gorzelany-Mostak. Special issue, *American Music* 35, no. 4 (2017): 435–45.

Grossberg, Lawrence. "Another Boring Day in Paradise: Rock and Roll and the Empowerment of Everyday Life." *Popular Music* 4 (January 1984): 225–58.

Hall, Kira, Donna M. Goldstein, and Matthew Bruce Ingram. "The Hands of Donald Trump: Entertainment, Gesture, Spectacle." *Hau: Journal of Ethnographic Theory* 6, no. 2 (2016): 71–100.

Harris, Jerry, and Carl Davidson. "Obama: The New Contours of Power." *Race & Class* 50, no. 4 (2009): 1–19. https://doi.org/10.1177/0306396809102993

Harris, Kamala. *The Truths We Hold: An American Journey*. New York: Penguin, 2019.

Hartley, John. *Digital Futures for Cultural and Media Studies*. Malden, MA: Wiley-Blackwell, 2012.

Hartley, John. "Silly Citizenship." *Critical Discourse Studies* 7, no. 4 (2010): 233–48. https://doi.org/10.1080/17405904.2010.511826

Hartley, John. *Uses of Television*. London: Routledge, 1999.

Havlena, William J., and Susan L. Holak. "'The Good Old Days': Observations on Nostalgia and Its Role in Consumer Behavior." In *Advances in Consumer Research* 18, edited by Rebecca H. Holman and Michael R. Solomon, 323–29. Provo, UT: Association for Consumer Research, 1991. https://www.acrwebsite.org/volumes/7180

Hess, Mickey. "Hip-Hop Realness and the White Performer." *Critical Studies in Media Communication* 22, no. 5 (2005): 372–89. https://doi.org/10.1080/0739318050034 2878

Higginbotham, Evelyn Brooks. *Righteous Discontent: The Women's Movement in the Black Baptist Church, 1880–1920*. Cambridge, MA: Harvard University Press, 1994.

Holbrook, Morris B., and Robert M. Schindler. "Echoes of the Dear Departed Past: Some Work in Progress on Nostalgia." In *Advances in Consumer Research* 18, edited by Rebecca H. Holman and Michael R. Solomon, 330–33. Provo, UT: Association for Consumer Research, 1991. https://www.acrwebsite.org/volumes/7181

Holbrook. Morris B., and Robert M. Schindler. "Some Exploratory Findings on the Development of Musical Tastes." *Journal of Consumer Research* 16, no. 1 (June 1989): 119–24.

Holt, Fabian. *Genre in Popular Music*. Chicago: University of Chicago Press, 2007.

Hörnqvist, Magnus. *The Pleasure of Punishment*. London: Routledge, 2021.

HoSang, Daniel Martinez, and Joseph E. Lowndes. *Producers, Parasites, Patriots: Race and the New Right-Wing Politics of Precarity*. Minneapolis: University of Minnesota Press, 2019.

Hutchison, Emma. *Affective Communities in World Politics: Collective Emotions after Trauma*. Cambridge: Cambridge University Press, 2016.

Jackman, Mary R. *The Velvet Glove: Paternalism and Conflict in Gender, Class, and Race Relations*. Berkeley: University of California Press, 1994.

Jackson, Jerma A. *Singing in My Soul: Black Gospel Music in a Secular Age*. Chapel Hill: University of North Carolina Press, 2004.

Jarman-Ivens, Freya. "'Don't Cry, Daddy': The Degeneration of Elvis Presley's Musical Masculinity." In *Oh Boy!: Masculinities and Popular Music*, edited by Freya Jarman-Ivens, 161–80. New York: Routledge, 2007.

Jeffries, Michael P. "Hip-Hop Authenticity in Black and White." In *Thug Life: Race, Gender, and the Meaning of Hip-Hop*, 117–50. Chicago: University of Chicago Press, 2011.

Jeffries, Michael P. "The King's English: Obama, Jay Z, and the Science of Code Switching." In *The Hip Hop & Obama Reader*, edited by Travis L. Gosa and Erik Nielson, 243–61. New York: Oxford University Press, 2015.

Jeffries, Michael P. "Obama as Hip-Hop Icon." In *Thug Life: Race, Gender, and the Meaning of Hip-Hop*, 199–206. Chicago: University of Chicago Press, 2011.

Jeffries, Michael P. "'Where Ya At?' Hip-Hop's Political Locations in the Obama Era." In *The Cambridge Companion to Hip-Hop*, edited by Justin A. Williams, 314–26. Cambridge: Cambridge University Press, 2015.

Johnson, Paul Elliott. "The Art of Masculine Victimhood: Donald Trump's Demagoguery." *Women's Studies in Communication* 40, no. 3 (2017): 229–50.

Jones, Robert P. *The End of White Christian America*. New York: Simon & Schuster, 2016.

Jordan, Matthew F. "Obama's iPod: Popular Music and the Perils of Postpolitical Populism." *Popular Communication* 11, no. 2 (2013): 99–115.

Kajikawa, Loren. "'My Name Is': Signifying Whiteness, Rearticulating Race." In *Sounding Race in Rap Songs*, 118–42. Oakland: University of California Press, 2015.

Karenga, Maulana. "Jesse Jackson and the Presidential Campaign: The Invitation and Oppositions of History." *Black Scholar* 15, no. 5 (September–October 1984): 57–71.

Kaskowitz, Sheryl. *God Bless America: The Surprising History of an Iconic Song*. New York: Oxford University Press, 2013.

Kasper, Eric T., and Benjamin S. Schoening. *You Shook Me All Campaign Long: Music in the 2016 Presidential Election and Beyond*. Denton: University of North Texas Press, 2018.

Katz, Jackson. *Leading Men: Presidential Campaigns and the Politics of Manhood*. Northampton, MA: Interlink, 2013.

Katz, Jackson. *Man Enough? Donald Trump, Hillary Clinton, and the Politics of Presidential Masculinity*. Northampton, MA: Interlink, 2016.

Keightley, Keir. "Reconsidering Rock." In *The Cambridge Companion to Pop and Rock*, edited by Simon Frith, Will Straw, and John Street, 109–42. Cambridge: Cambridge University Press, 2001.

Kellner, Douglas. "Barack Obama and Celebrity Spectacle." *International Journal of Communication* 3 (2009): 715–41. https://pages.gseis.ucla.edu/faculty/kellner/essays/2009_ObamaCelebritySpectacle.pdf

Kitwana, Bakari. *The Hip Hop Generation: Young Blacks and the Crisis in African American Culture*. New York: BasicCivitas, 2002.

Kitwana, Bakari, and Elizabeth Méndez Berry. "It's Bigger Than Barack: Hip Hop Political Organizing, 2004–2013." In *The Hip Hop & Obama Reader*, edited by Travis L. Gosa and Erik Nielson, 54–69. New York: Oxford University Press, 2015.

Klein, Bethany. *As Heard on TV: Popular Music in Advertising*. Farnham, UK: Ashgate, 2009.

Klein, Naomi. *No Logo*. 10th anniversary ed. New York: Picador, 2009.

Kuhn, Virginia. "Remix in the Age of Trump." *Journal of Contemporary Rhetoric* 7, nos. 2–3 (2017): 87–93.

Kun, Josh. *Audiotopia: Music, Race, and America*. Berkeley: University of California Press, 2005.

Larson, Jodi. "American Tune: Postwar Campaign Songs in a Changing Nation." *Journal of Popular Culture* 42, no. 1 (February 2009): 3–26.

Lawrence, Regina G., and Melody Rose. *Hillary Clinton's Race for the White House: Gender Politics and the Media on the Campaign Trail*. Boulder, CO: Lynne Rienner, 2010.

Lemelle, Anthony J., Jr. *Black Masculinity and Sexual Politics*. New York: Routledge, 2010.

Lemi, Danielle Casarez, and Nadia E. Brown. "The Political Implications of Colorism Are Gendered." *PS: Political Science & Politics* 53, no. 4 (October 2020): 669–73. https://doi.org/10.1017/S1049096520000761

Link, Stan. "Sympathy with the Devil? Music of the Psycho Post-*Psycho*." *Screen* 45, no. 1 (Spring 2004): 1–20. https://doi.org/10.1093/screen/45.1.1

Lohman, Laura. *Hail Columbia!: American Music and Politics in the Early Nation.* Oxford: Oxford University Press, 2020.

López, Ian Haney. *Dog Whistle Politics: How Coded Racial Appeals Have Reinvented Racism and Wrecked the Middle Class.* New York: Oxford University Press, 2013.

Lott, Eric. "All the King's Men: Elvis Impersonators and White Working-Class Masculinity." In *Race and the Subject of Masculinities,* edited by Harry Stecopoulos and Michael Uebel, 192–230. Durham: Duke University Press, 1997.

MacWilliams, Matthew C. "Who Decides When the Party Doesn't? Authoritarian Voters and the Rise of Donald Trump." *PS: Political Science & Politics* 49, no. 4 (October 2016): 716–21.

Marcus, Greil. *Double Trouble: Bill Clinton and Elvis Presley in a Land of No Alternatives.* New York: Picador, 2001.

Matos, Amanda R. "Alexandria Ocasio-Cortez and Cardi B Jump through Hoops: Disrupting Respectability Politics When You Are from the Bronx and Wear Hoops." *Harvard Journal of Hispanic Policy* 31 (2019): 89–93.

McIntosh, Janet. "Language and Trump's White Nationalist Strongman Politics." In *Language in the Trump Era: Scandals and Emergencies,* edited by Janet McIntosh and Norma Mendoza-Denton, 217–25. Cambridge: Cambridge University Press, 2020.

McIntosh, Janet, and Norma Mendoza-Denton, eds. *Language in the Trump Era: Scandals and Emergencies.* Cambridge: Cambridge University Press, 2020.

McLeod, Ken. *We Are the Champions: The Politics of Sports and Popular Music.* Farnham, UK: Ashgate, 2011.

Messaris, Paul. *Visual "Literacy": Image, Mind, and Reality.* Boulder, CO: Westview, 1994.

Middleton, Richard. "'From Me to You': Popular Music as Message." In *Studying Popular Music,* 172–246. Milton Keynes: Open University Press, 1990.

Middleton, Richard. "Introduction: Locating the Popular Music Text." In *Reading Pop: Approaches to Textual Analysis in Popular Music,* edited by Richard Middleton, 1–20. Oxford: Oxford University Press, 2000.

Miles, William. *Songs, Odes, Glees and Ballads: A Bibliography of American Presidential Campaign Songsters.* New York: Greenwood Press, 1990.

Miller, Karl Hagstrom. *Segregating Sound: Inventing Folk and Pop Music in the Age of Jim Crow.* Durham: Duke University Press, 2010.

Miller, Keith D. *Voice of Deliverance: The Language of Martin Luther King, Jr. and Its Sources.* New York: Free Press, 1992.

Misciagno, Patricia S. "Rethinking the Mythic Presidency." *Political Communication* 13, no. 3 (1996): 329–44.

Monson, Ingrid. "The Problem with White Hipness: Race, Gender, and Cultural Conceptions in Jazz Historical Discourse." *Journal of the American Musicological Society* 48, no. 3 (Autumn 1995): 396–422. https://doi.org/10.2307/3519833

Morris, Mitchell. *The Persistence of Sentiment: Display and Feeling in Popular Music of the 1970s.* Berkeley: University of California Press, 2013.

Mueller, Max Perry. "Religion (and Race) Problems on the Way to the White House:

Mitt Romney and Barack Obama's 'Faith' Speeches." In *Religion in the Age of Obama*, edited by Juan M. Floyd-Thomas and Anthony B. Pinn, 19–35. London: Bloomsbury, 2018.

Mulvey, Laura. "Visual Pleasure and Narrative Cinema." *Screen* 16, no. 3 (Autumn 1975): 6–18. https://doi.org/10.1093/screen/16.3.6

Murphy, John M. "Inventing Authority: Bill Clinton, Martin Luther King, Jr., and the Orchestration of Rhetorical Traditions." *Quarterly Journal of Speech* 83, no. 1 (1997): 71–89. https://doi.org/10.1080/00335639709384172

Neal, Anthony. *The Oral Presidency of Barack Obama*. Lanham, MD: Lexington Books, 2018.

Nielson, Erik. "'My President Is Black, My Lambo's Blue': The Obamafication of Rap?" *Journal of Popular Music Studies* 21, no. 4 (December 2009): 344–63.

Nietzsche, Friedrich. *The Genealogy of Morals*. Vol. 13 of *The Complete Works of Friedrich Nietzsche*, edited by Oscar Levy, translated by Horace B. Samuel and J. M. Kennedy. Edinburgh: Foulis, 1913.

Nietzsche, Friedrich. *Thus Spoke Zarathustra: A Book for All and None*. Edited by Adrian Del Caro and Robert B. Pippin. Translated by Adrian Del Caro. Cambridge: Cambridge University Press, 2006.

Obama, Barack. *Dreams from My Father: A Story of Race and Inheritance*. New York: Times Books, 1995.

Ogbar, Jeffrey O. G. "Message from the Grassroots: Hip Hop Activism, Millennials, and the Race for the White House." In *The Hip Hop & Obama Reader*, edited by Travis L. Gosa and Erik Nielson, 31–53. New York: Oxford University Press, 2015.

Omi, Michael, and Howard Winant. *Racial Formation in the United States*, 3rd ed. New York: Routledge, 2015.

Orey, Byron D'Andra, and Yu Zhang. "Melanated Millennials and the Politics of Black Hair." *Social Science Quarterly* 100, no. 6 (2019): 2458–76. https://doi.org/10.1111/ssqu.12694

Ossei-Owusu, Shaun. "Barack Obama's Anomalous Relationship with the Hip-Hop Community." In *The Obama Phenomenon: Toward a Multiracial Democracy*, edited by Charles P. Henry, Robert L. Allen, and Robert Chrisman, 218–35. Urbana: University of Illinois Press, 2011.

Ott, Brian L., and Greg Dickinson. *The Twitter Presidency: Donald J. Trump and the Politics of White Rage*. New York: Routledge, 2019.

Parry-Giles, Shawn J. "Mediating Hillary Rodham Clinton: Television News Practices and Image-Making in the Postmodern Age." *Critical Studies in Media Communication* 17, no. 2 (2000): 205–26. https://doi.org/10.1080/15295030000938 8390

Parry-Giles, Shawn J., and Trevor Parry-Giles. *Constructing Clinton: Hyperreality and Presidential Image-Making in Postmodern Politics*. New York: Peter Lang, 2002.

Pascoe, C. J. "Who Is a Real Man? The Gender of Trumpism." *Masculinities and Social Change* 6, no. 2 (2017): 119–41. https://doi.org/10.17583/MCS.2017.2745

Pascoe, C. J., and Jocelyn A. Hollander. "Good Guys Don't Rape: Gender, Domination, and Mobilizing Rape." *Gender & Society* 30, no. 1 (February 2016): 67–79.

Patch, Justin. *Discordant Democracy: Noise, Affect, Populism, and the Presidential Campaign*. New York: Routledge, 2019.

Patch, Justin. "This Is What Democracy Sounds Like." In *You Shook Me All Campaign Long: Music in the 2016 Presidential Election and Beyond*, edited by Eric T. Kasper and Benjamin S. Schoening, 19–50. Denton: University of North Texas Press, 2018.

Pérez, Raúl. "Racism without Hatred? Racist Humor and the Myth of 'Colorblindness.'" *Sociological Perspectives* 60, no. 5 (2017): 956–74.

Pham, Vincent N. "Our Foreign President Barack Obama: The Racial Logics of Birther Discourses." *Journal of International and Intercultural Communication* 8, no. 2 (2015): 86–107. https://doi.org/10.1080/17513057.2015.1025327

Phillips, Whitney. *This Is Why We Can't Have Nice Things: Mapping the Relationship between Online Trolling and Mainstream Culture*. Cambridge, MA: MIT Press, 2016.

Phillips, Whitney, and Ryan M. Milner. *The Ambivalent Internet: Mischief, Oddity, and Antagonism Online*. Malden, MA: Polity, 2017.

Philpot, Tasha S., and Hanes Walton Jr. "One of Our Own: Black Female Candidates and the Voters Who Support Them." *American Journal of Political Science* 51, no. 1 (January 2007): 49–62.

Pinn, Anthony B. "In the Wake of Obama's Hope: Thoughts on Black Lives Matter, Moralism, and Re-imaging Race Struggle." In *Religion in the Age of Obama*, edited by Juan M. Floyd-Thomas and Anthony B. Pinn, 142–51. London: Bloomsbury, 2018.

Popkin, Samuel L. *The Reasoning Voter: Communication and Persuasion in Presidential Campaigns*. Chicago: University of Chicago Press, 1991.

Pough, Gwendolyn D. *Check It While I Wreck It: Black Womanhood, Hip-Hop Culture, and the Public Sphere*. Boston: Northeastern University Press, 2004.

Prins, Annelot. "From Awkward Teen Girl to Aryan Goddess Meme: Taylor Swift and the Hijacking of Star Texts." *Celebrity Studies* 11, no. 1 (2020): 144–48. https://doi.org/10.1080/19392397.2020.1704431

Radano, Ronald, and Philip V. Bohlman. "Introduction: Music and Race, Their Past, Their Presence." In *Music and the Racial Imagination*, edited by Ronald Radano and Philip V. Bohlman, 1–56. Chicago: University of Chicago Press, 2000.

Richmond, Sanford K. "Paint the White House Black!! A Critical Discourse Analysis Look at Hip Hop's Social, Cultural, and Political Influence on the Presidency of Barack Obama." *Western Journal of Black Studies* 37, no. 4 (Winter 2013): 249–57.

Rivière, Joan. "Womanliness as Masquerade." In *Feminist Theory: A Reader*, 3rd ed., edited by Wendy K. Kolmar and Frances Bartowski, 131–35. Boston: McGraw-Hill, 2010.

Roberts, Philippa, and Jane Cunningham. "Feminisation of Brands." *Marketing*, September 2, 2008.

Rogness, Kate Zittlow. "This Is Our Fight Song." In *You Shook Me All Campaign Long: Music in the 2016 Presidential Election and Beyond*, edited by Eric T. Kasper and Benjamin S. Schoening, 215–38. Denton: University of North Texas Press, 2018.

Rose, Tricia. *The Hip Hop Wars: What We Talk about When We Talk about Hip Hop—and Why It Matters*. New York: BasicCivitas, 2008.

Ross, Andrew. *No Respect: Intellectuals & Popular Culture*. New York: Routledge, 1989.

Sanchez-Hucles, Janis V., and Donald D. Davis. "Women and Women of Color in Leadership: Complexity, Identity, and Intersectionality." *American Psychologist* 65, no. 3 (2010): 171–81.

Sasahara, Kazutoshi, Wen Chen, Hao Peng, Giovanni Luca Ciampaglia, Alessandro Flammini, and Filippo Menczer. "Social Influence and Unfollowing Accelerate the Emergence of Echo Chambers." *Journal of Computational Social Science* 4 (2021): 381–402. https://doi.org/10.1007/s42001-020-00084-7

Schoening, Benjamin S., and Eric T. Kasper. *Don't Stop Thinking about the Music: The Politics of Songs and Musicians in Presidential Campaigns*. Lanham, MD: Lexington Books, 2012.

Scott, Derek B. "The US Presidential Campaign Songster, 1840–1900." In *Cheap Print and Popular Song in the Nineteenth Century: A Cultural History of the Songster*, edited by Paul Watt, Derek B. Scott, and Patrick Spedding, 73–90. Cambridge: Cambridge University Press, 2017.

Sikanku, Etse, and Nicholas A. Yanes. "The Modern *E Pluribus Unum* Man: How Obama Constructed His American Identity from His Global Background." In *The Iconic Obama, 2007–2009: Essays on Media Representations of the Candidate and New President*, edited by Nicholas A. Yanes and Derrais Carter, 16–27. Jefferson, NC: McFarland, 2012.

Silber, Irwin. *Songs America Voted By: With the Words and Music That Won and Lost Elections and Influenced the Democratic Process*. Harrisburg, PA: Stackpole Books, 1971.

Small, Christopher. *Musicking: The Meanings of Performing and Listening*. Middletown, CT: Wesleyan University Press, 1998.

Smirnova, Michelle. "Small Hands, Nasty Women, and Bad Hombres: Hegemonic Masculinity and Humor in the 2016 Presidential Election." *Socius* 4 (2018). https://doi.org/10.1177/2378023117749380

Smith, Suzanne E. *Dancing in the Street: Motown and the Cultural Politics of Detroit*. Cambridge, MA: Harvard University Press, 1999.

Smitherman, Geneva. *Talkin That Talk: Language, Culture, and Education in African America*. New York: Routledge, 2000.

Sontag, Susan. "Notes on 'Camp.'" In *Against Interpretation, and Other Essays*, 275–92. New York: Picador, 2001.

Spence, Lester K. "Obama and the Future of Hip-Hop Politics." In *Stare in the Darkness: The Limits of Hip-Hop and Black Politics*, 157–76. Minneapolis: University of Minnesota Press, 2011.

Stauffer, John, and Benjamin Soskis. *The Battle Hymn of the Republic: A Biography of the Song That Marches On*. New York: Oxford University Press, 2013.

Stoever, Jennifer Lynn. *The Sonic Color Line: Race and the Cultural Politics of Listening*. New York: New York University Press, 2016.

Stow, Simon. "On the Existential Politics of Hip-Hop (Or, the Concept of Irony with Continual Reference to Eminem)." *Brolly* 2, no. 2 (2019): 103–24.

Stras, Laurie. "She's So Fine, or Why Girl Singers (Still) Matter." In *She's So Fine: Reflections on Whiteness, Femininity, Adolescence and Class in 1960s Music*, edited by Laurie Stras, 1–32. Farnham, UK: Ashgate, 2010.

Stras, Laurie. "Voice of the Beehive: Vocal Technique at the Turn of the 1960s." In *She's So Fine: Reflections on Whiteness, Femininity, Adolescence and Class in 1960s Music*, edited by Laurie Stras, 33–56. Farnham, UK: Ashgate, 2010.

Streeter, Caroline A. "Obama Jungle Fever: Interracial Desire on the Campaign Trail." In *The Iconic Obama, 2007–2009: Essays on Media Representations of the Candidate and New President*, edited by Nicholas A. Yanes and Derrais Carter, 167–83. Jefferson, NC: McFarland, 2012.

Studlar, Gaylyn. *Precocious Charms: Stars Performing Girlhood in Classical Hollywood Cinema.* Berkeley: University of California Press, 2012.

Tesler, Michael. *Post-Racial or Most-Racial?: Race and Politics in the Obama Era.* Chicago: University of Chicago Press, 2016.

Tien, Charles. "The Racial Gap in Voting among Women: White Women, Racial Resentment, and Support for Trump." *New Political Science* 39, no. 4 (2017): 651–69. https://doi.org/10.1080/07393148.2017.1378296

Tompkins, Joe. "Pop Goes the Horror Score: Left Alone in *The Last House on the Left.*" In *Music in the Horror Film: Listening to Fear*, edited by Neil Lerner, 98–113. New York: Routledge, 2010.

Umbach, Maiken, and Matthew Humphrey. *Authenticity: The Cultural History of a Political Concept.* Cham: Palgrave Macmillan, 2018.

Valentino, Nicholas A., Carly Wayne, and Marzia Oceno. "Mobilizing Sexism: The Interaction of Emotion and Gender Attitudes in the 2016 US Presidential Election." *Public Opinion Quarterly* 82, no. S1 (2018): 799–821. https://doi.org/10.1093/poq/nfy003

Vernallis, Carol. "Audiovisual Change: Viral Web Media and the Obama Campaign." *Cinema Journal* 50, no. 4 (Summer 2011): 73–97.

Vieregge, Quentin. "Ameritude." In *You Shook Me All Campaign Long: Music in the 2016 Presidential Election and Beyond*, edited by Eric T. Kasper and Benjamin S. Schoening, 185–214. Denton: University of North Texas Press, 2018.

Walters, Ron. "Barack Obama and the Politics of Blackness." *Journal of Black Studies* 38, no. 1 (September 2007): 7–29.

Watkins, S. Craig. *Hip Hop Matters: Politics, Pop Culture, and the Struggle for the Soul of a Movement.* Boston: Beacon, 2005.

Welter, Barbara. "The Cult of True Womanhood: 1820–1860." *American Quarterly* 18, no. 2, pt. 1 (Summer 1966): 151–74.

Wicke, Peter. *Rock Music: Culture, Aesthetics, and Sociology.* Translated by Rachel Fogg. Cambridge: Cambridge University Press, 1990.

Williams, Sherri. "Cardi B: *Love & Hip Hop*'s Unlikely Feminist Hero." *Feminist Media Studies* 17, no. 6 (2017): 1114–17. https://doi.org/10.1080/14680777.2017.1380431

Wilson, David. "'Pub Fight' Politics." In *You Shook Me All Campaign Long: Music in the 2016 Presidential Election and Beyond*, edited by Eric T. Kasper and Benjamin S. Schoening, 317–45. Denton: University of North Texas Press, 2018.

Wood, Amy Louise. *Lynching and Spectacle: Witnessing Racial Violence in America, 1890–1940*. Chapel Hill: University of North Carolina Press, 2009.

OTHER

Catalyst. "The Double-Bind Dilemma for Women in Leadership: Damned If You Do, Doomed If You Don't" [2007 Report]. July 15, 2007. https://www.catalyst.org/rese arch/the-double-bind-dilemma-for-women-in-leadership-damned-if-you-do-doo med-if-you-dont/

Center for Responsive Politics. "Donor Demographics by Gender." July 13, 2009. https://www.opensecrets.org/pres08/donordemCID_compare.php%7B?%7Dcycle =2008 (no longer available).

Dittmar, Kelly. "Black Women in American Politics, 2019." Center for American Women and Politics. https://cawp.rutgers.edu/sites/default/files/resources/black -women-politics-2019.pdf. Accessed June 25, 2021.

FiveThirtyEight. "Obama and the Rev. Wright Controversy: What Really Happened." n.d. https://fivethirtyeight.com/videos/obama-and-the-rev-wright-controversy -what-really-happened/

GovTrack.us. "Sen. Kamala Harris's 2019 Report." Last updated January 18, 2020. https://www.govtrack.us/congress/members/kamala_harris/412678/report-card /2019

Horowitz, Juliana Menasce, Kim Parker, Anna Brown, and Kiana Cox. "Amid National Reckoning, Americans Divided on Whether Increased Focus on Race Will Lead to Major Policy Change." Pew Research Center, October 6, 2020. https://www.pewre search.org/social-trends/2020/10/06/amid-national-reckoning-americans-divided -on-whether-increased-focus-on-race-will-lead-to-major-policy-change/

Jensen, Tom. "A Deeper Look at the Birthers." Public Policy Polling, August 19, 2009. http://publicpolicypolling.blogspot.com/2009/08/deeper-look-at-birthers.html

Kishi, Roudabeh, and Sam Jones. "Demonstrations and Political Violence in America: New Data for Summer 2020." Armed Conflict Location & Event Data Project, September 3, 2020. https://acleddata.com/2020/09/03/demonstrations-political-vi olence-in-america-new-data-for-summer-2020/

"Neurosurgeon Demographics and Statistics in the US." Zippia. n.d. https://www.zipp ia.com/neurosurgeon-jobs/demographics/. Accessed October 1, 2022.

Pew Research Center. "Growing Number of Americans Say Obama Is a Muslim." August 18, 2010. https://www.pewforum.org/2010/08/18/growing-number-of-ame ricans-say-obama-is-a-muslim/

"Protecting American Monuments, Memorials, and Statues and Combating Recent Criminal Violence." Executive Order 13933, Federal Register (National Archives),

June 26, 2020. https://www.federalregister.gov/documents/2020/07/02/2020-14509
/protecting-american-monuments-memorials-and-statues-and-combating-recent
-criminal-violence

Shelley, Braxton D. "Music, Memes, and Digital Antiphony." Paper presented at the
Radcliffe Institute for Advanced Study, March 23, 2020. YouTube video. 57:46.
Posted by Harvard Radcliffe Institute. https://www.youtube.com/watch?v=PYXX
wPdOpYA

Williamson, Vanessa, and Isabella Gelfand. "Trump and Racism: What Do the Data
Say?" Brookings, August 14, 2019. https://www.brookings.edu/blog/fixgov/2019/08
/14/trump-and-racism-what-do-the-data-say/

INDEX

Page numbers in italics refer to figures; page numbers in bold refer to tables.

Brackett, David, 4, 12–13
The Breakfast Club (radio show), 18, 68, 78–81, 82
Bush, George H. W., 6, 8, 25, 136n31
Bush, George W., 21, 30, 57

Cabaret (1972), 105–6
Camille & Haley: agency of, 108–10; background and self-presentation of, 94–98, *96*; "Game On," 94, 96; "Keep America Great," 18–19, 95–96, 98, *99*, 100, *101*, 102–4, 106, 108; responses to, 100, 102–7; vocal style of, 96, 103; and White girlhood, 19, 94–95, 98, 100, 102–4, 107–10
camp, 5–6, 8–9
campaign launch events, 53–57, **55**, 60–65, *64*
campaign playlists: Bill Clinton, 9–12, **11**, 70; Hillary Clinton, 21, 70, 73; Harris, 69–71, **72**, 73–74, 85; McCain, 41; Obama, 22, 33–35, **36–37**, 40–46, 47–48, 70, 147n70; Trump, 90
campaign soundscapes, 2–3, 16, 25, 33
Campbell, Karlyn Kohrs, 71
Campbell, Luther, 84
Cannen, Emma, 41–42
Cardi B, 76–78. *See also* "I Like It"
Carson, Ben: background of, 51–52, 62; blackness and, 17–18, 49–53; campaign launch event, 53–57, **55**, 60–65, *64*; Christianity and, 51–52; "Freedom" radio ad, 49–51, 151–52n14; remarks by, 50–51, 52, 62–63, 152n15
Carson, Candy, 54, **55**
Carter, Jimmy, 8, 21
Charlamagne Tha God, 79–81
Chisholm, Shirley, 52
Christian identity, 17–18, 19, 51–52, 57, 89–90, 91, 94–98, 107–8
Christian music, 54, 94–95, 97. *See also* gospel
Christian nationalism, 19, 63, 95–97, 98, 100, 104, 107–8
Chrysler, 58–60
civil rights movement, 17, 33–34, 35, 38, 41, 147n62

classical crossover, 17–18, 63–65. *See also* Veritas
classic rock, 9–11, 13, 21. *See also* rock music
Clinton, Bill: on *The Arsenio Hall Show*, 1–2, *2*, 5–9, 66, 133n4; campaign playlists, 9–12, **11**, 70; compared to Elvis, 1, 5–6, 8–9, 133n4, 135n20; compared to Obama, 34, 35, 39–40; criticized by Trump, 93; presidential identity of, 1–2, 5–12, 14; and race, 1–2, 6–9, 39, 66, 133n6; Sister Souljah incident, 25–26, 27–28
Clinton, Hillary: "basket of deplorables" comment, 111–12; campaign playlists, 21, 34, 70, 73; criticized by Obama, 30; and gender, 31–32, 40, 43, 66, 128, 148n80; perceived inauthenticity of, 34, 73, 78, 161n65; presidential identity of, 40, 42; in user-generated content, 31–32, 66, *67*
A Clockwork Orange (1971), 118–19
Coates, Ta-Nehisi, 15
code-switching, 30–31, 83
Colbert, Stephen, 89. See also *The Late Show with Stephen Colbert*
"colorblind" rhetoric, 14
colorism, 69, 85
Cooke, Sam, 35
Cooper, Frank Rudy, 41
Cordero, Johnnie, 83
country music, 4, 12–13, 21. *See also* Camille & Haley
Covid-19, 15, 98, 115
"Crazy in Love" (Beyoncé/Jay-Z), 29, 31
critical race theory, 15, 20, 139n68
"Crush on Obama" (Ettinger), 16, 17, 42–43
Cruz, Ted, 12–13, 71, 74, 158–59n37
Cyrus, Miley, 89–90

dancing, 31–32, 60, 66, 74–78, *75*, 86, 118–19
dehumanization, 117, 120–21, 131
Detroit, Michigan: Carson's campaign launch in, 53–57, **55**, 60–65, *64*; and Selected of God, 58–61, 62. *See also* Motown

32; in hip-hop, 27, 29, 30, 57–58, 85; in the Trump ethos, 93, 117
Monson, Ingrid, 7–8
Morrison, Toni, 1, 133n6
Motown, 35, 38, 47
MTV News, 29
Mulvey, Laura, 100
Murdoch, Rupert, 49

Nader, Ralph, 21, 23
Nazism, 105–6
Nielson, Erik, 28–29
Nietzsche, Friedrich, 126
nostalgia, 9–11, 17–18, 35, 88–90, 108, 136n36

Obama, Barack: background of, 22–24, 33, 46–47, 142n6, 147n62; blackness and, 16–17, 21–25, 33–34, 41–42, 46–48, 52–53, 83–84; campaign playlists, 22, 33–35, **36–37**, 40–46, 47–48, 70, 147n70; compared to Bill Clinton, 34, 35, 39–40; compared to Harris, 69, 71, 83–84, 85–86; dancing on *The Ellen DeGeneres Show*, 76; discussing music in interviews, 27–30, 34, **36–37**, 38, 147n70; and hip-hop, 16–17, 25, 26–32, 41–42, 46–47, 53, 83–84, 143–44n22, 144–45n32; marriage and family of, 42, 43; as "old school," 29, 34–35, 47–48, 83–84; and R & B, 17, 35, 47–48, 84; and US racial discourse, 14, 21–25, 33–34, 41–42, 52–53, 91; and YouTube, 15–16, 17, 31–33, 42–43
Obama, Michelle, 42, 43
"Obama Dirt off Your Shoulder Remix" (mashup), 31–32
Ocasio-Cortez, Alexandria, 76, 77–78
"One Nation Under a Groove" (Funkadelic), 70, **72**
online culture. *See* meme culture; troll culture
O'Rourke, Beto, 10
"Over There" (Cohan), 88

"Panderdom" ("Freedom" parody), 50–51
pandering, 12–13, 50–51, 77–78, 161n65. *See also* authenticity, perceptions of

parody, 50–51, 88–89, 111–13, *112*
patriotic songs, **55**, 61–62, 63–65, 95–97, 155n59
Pelosi, Nancy, 66, *67*
Peoples Temple, 106–7
Perry, Cal, 98, *99*
"Petty" (YouTube video), 66–67, *67*, 155n2
Phillips, Whitney, 118–19, 122
playlists. *See* campaign playlists
police: support for, 94, 108, 119–21; violence by, 106, 114–15. *See also* Harris, Kamala: "cop" image of
"Politics as Usual" (Ludacris), 30
Popick, Jeff, 89
Portland, Oregon, protest (September 5, 2020): Announcer video, 116–19, 121; events of, 113–14, 115–16, 172n24; "Footloose" video, 19, 113–14, 116, 118–21, **124–25**, 129, 130–31; other online responses to, 119–23, **124–25**, 126–27
postracial ideology, 14, 18, 52–56, 65
Pough, Gwendolyn, 76, 160n53
Powell, Adam Clayton IV, 26
presidential identity: of Carson, 53–56, 60–63, 65; of Bill Clinton, 1–2, 5–12, 14; of Hillary Clinton, 40, 42; of Harris, 68–69, 71, 73–74, 78, 82–87; of Obama, 15–16, 21–25, 30–32, 33–35, 40–43, 45–48
Presley, Elvis, 1, 5–6, 8–9, 133n4, 135n20
Prins, Annelot, 104
protests. *See* Black Lives Matter; Portland, Oregon, protest (September 5, 2020)

R & B, 17, 35, 47–48, 84, 86
racial discourse: and Obama's election, 14, 21–25, 33–34, 41–42, 52–53, 91; in the Trump era, 14–15, 20, 92, 114–15, 120–21, 126–29, 130–31
racialization of sound, 3–4, 6–8, 16–19, 41–42, 50–51, 56–57, 63–65, 103
racial transposition, 120–21, 127
radio: *The Breakfast Club*, 18, 68, 78–81, 82; Carson campaign ad, 49–51, 151–52n14
rally playlists. *See* campaign playlists

music, 12; discourses of, 6–9, 12, 84, 89–92, 103, 104–7; and Eminem, 51, 54–55, 58, 153n34; and Trump, 14–15, 90, 91–92, 128

White supremacy, 4, 92, 104–6, 127–29, 139n68

White womanhood, 88–90, 94–95, 100, 102–4, 107, 108–10, 128

Wicke, Peter, 44–45

Williams, Sherri, 76

Wilson, Jackie, 35, 48

Wonder, Stevie, 38–39, 40–41, 43–45, *44*, 47–48, 85

Woods, Phil, 7

"Work That" (Blige), 85, 87

Wright, Jeremiah, 23–24, 31

yacht rock, 119

"Yes We Can" (will.i.am), 16, 32, 49

Yon, Kevin, 58–59

"(Your Love Keeps Lifting Me) Higher and Higher" (Wilson), 35, 41, 43

YouTube: and the 2008 election, 15–16, 17, 21, 31–33, 42–43; and the 2020 election, 66–67, *67*, 100, 102–3, 106; comments on, 100, 102–3; participatory culture of, 15–16, 31–33, 106, 113